HEALTH PSYCHOLOGY SERIES
Gloria R. Leon, Series Editor

PSYCHOLOGY AND HEALTH

MYLES GENEST
SHARON GENEST

RESEARCH PRESS

2612 NORTH MATTIS AVENUE
CHAMPAIGN, ILLINOIS 61821

150
G32p

m.R.

Advisory Editor, Frederick H. Kanfer

Copyright © 1987 by Myles Genest and Sharon Genest

91 90 89 88 87   5 4 3 2 1

All rights reserved. Printed in the United States of America. No part of this book may be reproduced by mimeograph or any other means without the written permission of the publisher. Excerpts may be printed in connection with published reviews in periodicals without express permission.

Copies of this book may be ordered from the publisher at the address given on the title page.

Cover design by Jack Davis

Composition by Circle Type Corp.

ISBN 0-87822-280-4

Library of Congress Catalog Card Number 86-63680

TO

our parents: Kathleen Genest and the memory of Georges Genest
Audrey and Emerson Doney

and our children: Aaron and Anna Genest

University Libraries
Carnegie Mellon University
Pittsburgh, Pennsylvania 15213

Contents

Foreword

This excellent book by Genest and Genest is the inaugural text in the Research Press Health Psychology Series. Health psychology has become a substantive content area, reflecting a growing interest among researchers and clinicians in the interaction between psychological factors and physical health. Behavioral scientists are involved in developing and assessing interventions to change behaviors that are detrimental to health, and they also make significant contributions to the more effective management of physical diseases. As a result, specific psychologically based treatment techniques now can be applied to extremely challenging health problems.

Genest and Genest have nicely highlighted the areas in which psychologists can make unique contributions to enhancing the general health of our society. A major focus of their book is health promotion. They cogently document that traditional medical approaches have not been effective in modifying the rates of those diseases that have strong lifestyle influences. They also discuss the potent economic, institutional, and societal influences that have maintained the medical profession's orientation of treating existing diseases rather than directing efforts at prevention. The need for sensitivity to the psychological concomitants of illness is examined as well.

The authors provide detailed descriptions and evaluations of the efficacy of behavior-change procedures that have been implemented with a range of physical disorders. The thorny area of patient adherence to prescribed behavioral and medical treatments is explored and recommendations for enhancing compliance are presented. The area of stress and disease is considered as well.

In my view, the field of health psychology can be conceptualized within a risk-factor paradigm of health and disease, suggesting that there are combinations of factors that determine an individual's vulnerability for the development of a given disorder or a range of disorders. The implications for enhancing the efficacy of treatment programs for specific individuals are considerable. A future direction in psychology is the identification and study of biological and psychological vulnerabilities and strengths in given individuals. The type and strength level of particular risk factors, however, will differ from individual to individual. This conception of physical disease or psychological disorder is, of course, a statistical statement. It is an estimate of the probability that an individual will develop a particular disorder given the presence of identified risk variables. A person whose risk level is low might not be immune to a particular disorder, but the likelihood of developing that disorder is low. The role of the behavioral and biological sciences is to identify the factors that place an individual at risk for the development of a disorder. Then, treatment strategies may more effectively reduce the health risk if targeted to these vulnerability factors.

The influence of generalized stress on the immune system can also be accounted for within a high-risk paradigm. Stress can be viewed as serving a triggering or eliciting function, making people more susceptible to whatever environmental risks (e.g., upper respiratory viruses) or internal risks (e.g., dormant viruses) to which they are exposed (Jemmott & Locke, 1984). There may be individual differences in stress reactivity and how stress is manifested that are biologically as well as environmentally determined. Some people may be more likely to develop a physical disorder, others a psychological disorder, and still others a combination of the two. Some people will be stress resistant. The path of a particular disorder most likely depends on predisposing factors interacting with current influences and patterns of coping.

This book discusses a number of epidemiological studies that clearly demonstrate the influence of behavioral and lifestyle patterns on physical health. The impact of cigarette smoking on the incidence of cancer and cardiovascular disease is but one example. Patterns of dealing with conflict, nutritional practices, and the use of leisure time may all serve as risk or resistance factors for the development of particular disorders.

Genest and Genest conclude their book by surveying community programs developed over the past decade that are aimed at the modification of lifestyle patterns. The information about large-scale screening and intervention programs leaves one with a feeling of optimism; the behavioral sciences already are playing a major role in alleviating, as well as more effectively treating, physical disorders. The authors present a balanced view of the current status of the field of health psychology, examining present problems as well as providing direction for research and interventions in this emerging area.

Gloria R. Leon
University of Minnesota

References

Jemmott, J. B., & Locke, S. E. (1984). Psychosocial factors, immunologic mediation, and human susceptibility to infectious diseases: How much do we know? *Psychological Bulletin, 95,* 78-108.

Acknowledgments

It is a pleasure to acknowledge the help of Glenn Pancyr, Kiyoko Kato, and Harry van Eyck. Their efforts were invaluable. Aaron and Anna deserve thanks for their help, for waiting for this to be finished, and for learning to make their own snacks.

Introduction

Until the last few years when we have become more health conscious, staying healthy meant one thing—going to see the doctor when we got sick. We expected some medicine, and usually our expectations were fulfilled. Whether we took the drug properly or took it at all, we usually got better and invariably attributed our improved health to the visit to the doctor's office. Few of us considered that measures beyond these were necessary for our good health. Despite growing awareness of the importance of healthy lifestyles in staying well, this archaic, treatment-oriented view still underlies our attitude toward health.

It is not surprising that this attitude lingers. With fears of polio epidemics and first-hand knowledge of frequent pneumonia deaths still fresh in their minds, parents of those of us who missed these events firmly believed in the miracle of modern medicine. If something went wrong, the doctor could fix it. And if the problem could not be fixed right now, discovery of the method for "repair" was just around the corner.

As children of those awestruck parents, we are sadly disillusioned to learn that when things of consequence go wrong with bodies, they often cannot be fixed. We have trouble believing that cures for cancer, multiple sclerosis, diabetes, atherosclerosis, and other modern diseases are not imminent. As a consequence of our inherent faith, we endorse medical research as enthusiastically as did our parents, but with far less reason for

1

optimism. The health and longevity of the general population in North America and Europe has improved only insignificantly over the last several decades (National Center for Health Statistics, 1983) and most of the improvement seems due to nonmedical factors. For example, U.S. mortality rates from stomach cancer have fallen considerably during the 20th century (Silverberg, 1983), but the decline cannot be attributed to medical intervention (Goldman & Cook, 1984). The fatality rate for carcinoma of the stomach has not changed for several decades (Green & O'Toole, 1982). Rather, changes in diet or cooking habits seem to be responsible for a decline in the incidence of the disease (Urquhart & Heilmann, 1984). Richard Peto, a British epidemiologist and author of a major study of cancer mortality for the Congressional Office of Technology Assessment, was quoted by Boffey (1984) as saying that "there has been disappointingly little progress in curative treatment since the middle of the century" (p. C1) and that he saw no reason to expect substantial progress for the rest of this century.

In our complex Western culture, the health problems are also complex: too complex for answers from one source. Cancer-causing toxins in our air, water, and food produce tumors that may not be completely eradicated by medical treatment. A baby born with fetal alcohol syndrome is already sick and possibly permanently damaged before medical care can intervene. Stress may induce high blood pressure, which could lead to a fatal or damaging heart attack if an individual does not learn to cope with the stress. For the improvements to health we avidly seek, an extensive, liberal examination of the physical, social, and psychological environment is necessary. We need to know what makes us sick and how to avoid getting sick, because when we become ill, we too often cannot get better by going to the doctor. Even when a visit to the doctor can help us, we may ignore prescriptions for life-saving drugs or fail to alter our lifestyles to improve chronic conditions because of anger at long waits to see our doctors, confusion about the information and advice given, and, occasionally, alienation by the aloof professionalism we have encountered. The focus of biomedical research and the traditional practice of clinical medicine are clearly not broad enough to encompass all aspects of the cause of disease and the maintenance of health.

Psychologists first found a place in health treatment as an adjunct to standard medical practice when some of the unmet needs of patients were recognized: Illnesses that did not seem to have physiological bases were turned over to psychiatrists and psychologists for psychotherapy. In other instances, psychologists were asked to deal with the residual problems of medical treatment: Some patients were not taking their medicine and anxious children in hospitals were a problem for the busy medical staff. From these beginnings, a new area of specialization has evolved, best known as health psychology, or behavioral medicine.

A definition of the field of health psychology is provided by the Public Information Committee of the 3000-member Health Psychology Division of the American Psychological Association (1985):

> Health Psychology is the aggregate of the specific educational, scientific, and professional contributions of the discipline of psychology to the promotion and maintenance of health, the prevention and treatment of illness, and the identification of etiologic and diagnostic correlates of health, illness, and related dysfunctions, and to the analysis and improvement of the health care system and health policy formation.

As the Public Information Committee noted, "Many disciplines can aid this effort, but psychology, owing to its emphasis on the study of behavior, has a unique contribution to make."

Psychologists have become part of the health-care team in medical settings and in nonmedical settings concerned with health, where they provide services, teach, and carry out research. In fact, the largest single placement area of psychologists over the past decade has been in medical centers, where they work in rehabilitation medicine, pediatrics, cardiology, dentistry, family medicine, pain centers, cancer clinics, and other specialty centers. In these settings, they confront problems such as how to encourage a diabetic to exercise, to eat properly, and to administer insulin safely—problems quite different from the psychopathology that clinical psychologists have traditionally been trained to assess and treat. Training medical staff (for example, nurses, physiotherapists, and nutritionists) to carry out specific psychotherapeutic interventions for specific problems is probably the most visible contribution of psychologists in many medical settings.

One idealistic part of the psychologist's role in health involves attempts to build into the system an awareness of the complexities of the patient and health-care system interaction. Part of this task is alerting other health-care professionals to the emotional component in becoming ill, being ill, and being treated for illness. Some progress has been made in this area. Health-care professionals are increasingly recognizing that many of the problems patients present for medical solutions are emotionally based and they are referring these patients more frequently for psychological intervention. Further, clinical psychologists have generally received training in research methodology and can therefore undertake an assessment of the effectiveness of medical practice and the health-care system itself.

Thus, health psychology has developed out of an awareness of the psychological components of illness and of the interplay of human experiences and illness. As a result, the role of psychologists both within medical settings and as health-care professionals outside the medical system has expanded. As the complexities of illnesses are slowly unraveled, the role of human behavior is seen in a much broader perspective. The way people live, that is, whether they smoke cigarettes or consume alcohol excessively, exercise regularly, consume foods high in cholesterol, use seatbelts, or live in an industrial area, for example, influences their health. It is increasingly clear that continued expansions of purely medical treatments will offer fewer general benefits to health. Instead, it is recognized that there is a need to identify behaviors that increase the risk of ill-health and to assist people in altering their behaviors to be more health promoting. As a result, health research is no longer synonymous with biomedical research: Health psychologists have expanded the investigation of health maintenance to include the crucial role of human behavior.

This volume will examine the contributions of health psychologists and other psychological researchers in studying the parameters of healthy behavior, lifestyle change, maintenance of change, and development of the groundwork for effective programs of prevention and treatment. The fundamental issues of treatment of illness versus prevention of illness, factors influencing adherence to medical or lifestyle-change interventions, and social and cultural attitudes that have shaped the health-care system will be explored. Empirical literature and the behavioral applications of research on the following disorders will be presented: spinal cord injury, tension headache, hypotension, essential hypertension, chronic pain, acute stress (arising from invasive medical procedures), and chronic stress and its relation to peptic ulcers, cardiovascular disease, and cancer. Suggestions for lifestyle changes related to smoking, obesity, fitness, and substance abuse on an individual and community level conclude the volume.

Some areas of concern could not be discussed within the scope of this volume, among them birth control, dental care, prevention of accidents in the workplace, the roles of allied professionals in promoting health, psychological contributions to the treatment of many diseases, issues concerning minority groups and different social clusters, and the role of various risk factors with reference to specific diseases (e.g., lung disease, multiple sclerosis, venereal disease, diabetes). Succeeding volumes in this series will provide more detailed information on specific health psychology topics. Our goal here has not been encyclopedic; rather, we have attempted to illustrate the problems and solutions that are represented in health psychology, to provide glimpses of the action. Glimpses are all that are possible in a field expanding so rapidly. In 1984, Agras found that two-thirds of all the existing health psychology research had been published since 1973, and that the trend showed no signs of reaching a plateau.

Health promotion requires teamwork on a grand scale. Policy and funding from governments, cooperation of the media and educational institutions, and research and implementation by large numbers of people in a great many professions are fundamental to developing the knowledge base for change and influencing people toward positive, healthy lifestyles. We hope that readers will share our optimism for the future of the field, and will have been stimulated to continue its advance.

Chapter One

Determinants
of Health

Throughout recent history and probably throughout the history of the medical profession, there has been a preoccupation with disease. The causes of disease have been studied in great detail, but rarely have concerted, thoughtful studies of what contributes to good health been made. As a result, a great deal is known about the diseases which plague mankind, but little is known about the causes of good health in man. (King, 1974, p. 237)

MEDICINE'S ROLE IN HEALTH IMPROVEMENT

Since the 17th century, the medical approach to illness has been based on engineering: That is, in understanding and treating an illness, a specific etiological agent is posited, the physiological reactions and problems created by this agent are specified, and a specific procedure is used to stop the negative process. The medical profession therefore views health largely as the avoidance of specific diseases (Leventhal & Hirschman, in press). This approach, however, is seriously deficient as a conceptualization of the problems of human health because it does not adequately consider the complexity of modern diseases, nor, to any significant extent, the role of human behavior in maintaining health (McKeown, 1971a).

It is often assumed that modern medicine has increased life expectancy through eradication (by antibiotics and generally better medical care) of infectious diseases that used to be major killers (Burish & Bradley, 1983; King, 1974; McKeown, 1971a). This "better treatment" explanation for changing mortality patterns is a misleading one. In fact, specific medical advances have been of secondary importance.

The most dramatic improvements in health and longevity have arisen from improvements in general living conditions—in other words, from measures that *prevent* disease. The virtual absence of plague in the Western world is not a result of effective treatment of plague infections with antibiotics or other medical intervention. Rather, plague epidemics have ceased because people in Western societies live in healthier environments than did their forebears. They live in less crowded conditions, have fewer children, enjoy better housing and better nutrition, and are more mindful of hygiene and sanitation. Therefore, they do not become infected in the first place. Improvements in the standard of living were undertaken as humanitarian acts inspired by the utilitarian philosophy of such thinkers as Jeremy Bentham and a growing societal awareness of the appalling conditions created by the new industrial society, rather than as programs for improving health. The fight against poor living conditions was amazingly effective in increasing life expectancy from 40 years in 1850 to 70 years in 1950.

An examination of illness and health in modern times supports McKeown's (1971b) claim that further advances in health, like past improvements, will follow from modification of behavior and changes in the environment. For example, the highly touted recent reductions in mortality for heart disease appear not to have resulted from medical treatment, but rather from social, behavioral, and economic changes (Goldman & Cook, 1984; Wing, 1984). The medical profession, however, has traditionally been credited for those improvements and encourages the public view that the practice of medicine is the solution to all health problems. Consequently, medical research has been funded by an enthusiastic public, convinced that miracles will be the outcome (Bowers, 1971; King, 1974). Despite this outpouring of money and faith, the problems of health confronting us today have yielded little to attempts to cure, control, or prevent.

Death rates have not substantially decreased in the past several decades, cures have not been found for the major causes of death in our culture, and there is no substantial evidence that such cures are forthcoming. The grim situation is that we are virtually at a standstill in our fight against the life threatening, incurable diseases facing us today. Lifestyle, diet, and environmental variables are major factors in cardiovascular disease, cancer, and motor vehicle and other accidents, which are the leading causes of death in North America (Belloc & Breslow, 1972; Lalonde, 1974). In Powles's (1974) words, today we are faced with the diseases of civilization.

LIFE EXPECTANCY

A person born in the United States in 1900 could expect to live 47.3 years, on average (National Center for Health Statistics, 1983). He could expect to die from influenza, pneumonia, tuberculosis, gastroenteritis, chronic nephritis, or diphtheria, which were the major causes of death at the turn of the century (Lalonde, 1974). The next half-century changed this picture dramatically. With every year that passed, the average life expectancy increased by almost half a year. By 1950, life expectancy at birth was 68.9 years, an increase of almost 46 percent from 1900. For a time, the limits to the life-span appeared to be steadily receding. We remember optimistically thinking, as children in the 1950s, that there was a real possibility of living for 150 years or so, since the life-span seemed to have increased so much, so quickly, and the rate of increase did not appear to be slowing. Today's outlook is not nearly so optimistic. The once remarkable annual increases in life expectancy have diminished to small steps or no steps at all; the average life-span in 1900 was 47.3 years, in 1950 it was 68.9 years, and in 1982 it was 74.5 years. The average yearly increment in life-span, which was .42 in the first half of the century, slowed to .175 between 1950 and 1982 (National Center for Health Statistics, 1983). A decline in infant mortality was largely responsible for even these life expectancy increases.

Between 1900 and 1950, the life expectancy of a newborn increased by 21.6 years. The major gains during this period clearly resulted from changes in early life rather than later life. The beginning of this notable improvement in infant mortality is attributed to Jean Jacques Rousseau, who vigorously advocated a healthful approach to childcare, including the abandoning of swaddling clothes and a return to the practice of mothers breastfeeding their own infants. During the 19th century, the specialty of pediatrics emerged as an outgrowth of the philosophy of the Enlightenment, with its emphasis on humanitarianism, including the introduction of child labor laws. Infant and child mortality continued to decline with that of the adult population as living conditions improved. In 1950, 29.2 deaths occurred among every 1000 U.S. infants in their first year of life; by 1982, the number had fallen to 11.2, a decrease of 18. By comparison, the *overall* death rate during the same period fell only by 1 per 1000, from 9.6 to 8.6 (National Center for Health Statistics, 1983).

During the last several decades, our collective battle against death has advanced less and less (Figure 1). This disappointing advance of life expectancy contrasts sharply with wildly increasing expenditures on medical care. In 1960, personal health care expenditures comprised 26.9 billion dollars, or 5.3 percent of the Gross National Product (GNP) of the United States. By 1981 they had grown to 286.6 billion dollars, or 9.8 percent of the GNP; the prediction is that these costs will reach 12 percent of the GNP by 1990 (National Center for Health Statistics, 1983). The cost of treating illness is not just growing, it is outpacing the growth of the rest of the economy. The situation is the same in other Western nations. A key advisor in the Ontario government noted,

> The demands of the health service programme have become so extensive that everything else—in relative terms—has been pushed back somewhat. . . . Highways, for example, are getting less money in relative terms than was the case ten or twenty years ago. If universities— or anything else for that matter— were to have ridden up in relative terms in the same way as the health system, God knows what size of a budget we'd have in this province, and God knows where we would find the money to pay for it. (Edward Stewart, advisor to former Ontario Premier William Davis, quoted by Frum, 1984, p. 45)

The ever increasing rate of growth in medical expenditures is correlated with ever decreasing gains in life expectancy. We are spending more for smaller increases in longevity.

Causes of Death

The current primary causes of death are chronic diseases, much less easily treated than the major killers of past times (Matarazzo, 1982; Millon, 1982). According to Burish and Bradley (1983)

> the rate of death from infectious disease decreased from about 36 per 100 deaths in the year 1900 to the 1980 level of approximately 6 per 100. In contrast, the rate of death from chronic disease increased during the first 8 decades of this century from about 20 per 100 deaths to nearly 70 per 100. (p. 3)

In order of their impact, the major causes of death across all ages in 1982 (Figure 2) were heart disease, cancer, accidents, and cerebrovascular disease (National Center for Health Statistics, 1983). Suicide, pneumonia and influenza, cirrhosis of the liver, homicide, and diabetes are the next most frequent causes. Of all these causes, only pneumonia and influenza, accounting for 3 percent of the deaths, are related to infections.

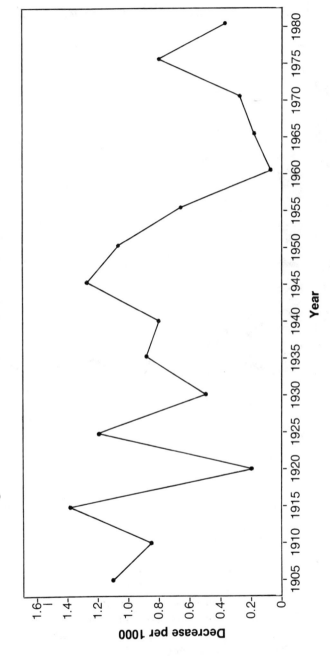

Figure 1.   Decreases in United States Death Rate from 1900 to 1980

Note. Figure is derived from data from *Health, United States, 1983* (DHHS Publication No. PHS 84-1232, p. 97) by the National Center for Health Statistics, 1983, Washington, DC: U.S. Government Printing Office and *Historical Statistics of the United States, Colonial Times to 1970, Bicentennial Edition, Part 2* (Stock No. 003-024-00120-9, p. 59) by the U.S. Bureau of the Census, 1975, Washington, DC: U.S. Government Printing Office.

11

Figure 2.   Major Causes of Death in the United States in 1982

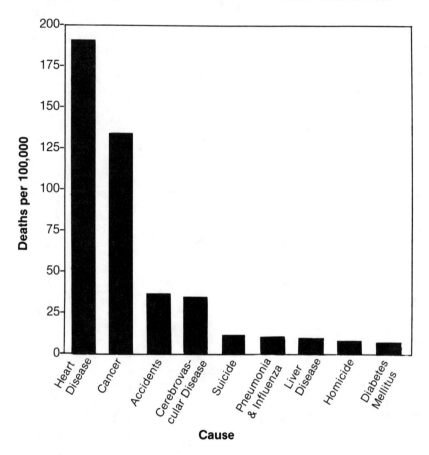

Note.   Figure is derived from data from *Health, United States, 1983*(DHHS Publication No. PHS 84-1232, p. 105) by the National Center for Health Statistics, 1983, Washington, DC: U.S. Government Printing Office.

One approach to determining how mortality can be reduced involves singling out "early deaths," that is, deaths that occur prematurely, generally defined as before 70 (4.5 years less than the average age of death). The statistics in Table 1 reflect the years of potential life that are lost as a result of the major causes of death. The table is based on statistics from a 1-year period (1975) in the United States.

**Table 1.   Years of Potential Life Lost in the
United States by Premature Death in 1975**

Cause	Total Millions of Person-years lost
Ischemic heart disease	4.5
Cancer	3.8
Motor vehicle accidents	1.8
All other accidents	1.6
Cerebrovascular diseases	0.9
Suicide	0.8
Homicide	0.8

Note.   Table adapted with permission from "Life Style and Health" by G.A. Goldsmith, 1981. In R.S. Chang (Ed.), *Preventive Health Care* (p. 36). Chicago: Year Book Medical Publishers.

Elusive "Cures"

The common response to mortality figures, as we have said earlier, is to call for more funding for research to find a cure for the diseases, despite a depressing lack of evidence that cures are imminent. Cancer provides the best example of this situation. Overall rates of cancer deaths from 1950 to 1982 have shown an increase from 125.4 to 133.3 per 100,000 people. This increase is not simply a result of the aging of the population, for the figures are adjusted to take that into account (National Center for Health Statistics, 1983). Similarly, deaths from lung cancer during the same period increased from 12.8 to 37.7 per 100,000 people (statistics adjusted for aging). These changes are generally attributed to a higher incidence of cancer, resulting from exposure to substances such as cigarette smoke and environmental pollutants.

The urgency of the need for a *cure* for cancer is felt by almost everyone—with "cure" usually defined as some pharmacological, surgical, or other invasive treatment or combination of treatments. This emphasis on cure is evident in the publicity and overwhelming public support given to Terry Fox in his attempted run across Canada in 1980 to raise money for cancer research. Terry, a 21-year-old whose right leg had been amputated because of cancer, eventually succumbed to a recurrence in his lungs before he made it much more than halfway across the country. He nevertheless raised 23.3 million dollars (or a dollar for every man, woman, and child in Canada) during his journey. The money was specifically designated by Terry and the Canadian Cancer Society for research into finding a cure. Each year since his run, there have been anniversary runs in thousands of communities across Canada, raising a further 10.5 million dollars in the first 4 years. In 1985, another young, one-legged cancer victim, Steve Fonyo, completed his own cross-country run, raising millions more. No other fund-raising campaign has been greeted so enthusiastically, no doubt because the hope for a cancer cure strikes a responsive chord in most people.

Yet cures remain elusive in cancer research. Even the meaning of "cure" has been changed to fit the unpleasant facts of the disease. The word is now understood to mean a 5-year survival rate after diagnosis (Haybittle, 1983). Despite claims of better success in treatment, it is clear that except in the instance of a few particular and generally rare cancers, such as Hodgkin's Disease and certain lymphomas, substantial gains have not been made. Earlier diagnosis may simply be starting the survival clock sooner (Bush, 1984). Using breast cancer as an example, Bush noted that women diagnosed early would automatically be more likely to survive the 5 years even without treatment. After 20 or 30 years, cancer patients are still more likely to die of their disease than are members of the normal population of the same age. In any case, earlier diagnosis is frequently not early enough: By the time most cancers are discovered, they have already spread to remain undetected for a time at other sites, where the tumor sequence begins anew (Bush, 1984).

The statistics demonstrate that cancer is not cured much more now than it was a generation ago. Changes in 5-year survival rates seem small when one considers that they reflect the aggregate impact of earlier detection, better surgical techniques, and the combined efforts of X-ray and chemotherapy advances. For endometrial cancers diagnosed between 1960 and 1963, the 5-year survival rate was 73 percent; between 1970 and 1973, it was 81 percent. Similar, modest changes are evident for numerous other cancers during the same period: breast cancer—from 63 percent to 68 percent; cervical cancer—from 58 percent to 64 percent; bladder cancer—from 53 percent to 61 percent; prostate cancer—from 50 percent to 63 percent; colonic cancer—from 43 percent to 49 percent (National Cancer Institute, 1981).

The message from cancer research seems clear: Primary prevention is the first line of defense. It is also worth noting that the emphasis on cancer cure is misplaced, if the intention is to increase longevity: "The *eradication* of cancer would add only one to two years to human life expectancy as compared with about ten years for all forms of arteriosclerosis" (Blumenthal, 1978, p. 21). By comparison, research with potentially much more dramatic and much broader consequences, that of the mechanisms of aging, has not received serious attention.

With the remaining leading causes of death, from diseases to accidents and suicide, one is again drawn to the conclusion that the focus must be on altering lifestyles toward health-promoting behavior (Belloc & Breslow, 1972). This conclusion is particularly compelling in the light of the impact of accidents and suicide on mortality figures. If, for example, every person in North America wore seatbelts and alcohol-impaired driving were reduced, it is estimated that deaths and injuries due to automobile accidents could be reduced by 50 percent (Lalonde, 1974). Yet seatbelts are worn by about 1 out of 7 U.S. drivers (Slovic, Lichtenstein, & Fischhoff, 1980), and alcohol impairment has been implicated in between 30 and 80 percent of all traffic accidents (Lalonde, 1974; McCarroll & Haddon, 1962; Myers, Taljaard, & Penman, 1977). Similarly, about 76 percent of mouth and throat cancers are attributable to the combined impact of smoking and alcohol consumption (Rothman & Keller, 1972). In other words, about 15 out of every 20 such cancers could be prevented by eliminating these exposures.

The reality of medical research is that most modern diseases do not have cures and are not likely to in the near future. Thomas (1977) pointed out that medicine has developed only halfway technologies—that research has developed the beginning of insight into the underlying processes in diseases, but until that insight is complete, medicine has to deal with illnesses at great cost and considerable waste. He emphasized that knowledge does not yet exist to rid us of diseases, even when we use broad screening to find them at earlier stages. His call is for research to elucidate the *mechanisms* of major diseases; this is a shift in emphasis from the perennial call for research to find cures, and is, as we shall discuss later, an important aspect of the preventive approach. But it is also necessary to ensure that the shift from cure to causality is more than a change within biomedical research. The scope of investigation requires broadening to explore the role of human behavior in health and illness. Perhaps the public's disillusionment with the search for cures will be the primary force toward a preventive approach to disease.

MULTIPLE CAUSATION OF DISEASE

Current scientific understanding of etiology has progressed little beyond the realization that illness is the result of more than a single pathogen in a healthy organism. Multiple causality is generally invoked in discussion of the complexities of current chronic diseases and environmental and lifestyle threats to health. But the presence of multiple determinants should not be overlooked for even simple diseases, such as the common cold. Ader (1977) summarized susceptibility to disease as including (1) the presence of a pathogenic agent, (2) the individual's vulnerability to a particular disease, which may be genetically determined, (3) whether the individual's perception of the psychosocial environment leads her to experience stress, and (4) the individual's ability to cope.

King (1974) discussed the complexity of susceptibility to disease with respect to only a few hypothesized causal factors:

> There are some intriguing correlations of various types of air pollution with the aggravation, at least, of certain acute and chronic diseases, such that the assumption of a relationship can be reasonably made. . . . The tradition of medical inquiry focusing on single causes for specific diseases has encouraged attempts to relate specific air pollutants, such as sulfur dioxide, to a specific disease. Such efforts have failed. It is probable that the SO_2 in the air must occur in a particular concentration and in certain combinations of humidity, temperature, and particulate size if it is to reach the vulnerable level of the respiratory tract. It may be that even then an adverse effect would only occur when the pulmonary field was already prepared for the insult by underlying disease or genetic predisposition. Measuring the level of oxides of sulfur in the ambient air and correlating that with any specific disease yields inconclusive findings . . . [yet] the association of sulfur dioxide and particulate pollution with serious increases in mortality and morbidity in a few specific disasters seems inescapable. (p. 243)

He noted further that the body may respond in nonspecific ways to a variety of insults, and tissue receptivity to diseases from inhaled agents may be enhanced by genetic predisposition, preexisting disease, or chronic cellular irritation from allergic or incidental occupational influences, fatigue, dietary or smoking indiscretions, stress, or age.

Attempts to sort out these relationships through simple, correlational studies can be misleading because they seldom take a sufficient number of variables into account and because correlational results cannot in themselves establish causality. Therefore, such studies lead to unproductive stalemates in policy arguments:

> Those who believe there is high risk from low exposures to environmental pollutants lobby with vigor for restrictive stan-

dards, standards which may be far beyond those necessary to protect human health. The industrial sector which contributes to much of the atmospheric and water pollution can similarly argue that no clear evidence has been developed which conclusively incriminates the current level of pollution. (King, 1974, p. 255)

Yet as Milsum (1980) pointed out, the type of research required to confirm causality is ethically difficult, if not impossible, involving as it would randomly assigned test and control groups, followed for several years, with specific lifestyle changes assigned to subjects who would be unlikely to be genuinely motivated to change. Converging evidence from various sources, some naturalistic and correlational, some analogue or animal experiments, is often the best that can be hoped for before undertaking trial interventions.

BEHAVIORAL CHANGE IN PREVENTION AND TREATMENT

Prevention of disease through behavioral and environmental change is the most promising means of controlling the chronic diseases prevalent in Western societies. Yet behavioral research has only recently been recognized as central to health programs. In a discussion of smoking, David Hamburg, president of the Carnegie Corporation, expounded on the historical emphases in research funding:

> In the past, support was given to epidemiological studies. More recently, money was given out for some biomedical research, and then for some behavioral research. But the behavioral approach has never been given "flagship" status, and people working in the field have never had the sense they are part of a vanguard that is working to solve the problem. (Quoted by Mervis, 1984, p. 7)

Some of the research issues that the newly created Institute for the Study of Smoking Behavior and Policy, Harvard University (funded by the Carnegie Corporation), plans to address now that they *have* been given flagship status are (1) the development of individual patterns of smoking and quitting and the demographics behind such patterns; (2) the social history of smoking, including the influence of peers, the role of non-smokers, and the social environment; (3) beliefs about smoking; (4) individual variables, including genetics, personality, and environment; (5) the relative effectiveness of various therapies and strategies for self-management; (6) the pharmacology of smoking and the nature of compensation for a change in smoking patterns; (7) effects of information and education campaigns; (8) the role of advertising; (9) the impact of price and differential taxation; and (10) regulatory alternatives in a variety of settings (Mervis, 1984). Such a comprehensive approach is the polar opposite to the medical model's engineering approach. The aim of the Harvard Institute is to develop an understanding of the complex interaction of influences on behavior, behavior itself, and illness, with a view to prevention of illness through alteration of illness-promoting behaviors.

The potential for improvement through behavioral and environmental change is evident. Among the best known current areas of investigation that may bear on mortality are (1) the role of elevated stress in the development of a variety of disorders, from cardiovascular disease to cancer and peptic ulcers, (2) the impact of the environment on the development of various cancers, and (3) the role of diet and exercise in such chronic diseases as coronary disease, hypertension, and cancers. There is more than sufficient epidemiological evidence to identify some populations at risk and to establish probable precursors to the development of these diseases. Nevertheless, medical researchers have rejected behavioral change as a technique for prevention, pointing to the lack of specific one-to-one causal relationships, the complexity of behavioral interventions, and the lack of technology for manipulation of behavior as significant roadblocks (Leventhal & Hirschman, in press).

Health care treatment has shifted somewhat in emphasis as an indirect result of mortality changes, but not, unfortunately, toward primary prevention. Partly because of the success in reducing infectious causes of death and because of advances in treatment of disease, we are keeping alive chronically ill and terminally ill patients longer. The Western population increasingly consists of aging and ailing individuals, and attention has of necessity turned toward the quality of life of such patients. This evolution in the population is reflected in the use of nursing homes: In 1963 there were 445,600 residents 65 years of age or older in nursing homes in the United States, or 25.4 per 1,000 people. By 1977 the total had grown to 1,126,000, representing 47.9 per 1,000, a proportionate increase of almost 100 percent (National Center for Health Statistics, 1983).

Low Back Pain

An illustration of the challenges of chronic disease is provided in the problem of chronic low back pain, which accounts for expenditures of 50 billion dollars a year in the United States, representing the most costly medical condition (Dengerink & Bakker, 1983). Yet medical attention is little help in most such cases. In 60 to 78 percent of patients who suffer low back pain, X rays and a thorough orthopedic examination fail to find any evidence of a physical condition that could cause the pain (Loeser, 1980). X-ray evaluations have been found to be of no diagnostic value in cases of nontraumatic backache, though they are routinely prescribed in about 25 percent of cases (Rockey, Tompkins, Wood, & Wolcott, 1978). Medical treatments, from surgery to injections, are correspondingly ineffective in the majority of instances (Melzack & Wall, 1982). In contrast to traditional medical approaches, the most effective means of treating these problems do not emphasize elimination of pain (Turk, Meichenbaum, & Genest, 1983). Instead, change is aimed at increasing activity levels and emotional adjustment and decreasing "pain behavior," the pattern of dependence on family and the health-care system in which pain becomes the central focus of the patient's life, leading to social isolation and overuse of drugs. Treatments of this sort provide some of the best examples of a multidimensional conception of health put into practice. Pain clinics have been developed to make use of the skills of a variety of medical and nonmedical therapists, who work together with the aim not of curing disease, but of improving health status (Block, 1982; von Baeyer & Genest, 1985).

An anecdote underscores the value of alternative treatment and preventive approaches to back pain. For several years both authors suffered chronic low back pain. Treatments prescribed and used over those years ranged from bedrest and chiropractic treatments to muscle relaxants, with varying degrees of temporary relief. Although some physicians were then recommending exercise to treat back pain, we were unaware of it and none of our physicians ever suggested it. Then both of us joined the current fitness trend: One began swimming and working out with weights regularly, and the other began practicing yoga and later switched to working with weights. The rewarding side effect to becoming trimmer and fitter was the disappearance of back pain which, even several years later, reappears only during infrequent backsliding into sedentary ways. Our gloating to family and friends revealed similar discoveries by others: one, a "noncompliant" patient who out of terror refused surgery to fuse some of his vertebrae and another who had worn a backbrace and curtailed normal physical activity for several years to limit painful episodes. Both have achieved and maintained normal levels of comfort and mobility for several years by becoming and remaining very active and fit. Neither had been prescribed muscle development through an active lifestyle as an antidote to back pain, though both had seen numerous professionals in the course of their search for relief. Even today, when the benefits of exercise for back problems are more widely known, we continue to come across many individuals for whom it was never prescribed until a friend or nonprofessional made the recommendation.

Cancer

Cancer provides another illustration of the need for a shift in etiolog-ical and treatment approaches. Recent cancer research emphasizes the multiplicity of causal factors; for cancer to develop in the human body, a series of rare events must occur. Development of the disease can be averted by the body's defense mechanisms at several stages (Rensberger, 1984). In light of this, the improbability of getting cancer seems over-whelming, but the fact that one out of four people eventually succumbs indicates that exposure to the causes must be common and persistent (Rensberger, 1984). To understand why some people develop cancer while others do not, we must look at a wide range of factors. Diet, for example, has been implicated. Blonston (1984) cites a Norwegian study that found the incidence of most forms of lung cancer to be six times higher among those whose diets were low in Vitamin A, compared to those whose diets were rich in Vitamin A. Deaths from cancer of all types, and from lung and digestive system cancers in particular, have similarly been found to be lower among Mormons, Seventh-Day Adventists, and members of the Reorganized Church of Jesus Christ of Latter-Day Saints (McEvoy & Land, 1981). These denominations discourage the use of tobacco, alcohol, and drinks containing caffeine and encourage well-balanced diets with whole grains, fruits, vegetables, and moderation in eating of meat.

Other work on cancer has stressed the interaction of factors involved in the development of tumors (e.g., Broitman, Vitale, & Gottlieb, 1983). Rothman and Keller (1972), for example, found evidence for a synergis-tic effect of alcohol and smoking in the production of mouth and throat cancers. Each of these substances individually increases the risk of such neoplasms: Either daily consumption of 1.6 oz of alcohol or smoking more than 40 cigarettes will more than double the risk. But combined, the effect is not simply additive; the risk for people who drink *and* smoke in these quantities is *15.5 times* the risk run by a nonsmoking non-drinker. Behavioral research has also emphasized the complexity of cancer etiology. Although the evidence is still far from definitive, certain psychological events and dispositions appear to interact with the other risk factors predisposing a person to cancer appearance and growth (Cunningham, 1985).

The examples of low back pain and cancer demonstrate that an approach to chronic disease based *solely* on physical medicine is no longer functional. Multiple elements interact to cause disease, and multi-ple treatment modalities for alleviation of chronic disabilities have begun to be advocated and practiced (Matarazzo, 1982). These modifications to the practice of traditional clinical medicine and the developing trend toward primary prevention through lifestyle modification offer the most promising avenues toward increased health in the population.

A PREVENTIVE PERSPECTIVE

Prevention has traditionally been subdivided into four categories: (1) *primary prevention*—interventions to prevent disease (e.g., vaccination, environmental and behavioral changes, or genetic interventions); (2) *secondary prevention*—early interventions that may include or lead to disease treatment, but also serve to minimize its seriousness (e.g., screening for early detection of breast cancer or venereal disease); (3) *tertiary prevention*—interventions to minimize the complications of established disease, which may constitute clinical medicine (e.g., dietary or insulin therapy for diabetes, which helps prevent organ damage from the disease); and (4) *quaternary prevention*—rehabilitation efforts that may discourage deterioration after the disease has been treated, with an emphasis on decreasing disability and increasing coping ability (e.g., speech or physical therapy or self-help support groups for patients who have suffered strokes or spinal cord injuries).

These traditional categories are broad enough to encompass an ambitious approach like that of the Harvard Institute, mentioned earlier, yet they have rarely before been interpreted this widely. Although this four-stage, preventive effort constitutes part of the practice of medicine, health promotion in this sense has not been in the forefront of medical endeavor. Many medical professionals believe that prevention is not a part of their normal responsibility because it requires intervention over and above the medical treatment solicited by a sick person from a health professional (Susser, 1975). They willingly relegate modification and control of behavior to governmental rules, group sanctions, or individual self-discipline (Leventhal, Safer, & Panagis, 1983). Psychologists are increasingly filling the void in advocating preventive actions.

Kaplan (1984) has provided perhaps the definitive analysis of the four basic assumptions in the clinical psychologist's practice of health promotion efforts: (1) Behaviors increase the risk of certain chronic diseases; (2) changes in behaviors can reduce the probability of risk of certain diseases; (3) behavior can easily be changed; and (4) behavioral interventions are cost effective. The regrettable difficulty is that the bases for these assumptions are somewhat shaky.

Arguments for large-scale measures outside of the realm of clinical medicine to promote better health in the population have been hampered by a lack of clear-cut evidence supporting their efficacy. Partly because research efforts and clinical medicine have been cure-directed, insufficient evidence exists to convince governments and the public of the potential of prevention. Even when there is good correlational evidence for a relationship between behavioral factors and disease states (for instance, the relationship between smoking and lung cancer), the function of the pathogen on the altered biological state of an organism may be challenged because it is not fully understood. This is particularly true if a large lobby group like the tobacco industry is invested in showing that the relationship has not been conclusively established. Similarly, the rudimentary state of knowledge concerning how to motivate individuals to change their behaviors from illness-producing to health-promoting and how to sustain such changes makes behavioral programs less attractive. The difficulty in motivating people to change is related to the lack of concrete evidence or the presence of conflicting evidence for causality; people are often unwilling to act without guarantees of positive outcome, especially if the actions are difficult or unpleasant.

Thus, three basic lines of research contribute to the emergence of a preventive orientation: (1) examination of pathogenic action on the human organism for particular disease states, (2) inquiry into behaviors and their associated risk of illness, and (3) the search for ways to encourage people to practice health-promoting behaviors.

Pathogenic Action of Hypothesized Causes

One of the means of establishing the etiology of an illness is the determination of biological pathogenesis. The origin of many major disorders is extremely complex and is based, as we have noted, upon the interaction of numerous factors over extended time frames. Consequently, despite rapid developments in such research as the biological mechanisms involved in cancer, comprehensive or conclusive explanations are unlikely to be forthcoming immediately.

It is not necessary, however, to await final word on the action of pathogens before instituting trial interventions based upon strong hypotheses. Lalonde (1974) recognized the need for a balance between intervention programs based on admittedly incomplete, but nevertheless strong, knowledge bases and continued efforts to resolve the causal and pathogenic relationships between health and such factors as smoking, weight, alcohol, fitness, and pollution.

Behavior and Risk

Empirical support for the relationship of smoking to lung cancer or alcohol use to liver diseases and traffic fatalities seems overwhelming, but the hypothesized relationships between diet, exercise, and heart disease, for instance, have less support (Friedewald, 1985; Inter-Society Commission for Heart Disease Resources, 1970). Establishing clear links between long-term or delayed behavioral factors (e.g., personality, childhood stress) and illness has proven even more difficult. Nor have changes in behaviors such as diet and exercise patterns been clearly shown to improve morbidity and mortality.

In his review of eight prospective studies on modifying dietary and exercise patterns in order to prevent heart disease, Kaplan (1984) noted a curious, unexplained finding in each of the studies: Mortality averaged over all causes was not affected by the experimental interventions. Reductions in deaths due to heart disease are associated with increases in deaths from other causes—in most cases, cancer. Four other studies reviewed by Kaplan (1984) reported that changes in dietary cholesterol had no impact on deaths due to heart disease. Though some intervention studies, for example the Lipid Research Clinics Program (1984), have demonstrated success in the reduction of serum cholesterol, the effects have been on the causes of death rather than the death rate. Kaplan's examination of the evidence led him to conclude that "the literature demonstrates that behavioral interventions may have modest rather than strong effects. Further, the long-term success rates for most interventions tend to be disappointing" (p. 761).

There is a danger, Matarazzo (1982) noted, in promising too much too soon, for if one expects miracles, then merely finding moderate relationships—even if these represent substantial advances over existing knowledge—can then seem disheartening. Given the early and methodologically rudimentary level of today's etiological studies, combined with the complexity of the causality under scrutiny, it is less surprising that the effects are modest than that they are obtained at all. Simple, behavioral programs are proving not to be the panacea that some had hoped for; yet they have pointed the way toward more sophisticated investigations and interventions.

Promotion of Health-Related Behaviors

One of the essential assumptions in the area of preventive medicine is the belief that once a link between certain behaviors and the risk of illness is established, those behaviors can then be changed, thereby lessening the risk of disease. Although behaviorally oriented clinical psychologists have demonstrated the success of their methods in managing difficult problems, the research to date indicates modest-to-disappointing results in long-term behavior change related to health (Kaplan, 1984; Stunkard, 1977). The high health risks of behaviors such as cigarette consumption, alcoholism, overeating, and dangerous driving are clear, yet people are slow to change their behavior.

> Year after year, the Surgeon General reports that smoking is the largest single preventable cause of illness and premature death in the United States. Successive reports from the U.S. Office of Smoking and Health have documented the role of cigarettes in causing various types of cancer, cardiovascular disease and chronic lung disease. *It is estimated that 340,000 people die each year because they smoke, the same number as the combined total of our dead during World War II and the Vietnam war.* (Mervis, 1984, p. 7, emphasis added)

In the United States injuries have replaced infections as the leading cause of death and disability among children and young adults, but research studies indicate that it is very difficult to influence parents to alter the environment to make it safer for children (Baker, O'Neill, & Karpf, 1984). Kane (1974a) suggests that primary prevention efforts may best be directed somewhere other than at individuals—making safer cars, for instance. Evidence indicates that passive tactics for accident reduction, tasks that require little effort (for example, turning the temperature of the hot water heater down or using airbags in cars) are more effective in accident prevention than promotion of active behaviors (such as monitoring a baby's bath water temperature or using seatbelts [Baker et al., 1984]). Passive tactics, however, are seen as a challenge to individual freedoms by those who argue that the inclusion of airbags in one's automobile, for example, or fluoridation of one's drinking water ought to be a matter of choice. Allman (1985) comments on the irrationality of most people in evaluating and acting upon the hazards in their lives:

> The general public . . . smokes billions of cigarettes a year while banning an artificial sweetener because of a one-in-a-million chance that it might cause cancer; the same public . . . eats meals full of fat, flocks to cities prone to earthquakes, and goes hang gliding while it frets about pesticides in foods, avoids the ocean for fear of sharks, and breaks into a cold sweat on airline flights. (p. 31-32)

Kane (1974a) further commented on the irony that the cry for stricter controls on environmental pollution coexists with continued smoking of cigarettes. He noted that people seem to depend on external controls to change their behavior. Measures such as increased taxation of cigarettes, laws regulating saturated fat in foodstuffs, and safety devices in cars are, however, severely impeded by industrial lobbies and the cultural emphasis on individual freedoms.

Interestingly, the lobbying efforts of some proponents of healthier lifestyles have recently overcome stiff opposition and resulted in more external motivation and support for positive changes. A strong antismoking movement has, for example, led to legislation requiring San Francisco businesses to provide smoke-free environments for workers. Comparable legislation is pending elsewhere, and some managers have voluntarily instituted similar programs. Legislation requiring automobile drivers and passengers to use seatbelts has also been enacted in many jurisdictions. The results of these new laws are consistent with Kane's emphasis on external controls. The amount of increased use of seatbelts has been dependent upon enforcement. In Puerto Rico, for example—the first U.S. jurisdiction to pass a mandatory seatbelt law—there was no enforcement and the usage rate climbed from 4 percent to only 6 percent. By contrast, in Ontario, where enforcement was intense, use of seatbelts soared from 17 percent to 77 percent a month after the law was passed, but later dropped back to 48 percent (Body Count, 1984). Similarly, alcohol-related accidents are affected by stiffer laws and their level of enforcement (Votey, 1984).

Motivation problems are also found in the reaction of people to exercise as a means of promoting health. Exercise, in the form of sustained increases in large muscle and cardiopulmonary activity (Caspersen, Powell, & Christenson, 1985), is widely considered to reduce cardiovascular risk and enhance quality of life. Nevertheless, polls indicate that roughly two-thirds of U.S. citizens do not exercise regularly and 45 percent may not exercise at all, even those cardiac patients who have been advised of the potential benefits to their health (Martin & Dubbert, 1982). Patients' adherence to clinically prescribed exercise programs is very low; one-half or fewer continue to exercise in individual or structured programs, after 3 to 6 months, despite almost universally favorable attitudes toward exercise (Martin & Dubbert, 1982).

In recent years, stronger public awareness of the links between fitness and health may have begun to move us from the sofas and television sets out to the racquet courts and swimming pools. The most recent Canada Fitness Survey found a 23 percent increase in sports participation in the 5-year period from 1976 to 1981, to over 75 percent of the population (Statistics Canada, 1983). Unfortunately, few individuals are considered to be actively engaged in activities at a minimum level sufficient for cardiovascular benefits (Dishman, Sallis, & Orenstein, 1985). Participation in such "exercise" rose by just 3 percent during this period. U.S. increases are generally smaller: During the decade ending in 1980, nationwide participation in all types of physical activity (not just that constituting "exercise") increased by only 4 to 14 percent, depending upon the type of assessment unit used, to a total of about 50 percent of the population (Dishman et al., 1985).

Milsum (1980) discussed the concepts of *threshold for change*—the point where enough awareness, appreciation, and concern has accumulated that one actually initiates changes—and Brown's *quantitative model for behavior change,* which involves five stages, each of which must be fulfilled before the next becomes possible—(1) awareness of risk, (2) acceptance that the risk applies personally, (3) integration of the knowledge into personal self-image, (4) effort (a decision to change behavior and the instigation of change), and (5) application of knowledge to produce change. These concepts recognize the complex, interactive nature of the various factors leading to behavior change and suggest the need for an integrated, comprehensive approach to motivate individuals to adapt lifestyles to promote health and prevent illness.

Lifestyle and lifestyle change have become a concern of many professional groups, thereby broadening the focus of both analysis and treatment of health problems. This complexity is reflected in developments such as the Health Hazard Appraisal (HHA) scale (Robbins & Hall, 1970; Sadusk & Robbins, 1968), which is a comprehensive instrument for assessing health risk on the basis of physiological, environmental, psychological, and social factors. The HHA assesses current health risks and estimates lowered risk levels arising from potential alterations in a person's behavior. Thus the HHA can be used to encourage healthful changes in lifestyle to prevent illness. Milsum (1980) claimed that the primary contributions of the HHA are that (1) it creates a "teachable moment" between a client and health counselor, with an emphasis on counseling rather than prescribing; (2) it encourages "self-responsibility" for adopting a lifestyle promoting better health; and (3) it sensitizes the counselor to lifestyle concerns, thereby encouraging her to model healthier patterns and to become involved in the development of follow-up community resources. A variety of similar instruments have become readily available, frequently with computer scoring and report-generating capabilities (Hettler, Janty, & Moffat, 1977). In addition to having clinical utility, they can serve as tools for further research on risk and assessment of the impact of risk-reduction programs (Goetz, Duff, & Bernstein, 1980). As we note in Chapter 8, changes in lifestyle-associated risk are possible, though efforts in this area are in their infancy and the issues are exceedingly complex.

PSYCHOLOGICAL FACTORS IN MEDICAL TREATMENT

It is becoming clear that any medical treatment is not simply a matter of the imposition of a physician's or other therapist's recommendations upon the patient. Instead, treatment involves *transactions* between therapist and patient and depends for its success upon a positive relationship.

The role of the health practitioner—from shaman to surgeon—is as ancient as society. Despite their limited effects on mortality and morbidity, healers have been revered because they meet the human need for responders to stress and invoke expectations of relief (Eisenberg, 1977; McKeown, 1971a). It has been noted that a primary element in traditional healing is the capacity of the healer to invoke changes that are produced by belief, ceremony, and expectation (Eisenberg, 1977; Frank, 1974). Norton (1982) refers to medicine as an "art" rather than a science in the sense that some people are better at it than others, relying as they must on psychologically creative elements in the absence of firm scientific answers to medical problems. However, Eisenberg (1977) has pointed out that modern medical practitioners have separated the element of "magic" from the "scientific," thereby losing the important interpersonal care aspect of medicine. Haney (1971) commented on the fact that modern physicians have a collegiate background in the sciences, rather than the humanities, and they are thus trained to make clear-cut, scientific decisions. When confronted with the need to make decisions about real people, where the situation is naturally ambiguous, physicians may be unprepared. They have been trained to find signs of disease and to do something about them; they have not been taught how to deal with such problems as having patients invested in being ill (e.g., to avoid responsibility or stressful situations), who might therefore mislead a physician or overinterpret the physician's response. Successful treatment, physicians are taught, is based solely on the things prescribed, rather than on working with the psychophysiological responses to the physician, elements of the patient-therapist relationship. Further, patient adherence to treatment regimens and appointment-keeping (discussed in more detail in Chapter 2) has been shown to be enhanced by a positive interaction between physician and patient (Litt & Cuskey, 1984; Sackett & Haynes, 1976), something all too often missing in the relationship between patient and physician.

Both Eisenberg and Frank encourage the physician's role as a "magician." This role makes it more likely that patients will reveal their problems and life stresses to the doctor, thereby increasing the physician's understanding of their illnesses. In support of this thesis, Eisenberg pointed out that three-quarters of people with minor illnesses treat themselves, whereas the other quarter seek care. Those who seek care are therefore responding to something more than physical discomfort. Eisenberg also cited Mechanic's (1972) finding that disproportionately large numbers of people who complain of illness are under stress. It may be because the physician has largely lost the role of magician that most patients with emotional problems do not confide in the physician, but instead report the physical symptoms (Wiggins, 1976). Thus, patients with disorders arising from emotional stressors may be routed through unpleasant, costly treatments and searches for physical causes of the physical symptoms arising from psychological stresses. When patients do reveal their emotional problems, physicians, untrained in psychology, frequently respond with prescriptions for psychiatric drugs that they hope will make the patients feel better.

It has frequently been reported that visits to a family physician are most often for minor conditions. Stoeckle, Zola, and Davidson (1963) described the striking differences among individuals and social groups in levels of symptoms that are necessary to lead to a decision to seek help. The majority of people visiting physicians are seeking reassurance that their problems are not serious. This majority also includes patients with emotional difficulties who report physical symptoms to their family physician (Wiggins, 1976). Eisenberg (1977) contrasted these needs with medical training in a university hospital where the opposite situation pertains; the medical student sees mainly serious cases. In fact, the emphasis on "interesting cases" leads to a curious reversal in training priorities, so that medical graduates may feel more assured in dealing with the rare and serious rather than the more frequently presented minor problems. Indeed, one new graduate, struggling in her first few days as a new member of a family practice, recently commented to the authors that she knows only "about life-and-death medicine and nothing about varicose veins and warts." Another specialist friend takes pride in being an expert on subacute sclerosing panencephalitis (a rare form of inflammation of the brain), yet this exotic disorder is so rare he has seen only one case in over a decade of practice. It has been found that the conditions most likely to be investigated by inquiry and tests are those that are least likely to exist according to base rate data. Conversely, the more frequently the disorder actually occurs, the less likely it is to be investigated (Olbrisch, 1977).

Eisenberg concluded that medical schools need to stress the intellectual challenges and satisfactions of the ability to understand the psychophysiological complexity of illness and the compassion and skill needed for primary care. He noted that specialists also should be taught the supportive aspects of care. Although specialized care deals with different biological problems, effective communication with patients is an important ingredient in management of those problems (Eisenberg, 1977; Mace, 1971).

An early report concerning the place of psychology in medical training from the committee of the American Psychological Association (Franz, 1913) revealed a basic lack of understanding of the goals of psychology as a profession on the part of those responsible for training medical personnel and a corresponding dearth of psychological sophistication in medical training programs. Though much has changed since 1913, Franz's report indicates how firmly the orientation of medical training is rooted in long-established traditions (Cassell, 1979; McKeown, 1971a). Nevertheless, changes are being undertaken. Cassell (1979) pointed out that in the United States the National Board of Medical Examiners has become concerned about finding ways to test interpersonal skills of new physicians. New behavioral science material has been introduced into their examinations, and psychologists are playing increasing roles in teaching hospitals (Thompson & Matarazzo, 1984). Cassell (1979) cautioned, however, that change occurs very slowly in medicine: "Whenever fundamental new concepts enter medicine, existing concepts must change and new tools for actions must be formed because medicine is, ultimately, a profession of action" (p. 729).

At issue is not only the physician's lack of training in interpersonal skills but also the problems caused by burgeoning malpractice suits and third-party payment of health-care costs. Eisenberg (1977) emphasized that the patient's need for attention, sympathy, and concern may be at odds with the physician's concern for time, money, and protection from malpractice suits through accuracy of diagnosis and treatment. In medical schools the premium is on diagnostic sophistication and management of life-threatening situations rather than on supportive care. In clinical practice, third-party reimbursement schemes make *procedures* profitable and penalize time spent listening and explaining. The danger of malpractice suits makes it safer to use every test that might be at all relevant rather than focusing on what is likely to be best, in all respects, for the health of the patient.

SUMMARY

Extended life expectancy and reduced number of deaths from the diseases endemic to modern Western society will arise from preventive efforts, aimed at promoting healthy lifestyles, rather than miracle medical cures (at least in the near future). Health psychologists must catalyze the medical profession (especially medical educators) and the public into recognizing the need for health-promoting activities and attention to psychological factors in the genesis of illness.

Motivation and adherence to health regimens are the major determinants in the success or lack of success in preventive and health-care interventions. Because attention to these behavioral components necessarily underlies all psychological contributions to the fields of health promotion and of health care, the following chapters will examine these elements more closely.

Chapter Two

Adherence

Adherence is an issue that cuts across most disciplines and pursuits of health-care professionals. Health-care interventions assume that the patient will actually carry out prescribed programs. Unfortunately, this assumption is frequently unwarranted: The incidence of noncompliance with prescribed regimens to treat disease or promote health is notoriously high. People do not take their prescribed drugs, cardiac and pulmonary patients do not exercise to prevent further deterioration of their health, and people everywhere refuse to use their seatbelts. In this chapter, we will describe the problem of adherence to health-care regimens, indicate some of the contributing factors, and review approaches that have tried to improve adherence.

THE PROBLEM OF ADHERENCE

The medical control of hypertension has been possible for years and requires only that patients take their medicine faithfully. Dilantin can reduce the occurrence of seizures in most epileptics, often to zero, but they must take the drug on schedule. Why, then, do epileptics still have fits and hypertensives still have strokes? No matter how efficacious a medication, it can do no good in the bottle. Getting medicine into the patient is a behavioral event, subject to behavioral principles. (Norton, 1982, p. 136)

Although Norton may be accused of oversimplifying the treatment of hypertension and epilepsy, his point is legitimate. There are effective medical treatments available for many health problems, yet those treatments do not have their full effect because they are not adequately carried out. Even the experimental testing of treatments is founded on the premise that the regimens are actually followed. If a new drug fails to provide relief in an experimental trial, but has not been taken on schedule by many of the patients in that trial, the net information gained is zero; the experimenter cannot tell whether the lack of results arose from failure of the ingredients in the drug or failure to achieve therapeutic doses over sufficient time.

Nonadherence is a relatively recent problem for medicine. Prior to the 1800s, many treatments were administered rather than prescribed. From trephining (removal of a circular disk of bone from the skull, carried out in ancient Egypt to allow evil spirits to escape the body) to bloodletting, interventions used force when necessary to ensure their effect (Davidson, 1976). Since the change toward a prescriptive form of treatment, patients have fortunately had more choice in the matter. This freedom, however, leads to reasons for concern. Adherence is generally dismal and the consequences of nonadherence are frequently serious or even fatal. This pervasive problem is one of the most important sources of physicians' dissatisfaction with their profession (Ort, Ford, & Liske, 1964).

Rates and Consequences of Nonadherence

An average noncompliance rate of 30 percent has been commonly reported in varied settings with different populations and problems although the rates vary widely from one investigation to another—as much as from 7 to 80 percent (Blackwell, 1976; Haynes, 1982; Sackett, 1976). Turk et al. (1983) summarized information from several sources, noting that 20 to 50 percent of patients fail to keep appointments, 20 to 80 percent make errors in taking medication, 25 to 60 percent stop taking medications too soon, and 20 to 80 percent drop out of long-term treatments. The range of compliance in each instance is dependent upon a variety of factors— the type of program prescribed, patient population, type of problem, and so forth.

There is a tendency on the part of care providers to "offer" treatment advice, leaving it to the patient to choose whether or not to follow the advice and shrugging off nonadherence as a matter of individual choice. This attitude may be a self-protective response, both for the psychotherapist whose client fails to return after one appointment and for the family physician who feels unable to monitor medication usage of all patients.

But the potential consequences of nonadherence make such an attitude border on callous and irresponsible. The problem is illustrated by a report from Vincent (1971), who followed patients treated for glaucoma. These patients were warned that "they must use eye drops three times a day or they would go blind" (p. 511). Nevertheless, only 42 percent of the patients adhered sufficiently to prevent complications. Once nonadhering patients had become legally blind in one eye, compliance in this subgroup increased only to 58 percent. Similar reports from other investigators drive the point home. Watkins and associates (Watkins, Roberts, Williams, Martin, & Coyle, 1967) reported that 58 percent of diabetics made errors in the use of insulin. Of their sample, 21 percent erred by injecting themselves with half the required amount or twice the necessary insulin by using the wrong scale on the syringe. Rates of error were similar in patients at a university clinic and those seen in private practices. Whereas one might expect that frequency of errors would decrease as patients became more familiar with the prescribed regimen, the opposite was found: Errors increased with duration of the disease. Stewart and Cluff (1972) found that up to 35 percent of patients misused medication in ways dangerous to their health.

In the context of prevention, adherence to treatment regimens is frequently essential to stopping relatively minor situations from developing into serious, potentially life-threatening illnesses. Chronic diseases such as high blood pressure and diabetes can be maintained relatively well through adherence to diet and medications. Yet treatment of such diseases suffers even worse adherence problems than treatment of acute disorders. Baseline assessments of long-term hypertension treatment at Henry Ford Hospital in Detroit, for example, found that 50 percent of the patients dropped out by the 11th month, and only 17 percent of those who still required treatment were continuing it after 5 years (Caldwell, Cobb, Dowling, & de Jongh, 1970).

Patients with insulin-dependent diabetes mellitus (IDDM) should test their blood glucose four times daily or more to properly monitor and adjust their self-treatment in order to reduce the risk of serious and life-threatening complications. Follow-up reports of diabetics trained in self-monitoring have found that only about half test themselves frequently enough to make adjustments to treatment (Gonder-Frederick, Cox, Pohl, & Carter, 1984). One investigation even found 50 percent testing themselves less than once per week (Hirsch et al., 1983). The longer diabetics have been monitoring their blood glucose levels, the less frequently they take measurements, though the need to monitor does not change (Gonder-Frederick et al., 1984).

FACTORS INFLUENCING ADHERENCE

Information on the factors influencing adherence is derived from two sources: (1) data from relatively straightforward clinical interventions, primarily from studies of appointment keeping and medication use; and (2) data from more complex, behavioral interventions. Although these two sources overlap, by and large they deal with different levels of adherence, and therefore will be dealt with separately. We will first consider information and issues related to the former, leaving the more complex topic of lifestyle changes to the section on preventive interventions (Chapter 8).

Patient Characteristics

The word most often used in medical settings to describe the problem of lack of adherence, "noncompliance," captures the patient-blaming attitude that has often characterized both writings and clinical practice (Gillum & Barsky, 1974; Stimson, 1974). Physicians frequently believe that they can predict from their patients' personalities which ones will and will not follow treatment recommendations. The evidence, however, is that these predictions are no better than chance (Caron & Roth, 1968). This conception of the problem as belonging to the patient has also led to extensive studies attempting to define personality characteristics of "noncompliers." Reviews of this literature have concluded that, other than the information that adherence is lower among psychiatric patients, no conclusions about general personality characteristics related to compliance can be drawn (Blackwell, 1976; Haynes, 1976; Stunkard, 1979). It is easy to "blame" the patient, more difficult to change the situation to enhance adherence.

Patient Attitudes and Beliefs

There have, however, been some attitudinal factors related to treatment adherence. These factors are clearly not solely the property of the patient, but result from an *interaction* among the patient, environment, and caregiver. The main thrust of this work has indicated that patients' perceptions of the problem and the treatment are critical components of adherence. In the context of behavioral interventions, Cameron (1978) put it this way:

> The important issues of therapeutic compliance and resistance reduce to two key questions. What sorts of cognitions regarding

the therapeutic process would facilitate therapeutic change (and, conversely, what sorts of cognitions would impede or preclude change)? If we can answer this first question, we are immediately faced with a second: What can we do to ensure that our clients' cognitions about the therapeutic process are positive rather than negative? (pp. 235-236)

The research literature appears to support the importance of several types of cognitions: (1) beliefs concerning the likelihood of personally succumbing to a disease; (2) perceived severity of the condition; (3) beliefs concerning the efficacy of the particular form of therapy; and (4) subjective evaluation of the feasibility and efficacy of the therapy weighed against perceived costs and disruptions involved (e.g., financial, social, physical); and (5) patients' expectations concerning the type of treatment likely to be offered (Carr & Maxim, 1983; Francis, Korsch, & Morris, 1969). Whereas *objective indices* of most of these variables (e.g., severity of disease or proven efficacy of treatment) bear little relationship to adherence, the patient's *perceptions* of them do have an impact (Becker, 1976; Francis et al., 1969).

Studies in the general medical literature reviewed by Blackwell (1976) illustrate the influence of attitudes and beliefs on adherence to prescribed medical regimens. One study found that farmers with heart disease were less likely to comply with treatment recommendations if they held beliefs incompatible with a medical intervention, such as the belief that time is all it takes to recover from any illness, or that illness is one way God shows his displeasure (Davis, 1967). Stimson (1974) noted other beliefs associated with lower adherence, such as the view that one should only take medicine when one is ill, not when one gets better (whereas complete drug regimens often require treatment well into a nonsymptomatic stage or for one's entire life), or that one's body needs a "rest" from drugs once in a while so it won't become dependent on or immune to the drugs. Similarly, Hyland, Novotny, Coyne, Travis, and Pruyser (1984) noted beliefs that can lead cancer patients to become despondent or to refuse treatment, such as the misconception that cancer progresses more rapidly when the tumor is exposed to the air, making surgery inadvisable.

Such variables are amenable to influence, if they are recognized as important. In fact, they are unwittingly influenced by health professionals and others all the time. Stimson (1974) noted, for example, that receipt of a prescription results in discussion and appraisal of the prescription between the patient and his friends. Decision-making based on this appraisal then influences treatment adherence.

A Cognitive Perspective

The patient's cognitions concerning the disease and treatment provide a unifying perspective from which to consider factors that bear on adherence (we will return later to this point in our discussion of theories). For, as we noted, the evidence strongly underscores the influence of subjective, rather than objective, factors. Modification of adherence patterns through provision of information, change in the treatment regimen, or attention to the patient-therapist relationship can all be seen as having their primary impact on the patient's belief system, which in turn determines the degree of adherence. The health belief model (Becker, 1976) has elaborated how the patient's personal beliefs affect therapeutic adherence. One of the most important considerations in adherence is communication between the caregiver and patient. If the patient's perceptions, beliefs, and attitudes are determinants of his adherence, then attempting to understand these and deal with them appropriately should help improve adherence.

From "Compliance" to "Adherence"

This view of the patient's participation in deciding the course of treatment also alters the way in which the adherence issue is phrased. The focus shifts from the traditional emphasis on the defaulting patient, exemplified by terms like "noncompliant" and "resistant," to determining what factors, under what conditions, encourage or discourage patients from following treatment regimens. To avoid identifying our discussion of this issue with a blaming perspective, we prefer the term "adherence" to "compliance." "Compliance" also has overtones of the ideal patient as an obedient recipient of instructions, whereas we prefer to consider patients as consumers (Hughes & Kennedy, 1983), people who approach health professionals with decision-making abilities, values, and ethics of their own and who make use of those in determining their actions (Janis, 1984). Consumers in the health-care system may make errors in the decision-making process (Janis, 1984), but a more independent and active role in interactions with all social institutions is increasingly valued in Western cultures.

Characteristics of the Treatment

One generalization is apt in describing aspects of treatment that are related to adherence: The more complex the treatment, the worse the adherence. A corollary is that the longer the treatment regimen continues, the lower the adherence.

In a study of a pediatric population, Francis et al. (1969) found that prescription of more than two medications or more than one treatment method (e.g., medication and diet or daily routines) reduced adherence. In another investigation, increasing the frequency of drug dosages from one to four times daily resulted in a halving of the adherence rate (Gately, 1968). Norton (1982) pointed out the important implication of such findings for general clinical practice: In prescribing a drug or any other treatment, the practitioner must consider that the potentially beneficial consequences of a more complex regimen, such as optimal dosages four times daily or use of a second drug to offset side effects of the first, may be significantly offset by the decreased likelihood that the regimen will be complied with at all.

> In practice, this means that the physician must calculate the relative *biological* advantage of a complex regimen with the *psychological* risk factors of noncompliance. . . . The physician must consider the absolute gravity of various secondary problems relative to the fact that treating them—adding medicines to the regimen—increases the risk of noncompliance and thus puts treatment of the primary problem at hazard. (Norton, 1982, p. 142)

Unfortunately, doctors and other health-care professionals, like people in general, have difficulty estimating or using probabilities in making decisions (Tversky & Kahneman, 1974) and are likely to give more weight to their subjective feelings about whether a given patient will comply than is warranted by base-rate data (Caron & Roth, 1968).

Interestingly, side effects associated with a treatment do not have an invariant impact upon adherence (Sackett & Haynes, 1976). Although psychiatric patients who stop taking their medication invoke side effects as the reason (Blackwell, 1976), for other groups side effects do not seem to be implicated in nonadherence (Norton, 1982).

Health-Care Practitioner's Behavior

There is more evidence that factors under the direct control of the health-care practitioner affect adherence than there is that patient variables do (Doyle & Ware, 1977). The general reluctance of care providers, particularly physicians, to recognize their own contributions to adherence constitutes a major obstacle to effective problem management (Blackwell, 1976). Gillum and Barsky (1974) found that whereas two-thirds of physicians attributed poor adherence to their patients' personalities, only one-quarter thought physicians might contribute to the difficulty.

An important practitioner characteristic influencing adherence is her enthusiasm concerning the treatment being recommended. There is much evidence that patient expectancy, which is affected by the practitioner's communications, influences both the potency of treatment and adherence. Placebo effects are an example of this relationship; experimental double-blind procedures were devised because of the necessity to control for the impact of the practitioner's expectancies on treatment effectiveness. Shapiro (1974) found that families who dropped out of treatment in a child guidance clinic did not differ in psychopathology from those who remained, but that their therapists' behaviors differed: Those who remained in treatment had therapists who showed more positive emotional responses, and who also had made a more optimistic initial prognosis. Similarly, Reynolds, Joyce, Swift, Tooley, and Weatherall (1965) reported better adherence and fewer side effects with a drug regimen when the therapist more actively promoted treatment.

An enthusiastic, upbeat attitude may be natural to faith healers or proponents of trendy new therapies, but it tends not to fit with the scientific skepticism and objectivity that is encouraged in other health-care practitioners. It is often thought to be unprofessional or unethical to promote faith in a therapy. Nevertheless, the empirical data are clear: If health-care practitioners persist in going to the extreme of maintaining an uncommitted, aloof stance regarding treatments that they implicitly endorse, on the other hand, by offering them to patients, they fail to capitalize on some of the most powerful aspects of the therapeutic interaction (Frank, 1974). It is important, nevertheless, to be mindful that unrealistic expectations upon initiation of a treatment may lead a patient to become discouraged and lose confidence if changes are too small or delayed. The practitioner has to be sensitive to the cognitions of the individual patient and tailor the approach accordingly (Cameron, 1978).

Practitioner-Patient Interaction

Many of the factors influencing adherence are best conceptualized as an interaction between the health-care practitioner and patient. A very simple variable that has consistently been found to bear a strong relationship to adherence is the length of time that a patient is kept waiting in the office before being seen by the physician. Davidson and Schrag (1969), for example, found that if patients were kept waiting in the office more than an hour, adherence dropped 40 percent below what it was with less than a half-hour wait.

The wait for a referral appointment also seems to make a difference. Haynes (1979) reviewed numerous studies that showed nearly double the compliance rates when referral delays were short (e.g., a few days) rather than long (e.g., a few weeks). These results are problematic for many specialty treatment centers, in which delays of several months are the rule rather than the exception.

Sackett and Haynes (1976) established that patient satisfaction is the single most important determinant of appointment-keeping and medication adherence. Numerous studies have indicated a relationship between satisfaction with treatment and the patient's interaction with the practitioners and the health-care system (Doyle & Ware, 1977).

One extensive study of 800 outpatient visits to Childrens' Hospital of Los Angeles related mothers' perceptions of the visit to aspects of the physician-family interaction (Francis et al., 1969). It is rather alarming that 24 percent of mothers were found to be "grossly dissatisfied" with the care provided. Although no significance test of the relationship was reported, the descriptive data suggest a relationship between level of satisfaction and adherence. Among those mothers who were highly satisfied, 53 percent were considered to have complied well with treatment recommendations for the next 10 days. This proportion diminished monotonically with decreasing levels of satisfaction: 43 percent for moderate satisfaction; 32 percent for moderate dissatisfaction; and 17 percent for high dissatisfaction. Specific factors associated with low adherence were also related to level of satisfaction: The extent to which a patient's expectations concerning the visit were left unmet, lack of warmth in the physician's behavior (i.e., mother defined the physician as businesslike instead of friendly), and failure to receive an explanation of the diagnosis and causal explanation of the illness all corresponded with lower adherence. Physicians who were seen as friendly, effective communicators and who conveyed an understanding of the mothers' concerns provided treatment that was rated as more satisfactory by mothers (Korsch, Gozzi, & Francis, 1968).

Along the same lines, physicians who are judged by trained observers to be more accurate in identifying the affective meaning of patients' body movements (e.g., the anxiety indicated by hands held close to the chest, or the exasperation of a heavy sigh and shoulder shrug) are rated by patients as more caring and sensitive than physicians with lower levels of this skill (DiMatteo, Taranta, Friedman, & Prince, 1980). A study of 24 physicians in audiotaped interactions with 140 patients found a high frequency of patient-centered behavior by the physician to be related to significantly higher reported patient compliance 10 days later and close to significantly better pill counts and levels of satisfaction (Stewart, 1984).

Similar findings have been reported with adolescent samples (e.g., Litt & Cuskey, 1984; Sternlieb & Munan, 1972). Adolescents who are satisfied with their health care are likely to be seeing physicians who are described as understanding, friendly, and informal, and who take the time to explain medical problems and laboratory tests to their patients (Stern-lieb & Munan, 1972).

This last point, taking the time to explain, deserves underscoring. One study with inpatients provided one experimental group with extra time with the physician, which was limited to general discussion of matters like food and hospital comfort, and a second experimental group with extra time during which the physician asked the patient about his understanding of information he had been provided and responded to the patient's questions (Ley, Bradshaw, Kincey, & Atherton, 1976). A third group received no special attention. Similar proportions of the control and "time-only" groups expressed satisfaction with hospitalization (48 percent and 41 percent, respectively), but almost twice as many of the group who received information reported satisfaction (80 percent). These findings highlight the importance of viewing patients as having an active role in seeking to understand their situations, rather than seeing them simply as passive "recipients of care."

Although in many social situations surveillance over someone's behavior leads to a reduction in compliance (reactance), in medical situations the reverse seems true (Davidson, 1976; Gillum & Barsky, 1974). Use of systematic self-monitoring also has an impact, although not a dramatic one (Epstein & Masek, 1978).

More significant results are obtained from a procedure called response-cost, developed in behavioral treatment programs. In this procedure, the patient deposits something of value, usually money, with the therapist, and forfeits standard portions of it for failing to perform some prearranged behavior. Epstein and Masek (1978) found that compliance with a regimen of taking vitamin C four times per day prophylactically for colds was raised from a baseline of about 35 percent to 78 percent by use of a response-cost manipulation. Response-cost manipulations have also been used in smoking and weight control programs, and in treatment of other difficult habit problems.

Communication Problems

A critical aspect of practitioner-patient contact involves the communication of information. The content and structure of this communication often is detrimental to patients' understanding and adherence.

Patients cannot carry out treatment recommendations that they do not remember, and they are reluctant to comply with those they do not understand. It is therefore disturbing to find that immediately upon leaving the physician's office, patients forget from 30 to 50 percent of what they have been told (Ley, Bradshaw, Eaves, & Walker, 1973). Fortunately, the information appears not to decay much more than this. Recall at 4 weeks (46 percent) was found to be comparable to that immediately following an office visit (48 percent) (Joyce, Caple, Mason, Reynolds, & Mathews, 1969).

One of the problems in communication is that physicians frequently use technical language beyond the comprehension of their patients (Korsch & Negrete, 1972; Ley & Spelman, 1967). Silver (1979) illustrated the problem thus: "One patient thought that being on a low-salt diet was bad enough. Then, in the hospital, she discovered to her dismay that she was also put on a low-sodium diet" (p. 4). Ley (1977) noted that the physician may assume too much about the possession of medical knowledge on the part of the patient, or the patient may have mistaken beliefs that impede comprehension.

This kind of problem underscores our earlier point that communication aimed at an understanding of the patient's perspective is critical. For example, the National Institutes of Health (1981) reported that the term "hypertension," the technical term for high blood pressure, is regularly misunderstood by the general public to mean "high levels of nervous tension." Obviously, such a mistake can have serious consequences for the patient's conception of the disorder and can fatally interfere with appreciation of the need to adhere to treatment regimens.

Unfortunately, physician-patient communication is frequently antithetical to the development of clear understanding. West (1983, 1984) has carried out detailed studies of the dialogues between patients and family physicians during routine visits. Her careful methodology involved fine-grained analyses of recorded conversations. She found that patients answered virtually all questions posed by their physicians (98 percent), but physicians, who were asked very few questions by their patients in the first place, responded to fewer of those that were asked (87 percent). Further, most of the questions asked by patients were stuttered, reformulated midway, and generally rendered ineffective by marked speech disturbances. Patients sometimes avoid mention of the primary reasons for their visits until it is time to leave, at which time they begin an exchange with "by the way, doctor" or "while I'm here" (Byrne & Long, 1976; Stewart, McWhinney, & Buck, 1975). This is hardly an ideal way to exchange information.

Noting the patient's role in the poor communication, Janis (1984) wrote that "another major difficulty is that when physicians are willing to answer questions, patients are so ineffective at interviewing that they might elicit little more than reassuring answers biased in the direction that the physicians think the patients want to hear" (p. 353). West (1983) noted that dialogues are almost all (91 percent) initiated by the physician. The interaction is clearly asymmetrical, and characterized by what West (1984) has called "medical misfires: mishearings, misgivings, and misunderstandings" (p. 107). Szasz and Hollender (1956) claimed that a mutual participation model of interaction is essentially foreign to medicine.

Beckman and Frankel (1984) focused on the physician's influence on initial patient-physician communications in a study of 74 office visits to 15 different physicians. Their findings were striking. In only 23 percent of the initial exchanges did the physicians permit their patients to complete their opening statement of concerns. Instead, physicians generally interrupted patients an average of 18 seconds after they had begun to speak and took control of the visit by asking specific, closed-ended questions. The results on the flow of information were disastrous; only 1 of the 52 interrupted patients went on to complete his description of his problems. It would appear that the physicians were attempting to identify and collect data concerning a chief complaint and may have been acting out of consciousness of time constraints. Unfortunately, as Beckman and Frankel pointed out, patients are *not* medically trained and may in fact be seeking a physician's assistance in identifying problems from a set of undifferentiated distressing concerns. There is no evidence that the ordering of the patient's stated concerns is related to medical importance or severity. There is, however, evidence that the patient's self-defined chief complaint agrees with the physician's determination of the primary problem in only 76 percent of somatic and 6 percent of psychosocial problems. Early closure may therefore result in loss of important data (Burack & Carpenter, 1983). It also seems that time need not be a concern; most of Beckman and Frankel's patients who *did* complete their opening statements (those who were not interrupted) took less than 60 seconds and none took longer than 150 seconds.

Data concerning the amount of time physicians spend providing explanations to patients is revealing in light of Francis et al.'s (1969) finding that patient satisfaction increases when patients receive adequate explanations. Wallen, Waitzkin, and Stoeckle (1979) found that less than 1 percent of the total talking time during a visit is spent in physician's explanations to patients. Similarly, Korsch et al. (1968) indicated that mothers' queries were commonly ignored or met with vague responses. Norton (1982) pointed out that much of the explanatory speech that physicians do engage in is ineffective, consisting of free-flowing discussion of general topics and principles (Bradshaw, Ley, Kincey, & Bradshaw, 1975; Ley, 1977). Stewart and Cluff (1972) suggested a disturbing analogy: "In our society, better instructions are provided when purchasing a new camera or automobile than when the patient receives a life-saving antibiotic or cardiac drug" (p. 467).

Leventhal, Zimmerman, and Gutmann (1984) described preliminary findings by Svarstad about physician-patient communication gathered in a clinical setting: (1) the physician actually failed to state the treatment regimen 17 percent of the time; (2) Svarstad often could not understand the regimen herself from observing and listening to the interaction; (3) regimens that were both written and stated orally (e.g., in providing a drug, the physician might describe the regimen as well as have it written on the label) were contradictory 20 percent of the time. Remedies for such problems are neither subtle nor difficult.

A sample exchange provided by West (1984) demonstrates how the physician-to-patient exchange can go awry. In this brief segment, the physician is attempting to alter the patient's diet, substituting nutritious foods, such as fruit, for an apparently unacceptably high level of sweets. (These quotations from West, 1984, p. 124, have been edited for readability, since in the original they were written in a phonetic code.) The physician's first communication is as follows: "And those are the different food groups that you want to try to get. You know, go light. And they all have nutritional value for you. And you notice that sweets aren't on that list at all. Okay?" The patient's reply is less than enthusiastic: "Oh, you got fruit here, right?" The physician follows with, "Um-hmm. Instead of having a Pepperidge Farm cookie, you can have an orange." At the same time, the patient says, "I don't eat a lot of fruit," but the physician may miss it because of her simultaneous speech. The patient tries again, beginning, "I don't . . . ," but leaves off as the physician plunges ahead, apparently trying to be convincing: "You know, which [referring to the orange] has calories in it but it has some nutritional value too. But the thing is, Mr. Malloy, I don't want you to deny yourself. What do you say?" Mr. Malloy is mildly compliant: "Mm. It's okay." West commented:

> For a patient who does not eat "a lodda fruit," the substitution of an "awr::unge" for a Pepperidge Farm cookie will probably be less than successful. Consequently, the diet plan also may be less than a success. . . . Disconfirming materials . . . may have passed unheard by the physician . . . in states of simultaneous speech. (p. 124)

In addition, the physician appears to ignore the clues that are available; by barreling ahead in her apparent determination to *convince* the patient through sheer force of logic, she overlooks the information that is flowing the other way. The patient's indications that he is unlikely to follow through on the treatment plan, and the reasons for this, are ignored.

Mace (1971) noted the common view of patients that they should not "bother the doctor" by asking questions. Complementing this silence and passivity is the physician's interpretation of such behavior as indicative that patients have no immediate problems. They therefore see little need to elicit from patients whatever may be troubling them. Further, Mace claimed, physicians are actively encouraged in medical school to see themselves as single-mindedly pursuing a science and consequently come to view communication with the patient as having low priority. Their task is to know facts, solve problems, and treat disease. This has little to do with something as vague as a "relationship."

The tendency for physicians to structure patient interactions in a hard-sell, expert-to-recipient fashion (it was evident in West's example that the patient's attempts, meek though they were, to change the nature of the communication were rebuffed) probably results partly from absence of knowledge concerning alternative approaches. What could the physician in this example do if she were to acknowledge the patient's reservations and the likelihood that he will ignore her prescribed course of action? It might lead to the admission of the need for a structured behavioral assessment and detailed, long-term program to alter engrained dietary habits. It is surely easier and more in keeping with her training to prescribe, to provide some brief explanation, and to leave the follow-through to the patient. It is unlikely that the physician feels she has the time or ability to deal with the attitudinal, habitual, and environmental factors that may interfere with adherence (Mace, 1971). Mace quoted Bird on this point: "In medical school a student spends hours learning to dissect, to percuss, etc.—all essential things—but he is presumed to know how to talk. This is not necessarily so" (p. 391). The distant professionalism of some physicians may constitute a self-protective style, in the absence of these social skills (Korsch et al., 1968).

As the "Pepperidge Farm" cookie example illustrates, patients themselves sometimes provide information concerning the likelihood of their adhering to treatment. In fact, an unpublished study by Berg, Maxim, and Brinkley (described in Carr & Maxim, 1983) suggests patients are mines of untapped information. In this study, patients were asked at the time medication was prescribed about their willingness and ability to take it. Of those who did not adhere to the prescribed dosage of medication, 75 percent had originally replied to these questions with negative or equivocal answers. They had also given clear reasons why they probably would not comply: "They felt they were being coerced; they have no money; they thought they were getting too little or too much medication; or they predicted that they would forget to take it" (Carr & Maxim, 1983, p. 154). Hall, Roter, and Rand (1981) had naive judges rate samples of patients' speech on seven affective dimensions. They found that a patient whose voice quality was rated as "satisfied" was more likely to have kept past appointments and was more likely to keep future appointments.

Behavioral therapists are accustomed to eliciting information related to adherence and to evaluating potential impediments to treatment effectiveness, but most medical practitioners are not, believing such activity to be outside of their mandate. But as Carr and Maxim (1983) noted, many of these stumbling blocks for patients are probably correctable by active intervention and negotiation if they are elicited and discussed as part of treatment.

Improving Communication

Several studies have documented the ways in which physicians may take into account information conveyed by patients. Gerbert (1984) found that when physicians were presented with patients in videotaped simulations of medical examinations they proposed different treatments for the same problem based on patient attributes that had been manipulated by the experimenter. Thus, with patients who were portrayed as pleasant but relatively incompetent (i.e., those who appeared unintelligent, did not seem conscientious, and did not pay close attention to the instructions given nor try to understand the treatment), physicians were likely to discuss diet and medication more extensively and to repeat information. For patients who made statements antithetical to medication use (e.g., "I want to work within my body. . . . I think a lot of this medication business is monkey business"), physicians were less likely to provide medication.

Physicians may avoid some types of communications with their patients because of a lack of effective means to deal with the information that might result. Whereas the "Pepperidge Farm" physician ignored data that might have proven difficult to handle, in Gerbert's (1984) study, physicians responded more to their patients' data because they could deal with them in ways compatible with their training and orientation (e.g., adjusting medication, giving more information). It would be informative to investigate this hypothesis by comparing simulated exchanges that brought to light information that could be handled readily through regular medical methods and exchanges that revealed the need for approaches less usual in medical practice (e.g., instituting behavioral programs or dealing with emotional material).

Other critical problems with practitioner-patient communication can be rectified by physicians fairly easily. For example, if physicians wish to find out more from their patients, a simple bit of information provided by Beckman and Frankel's (1984) study can be useful. These investigators found that patients were most likely to finish opening statements of their concerns when the physician responded to their initial sentences with what they called "continuers," that is, "mmh hmm," "go on," "I see," and the like. They noted, "Far from being inert, these linguistic devices appear to play a major role in facilitating all patient concerns" (p. 694).

Some measures are available to assist the practitioner in improving communication without dealing intensively with adherence problems that result from the patient's cognitions concerning treatment. Several experimental studies have demonstrated that the organization and presentation of information have a strong impact on its recall (Bradshaw et al., 1975; Ley, 1977; Ley et al., 1976). Ley and associates have made six suggestions based upon their empirical findings:

1. Whenever possible, present instructions and advice at the start of the information session; that is, make the critical points near the beginning of the interaction.
2. Stress the importance of any course of action that is recommended.
3. Use short words and short sentences.
4. Explicitly categorize topics whenever possible, rather than engaging in free-flowing speech.
4. Repeat information whenever possible.
6. When giving advice, make it specific (e.g., "Don't eat candy," rather than, "Be careful about your diet"), detailed, and as concrete as possible.

Ley (1977) reported that patients of four physicians who had read a leaflet with a summary of the previous points had recall of information about proposed treatment regimens 9 to 21 percent greater than that of patients who had met with these physicians prior to their reading the leaflet. This is a rather remarkable change from a minimal intervention. Comparable benefits were reported following a single tutorial session for physicians managing hypertensive problems (Inui, Yourtee, & Williamson, 1976).

Another approach to improving communication has been directed toward the patient. Roter (1977) found that patient satisfaction and adherence were improved by teaching patients to ask more questions of physicians. Both general educational efforts to enhance the consumer consciousness of patients and specific programs to encourage active participation may offer hope for better communication and, therefore, for better health services.

Adjunct Resources

Physicians who try to anticipate adherence problems are likely to discover that most hospital and clinic settings do not have resources that they can readily rely upon to manage problems involving behavioral interventions. Although programs for some specific populations and problems have been established, such as cardiac rehabilitative or low-back-pain groups, it is rare for there to be a unit accustomed to handling general referrals for specific dietary or other habit changes. The tendency to view the patient-physician interaction as a prescriptive, advice-following one also inhibits use of existing resources and development of further ones.

The problem facing the "Pepperidge Farm" physician is not minor. Although we might suggest that she attempt to assess the extent of the adherence problem rather than simply conveying her advice, we do not intend to suggest that she ought to undertake (or would have the appropriate skills to undertake) treatment of it. In this instance, a referral for psychological assistance to deal with a delineated problem would be in order. Practicing psychologists are accustomed to devising programs to change difficult behaviors and to dealing with adherence problems as a matter of course. Such specific referrals are only rarely received by most psychology departments, which more typically deal with psychiatric problems. Psychologists are partly to blame, for failing to educate other professionals about the wider use of their services. The rising profile of health psychology may change this situation.

PROBLEMS WITH THE ADHERENCE LITERATURE

Some general conclusions can be drawn from the extensive adherence literature, but beyond what we have described, it is difficult to evaluate much of the information because of serious methodological problems and inconsistencies. Many studies have used inadequate controls and measures with unknown reliability and validity or have failed to use inferential statistics to determine whether effects that were obtained were unlikely to be chance results.

Defining Adherence

One of the most serious difficulties in evaluating the literature results from the lack of a common definition of adherence. Carr and Maxim (1983) noted that some reports define noncompliance in terms of any deviation from a prescribed regimen of treatment, whereas others consider compliance with 75 to 80 percent of the treatment program to be an unqualified success. "In calculating non-compliance you can score as high for failing to make one phone call to a consultant's secretary as for failing to inject yourself with insulin 3,000 times over a period of years" (Davidson, 1976, p. 250). Although a standard definition is not feasible for the multiplicity of treatments and circumstances that are studied, the range and frequent lack of specificity of assessment methods makes comparison of results difficult. Similar measurement problems are present with other variables assessed in adherence research, such as level of satisfaction, patients' perceptions of the physician, and so forth.

The difficulty in comparing studies is significant because of the many variables that have been examined and the inconsistency of findings (Leventhal, Zimmerman, & Gutmann, 1984; Sackett & Haynes, 1976). Even those relationships between a variable and adherence that have been consistent are modest. For example, Francis et al.'s (1969) most highly satisfied group of patients nevertheless adhered to treatment in only 50 percent of the cases. In some instances, satisfaction and adherence have been unrelated (Hulka, Cassel, Kupper, & Burdette, 1976).

In Search of Theory

What are the causes of the behaviors that look adherent or nonadherent? Does it matter whether a change in behavior is *intended* to be compliant? Davidson (1976) described a personal example:

> I started to suspect I was developing ulcers. . . . The doctor sat me down . . . and said, "Dr. Davidson, I think we can solve your problems for you. You should quit smoking, lose 20 pounds, cut your coffee consumption to 2 cups a day, get some exercise and try to relax more often!"
>
> I no longer smoke, I lost 25 pounds, took up cross country skiing, and manage to sleep through at least some of my lectures, but increased my coffee consumption to 8 cups a day; and incidentally no longer have stomach problems. Sounds like an 80% compliance rate on a single case study, doesn't it? Does it make any difference that I quit smoking when a dentist removed 4 impacted wisdom teeth simultaneously? I lost 25 pounds 2 years later on a bet with my wife, took up cross country skiing when we moved to Calgary and increased my coffee consumption when I was given a filter coffee maker for my office. And what about the fact that my stomach problems disappeared when my wife quit putting nutmeg in desserts . . . ? I would say I was non-compliant . . . but my physician is, I am sure, convinced that my case represented a successful example of efficacious prescription on her part and high compliance on mine. (p. 250)

The difficulty in discerning the causes of adherence or nonadherence is not limited to the examination of a specific instance. For the most part, the theoretical literature has failed to provide a unifying framework from which to evaluate and understand the many empirical findings and inconsistencies. This led Haynes (1982) to undertake a "baldly empirical review" (p. 57), eschewing theory entirely. His review and his work with Sackett (Haynes, 1979; Sackett & Haynes, 1976) provided specific and practical suggestions to maximize compliance, similar to those of Ley and others, noted earlier.

By contrast, Becker (1974, 1976), Janis (1984), and Leventhal and his colleagues (Leventhal, 1973, 1984; Leventhal & Hirschman, in press; Leventhal et al., 1984) have concentrated on formulating theoretical positions that can guide both research and clinical practice. Leventhal et al. (1984) claimed that what is described as a failure of "technology" when patients fail to adhere to long-term treatment regimens is in reality a failure of theory. Without adequate theoretical understanding of the factors crucial to adherence and maintenance of treatment effects, the interventions themselves are improperly directed, lacking in critical elements.

Inadequate theoretical treatment of adherence problems may also lead to an overemphasis on main effects (Leventhal et al., 1984). Most of the research we reported investigated variables independently (e.g., patient attitudes, complexity of treatment, length of time in waiting room), without examining interactions among variables. Evidence points toward the patient's cognitions as central in the treatment process, and cognitions, whether they concern treatment, prognosis, or other aspects of health, have been shown to be multidetermined through complex interactions (Merluzzi, Glass, & Genest, 1981; Turk et al., 1983). An atheoretical approach will not even lead to a search for, much less an understanding of, these complex interactions (Leventhal et al., 1984).

Leventhal and his colleagues have reviewed three broad theoretical perspectives that have informed and guided work in the area of adherence (Leventhal, Meyer, & Gutmann, 1980; Leventhal et al., 1984): (1) The *medical model* has primarily searched for personality characteristics of the noncompliant patient. As we noted earlier, this work has largely been fruitless. (2) The *behavioral viewpoint*, with its redefinition of compliance as adherence, has led to more attention to the characteristics of the *situation* rather than the *person*. Although this has led to much greater initial success in altering behavior, the long-term results have in many instances been disappointing (Kaplan, 1984; Stunkard, 1977). (3) The "control theory" proposed by Leventhal et al. (1984) is a *cognitive approach* that treats patients' behaviors as goal-directed, rather than as simply reactive to external stimuli.

When applied to health and illness behavior, control theory has emphasized that people generate their own representations of

health threats, and plan and act in relation to their representations. . . . The representation of a health problem is built up from
information from media, friends, health practitioners and family
members, as well as from symptoms and sensations from the
body. Information from all of these sources is integrated into a
representation of a current illness episode or a future illness
threat. The representation then guides planning and action.
(p. 373)

Other writers have similarly emphasized cognitive views of the patient-
health system interaction (Becker, 1974, 1976; Cameron, 1978; Janis,
1984; Turk et al., 1983).

There have been significant advances in the investigation of adherence issues, despite the remaining problems in the literature. Perhaps the
most important advance is a change in attitude; the once pervasive
patient blaming evident in writings on "compliance" has evolved into a
less defensive posture, which leads to consideration of patient, therapist,
treatment, and setting variables in attempting to understand adherence.
Attempts to include interactions of these factors and to build a theory of
adherence hold promise for practical advances in effectiveness of both
preventive and treatment interventions. In particular, the emphasis on
communication patterns between health-care professionals and patients
is an exciting direction in current work.

SUMMARY

The issue of adherence is an essential concern in devising programs
for intervention to alter lifestyles and in dealing with treatment of traditional medical problems. In both these areas, enhancing adherence
involves recognition and attention to the extremely complex interactions
between caregivers and consumers in the health-care system.

Chapter Three

Psychological Intervention in Physical Disorders

Psychological interventions offer ways of dealing with what have traditionally been considered medical problems. The pharmacological or surgical solutions for problems like diabetes, spinal injury, loss of bladder control, epilepsy, and pain offer less than totally satisfactory outcomes. Furthermore, nonphysical components of disease—the anxiety, depression, and adherence problems—do not yield to medical management. This chapter will outline major elements in psychological interventions for the treatment of physical disorders.

Psychosomatics, the study of the relationship between physical illness and the mind, has historically been the arena within which psychological factors met physical medicine. Although health psychology owes some of its database and impetus to this field, psychosomatic medicine's roots in Freudian theory and its focus on a relatively narrow range of disorders and treatment modalities distinguishes it from most approaches we will describe. Some contemporary psychosomatic theorists would prefer their discipline to be more broadly conceived (Lipowski, 1977; Weiner, 1984). In fact, a content and citation analysis of the field's major forum, the journal *Psychosomatic Medicine*, found considerable variety in publications from the last 2 decades (Rose, 1983). Behavior therapy papers now outnumber those in psychodynamics by seven to one. The indications are that psychosomatics is merging with health psychology, although retaining a stronger biomedical orientation.

The most recent and currently most influential contributions of psychology to medical treatment have evolved from the application of principles derived from learning theories. These generally fall within the broad rubric of *behavioral interventions*. Initially, behavioral interventions were based on principles of either classical or operant conditioning.

APPLICATION OF CLASSICAL CONDITIONING

There have been very few applications of the classical conditioning paradigm to health-related problems, primarily because the method requires targeting a single behavioral event, which is seldom useful. This approach, familiar as Pavlovian conditioning, involves the pairing of a neutral stimulus with a stimulus that automatically and reliably elicits the desired behavioral response. Repeated pairings result in the association of the two stimuli: The previously neutral stimulus acquires the properties of the unconditioned stimulus in eliciting the response.

In one series of studies, conditioning was used to assist spinal-cord-injured patients who had no control over urination to achieve bladder control (Ince, Brucker, & Alba, 1977). A neutral stimulus, a mild electric current applied to the leg, was paired with an unconditioned, eliciting stimulus, a stronger electrical stimulation to the lower abdomen over the bladder, which did produce urination. Before pairing, the neutral stimulus alone did not produce urination, whereas the eliciting stimulus did. Repeated pairing of the mild leg current with the stronger stimulus led to voiding upon presentation of only the previously neutral stimulus.

In this study, careful observation and early tests of the neutral stimulus without effect established quite firmly the success of the classical conditioning approach. Brucker (1983) noted the practical implication that other functional control may be developed with spinal-cord-injured patients through conditioning and the theoretical importance of establishing for the first time that a human spinal reflex can be regulated in the absence of brain control.

Because of the complexity of most human behavior, such classical paradigms have found little application in health psychology. Significant gains seldom can be accomplished by targeting a single behavioral event (such as urination), and it is equally rare to have a stimulus readily available to elicit the desired response reliably (as did the lower abdominal shock). In most cases, health-related problems demand control over complex interaction patterns in human activity. Such patterns involve both reflexive and intentional behaviors and internal and external influences. Consequently, behavior is more amenable to being *shaped* through operant conditioning paradigms, described in the next section, or through other broadly based psychological approaches that will be discussed later. The classical conditioning, or associative, approach may nevertheless provide the means for control over otherwise intractable problems involving discrete and relatively circumscribed sequences of behaviors.

APPLICATION OF OPERANT CONDITIONING

Applications of behavioral methodology to health problems are based on the assumption that disease states or dysfunctions are maintained by the operation of unrecognized rewards and punishments. Recognition of these contributions can lead to the development of a behavioral program of other rewards and punishments that would enable more desired healthy states to replace dysfunctional ones. An example is provided by pain behavior—a pattern of dependence on family and the health-care system, social isolation, and overuse of drugs, with pain as the central focus in the patient's life (LeShan, 1964; Sternbach, 1974). This pattern becomes a problem separate from the chronic pain itself, and may actually exacerbate pain. For example, low back pain frequently leads the patient to reduce exercise level, thereby decreasing muscular strength in the back and increasing vulnerability to further pain-producing problems. Or chronic pain may lead a patient to circumscribe his life to the point where the major focus is pain, which, in and of itself, can intensify the experience of pain. Pain behavior is thought to develop and persist partly because it is rewarded and activity is discouraged. The classic example of this situation is the child who is allowed to stay home from school because of a stomachache. In instances of chronic pain the circumstances become infinitely more complex.

It is not always assumed that learning played a role in the *origins* of the physical dysfunction. Regardless of the etiology of health problems, in many instances reconditioning may be undertaken as a treatment in the belief that operant techniques can contribute to positive change.

As we shall see, there are instances in which behavioral means to improve health-care practices are available but have not been widely adopted (e.g., procedures to prepare patients for surgery). In other instances, enthusiasm for the potential of procedures has outpaced evidence of their efficacy and a clear understanding of their mechanisms of action (e.g., in some applications of biofeedback). The rush to bring new procedures to bear on pressing clinical problems is understandable. But overeagerness without sufficient information is likely to lead to some inappropriate and unsuccessful applications. General disenchantment with the behavioral approach can result and, as Mahoney and Kazdin

(1979) caution, possibly even abandonment of this line of treatment by the health-care system before it has been allowed to prove itself.

The following sections provide examples of the applications of operant training to health-related problems. These examples are by no means exhaustive, but they illustrate the potential as well as some problems in the area.

Muscular Strength

One study in this area illustrates clearly the potential straightforward application of operant techniques and some methodological pitfalls of investigating such applications. This program was designed to increase mobility and self-care (e.g., propelling a wheelchair, using crutches) of spinal-cord-injured patients by strengthening normal arm muscles. Trotter and Inman (1968) assigned 12 quadriplegics and 12 paraplegics to two groups, one of which received rewards contingent upon achieving specific gains in strength. In other respects, both groups received the same physical therapy program. The therapist gave the experimental group subjects rewards in the form of (1) verbal praise for gains, (2) attention during reviews of each patient's record of weight-lifting achievement, and (3) encouragement, by relating improvement to functional goals (e.g., use of crutches). In contrast, therapist-patient interactions in the control group were left to occur as usual in physical therapy; in the data collection for these subjects, their records were made discreetly, not discussed with them, nor related to their long-term goals. The intention of the researchers was to determine whether a planned program of positive reinforcement would enhance gains in strength. The general point being addressed was whether an operant conceptualization of physical therapy would help to maximize the therapy's effectiveness.

Over 4 weeks, the control subjects gained an average of 2.40 pounds in weight-lifting capability, whereas the experimental group gained an average of 10.29 pounds in capability. The difference between these changes was statistically significant.

These results appear to validate an operant approach in a physical therapy setting. Unfortunately, the systematic application of operant principles did not constitute the only difference between the two groups: Although the physical therapy program was identical for both groups, the experimental group was led by a physical therapist, whereas the control group had a nonprofessional assistant as a therapist. Trotter and Inman (1968) recognized the problem this caused, for in addressing potential explanations for group differences they wrote:

Possible reasons . . . include the presence of the physical therapist, and the status of a physical therapist versus a nonprofessional assistant. Certainly the knowledge and experience of the physical therapist versus those of the nonprofessional worker were important factors. Other possible factors may have included age and sex differences, and personality variables. (p. 350)

Clearly, the intended difference between the groups in this study, that of operant training, is seriously confounded with several other potentially powerful factors. Yet the study's results (attempts to replicate the study have not been reported) have often been treated as evidence for the efficacy of operant training, with no attention to its serious methodological problems (e.g., Brucker, 1983; Middaugh, 1982). We have described the details of this research both to illustrate how operant procedures may be applied in innovative treatment programs as well as to demonstrate the difficulty of drawing clear conclusions from much of the extant literature and the need for careful research in the area.

Before discussing interventions with other physical disorders, it is important to note that while we are suggesting that controlled group studies can provide the best evidence for the usefulness of operant procedures, those who have published the single-case studies that predominate in the literature can hardly be faulted for their efforts. Controlled outcome studies require large numbers of patients and conditions for investigation that frequently are impossible in the settings in which patients seek help. Problems such as quadriplegia, seizure disorders, and postural hypotension (which we describe later) rarely come to the attention of psychologists, and when they do, there is generally an urgent need for treatment. Those who respond by creatively improvising treatments to fit the problem may never have treated such problems before and may never again. Criticizing the research in the field for its methodological shortcomings is a bit like being an armchair quarterback. Nonetheless, the problems we raised with Trotter and Inman's study (and which we note in succeeding studies) do interfere with reaching clear conclusions concerning the effective ingredients of the intervention. One strategy that might help in future investigations would be more extensive use of rigorous single-case-design methodology. By means of such procedures as implementation of one component of treatment at a time, continuous or intermittent behavioral data-collection, and replication of the study across subjects, each with a different baseline (no-treatment) assessment period, investigations of single cases can achieve a high degree of reliability and validity (Hersen & Barlow, 1976; Kazdin, 1981).

Muscular Coordination

Trombly (1966) applied operant principles to facilitate increases in muscular coordination, rather than strength. Orthotic devices are motorized splints used to enable quadriplegic patients to achieve functional control over their paralyzed hands. The devices are controlled by movements produced by normally enervated muscles. Unfortunately, achieving control over an orthosis is frequently very difficult, and many patients give up in frustration. With two quadriplegic patients, Trombly rewarded successive approximations of the control required, beginning with praise for attainment of gross movements and gradually requiring more complete mastery. This method follows two of the main principles of operant conditioning: (1) that mastery of complex behaviors is achieved by mastery of each individual step, one at a time, eventually leading to full performance, and (2) that performance is reinforced by rewards. Trombly reported that both patients achieved success in controlling their orthotic devices with this training program.

Individual treatment cases, such as Trombly's, can be useful in suggesting directions for further investigation and, if carefully controlled, can provide evidence of treatment efficacy. The treatment reported in this instance, however, did not include controls for nonspecific factors. The cases presented were not treated using any recognized single-case experimental design. It is therefore not possible to conclude that the effectiveness of Trombly's treatment was a result of giving contingent rewards, rather than of other influences, such as simply breaking the task into manageable units, providing general (i.e., noncontingent) encouragement (not related to the achievement of specific goals), and spending more time with the patients. Similar problems in identifying the active ingredients of programs exist in other, similar reports (e.g., Horner, 1971; Kalb, 1978; Sachs, Martin, & Fitch, 1972). Nevertheless, it is noteworthy that the few studies that have been reported seem to be quite successful in achieving change and as such indicate promise for future work. It is therefore quite disappointing that there has been very little research activity in the area.

The assumption that operant treatments are effective *because of contingent reward* (and in some cases, punishment) is highly questionable. This is not to deny that numerous operant-based programs have produced results. But if we are to benefit the most from such programs and be able efficiently to develop new ones, the basis for their success must be understood. That understanding is still wanting in many instances. In our discussion that follows, we will return to this issue.

Other Applications

Operant programs constitute one of the most prevalent contributions of psychologists in health-care settings. Proliferation of operant regimens has been stimulated by their acknowledged success in treating psychological problems such as phobias (Wilson, 1984). Parallel treatment applications are possible for many health problems.

For example, Sand, Fordyce, and Fowler (1973) investigated the prevention of urinary tract infections. These infections are a leading cause of death among those with spinal cord injuries (Brucker, 1983). A goal with such patients is therefore to maintain a high daily fluid intake, which reduces risk of infection. Sand et al. (1973) assigned 93 spinal-cord-injured patients into two groups: (1) a verbal explanation group (n = 69), which received only the usual explanation from staff concerning the importance of fluid intake and a daily intake quota to aim for and (2) a reinforcement group (n = 24), which received, in addition to the standard explanation and quota, praise from staff when they achieved the quota, and whose daily records of intake were displayed in public. (Public records are frequently used to encourage self, peer, and supervisor rewards and censure in operant programs.) Sand et al. found that the reinforcement program resulted in significantly greater fluid consumption than did the regular program for subjects who had initially low levels of fluid intake. Among subjects with initially high intake levels, no significant difference was reported. Unfortunately, no follow-up assessment was carried out and, therefore, it is not known whether the improvement was maintained.

Another significant limitation of this report is that the two groups of patients were not treated at the same time. The control group received regular treatment in the rehabilitative medicine inpatient service, and their records were obtained retrospectively for comparison purposes. The experimental group, on the other hand, was treated during an experimental period, when the study was initiated. Since their records were prospective, the staff was aware of participating in an experimental investigation— quite a different situation from the control group's participation. Consequently, it is impossible to attribute the differences in the two groups unequivocally to the systematic use of rewards for desired behaviors. A significant role may have been played by the nonspecific factors related to the staff's and patients' participation in an identified experiment during one period but not the other, with the differential expectancies involved. Nevertheless, the apparent enhancement of the treatment goals is encouraging and warrants further investigation.

A similar comparison of an operant program with a traditional instructional program was reported by Rottkamp (1976). The program was intended to prevent bedsores (decubitus ulcers) in partially paralyzed patients. Such patients are particularly prone to pressure-related sores because absence of sensation leads them to remain in the same position for long periods, without any shifts in weight or position. The control subjects in Rottkamp's study received regular instruction in and demonstration of proper body positioning. Experimental subjects received, in addition, positive reinforcement for changes in body position. Only subjects in the operant program demonstrated the desired changes in positioning; some improvement in ulcers seemed to occur for these patients as well, although statistical group comparisons were not presented.

Attempts to achieve behavioral control over seizures provide a final prototypical instance of the need for further good research in the application of psychological treatments to physical disorders. The literature on operant treatment of seizures is full of promise but almost devoid of definitive findings. The numerous reports of success have been in uncontrolled single cases.

Stevens's (1966) report of the treatment of a teenage girl with paroxysmal choreoathetosis is an encouraging case-study example. This disorder, although known for over 100 years, is a poorly understood disease, commonly regarded as a form of reflex epilepsy (Mostofsky, 1981). When she was first seen, the girl was experiencing periods of movements beginning in the extremities and eventually including most of the body in bizarre writhing movements with grotesque posturing. Her activities were severely restricted because of the disease and eventually she was hospitalized. Behavioral treatment was instituted, with rewards such as praise and encouragement contingent upon reduced episodes and training in practice of normal movements (e.g., walking with a coin carried in a mouth-held spoon). A substantial decrease in abnormal movements occurred over a few days. Day passes from the hospital were then used as rewards; these were granted following days without unwanted movements. At an 18-month follow-up, some choreic movements had returned, but their frequency and severity were considerably below baseline levels (Mostofsky, 1981).

As Mostofsky and Iguchi (1982) noted, when improvement is reported in these instances it is probably better understood in terms of the broad impact that the treatment intervention has on the patient, rather than narrowly attributed to the limited, specific operant components of treatment. The potential for change is nonetheless noteworthy and encouraging.

Another approach has been to attempt psychophysical habituation to critical stimuli that trigger seizures, that is, helping patients to gradually become physically accustomed to experiencing the stimuli without a seizure response (Forster, 1978). Although this treatment requires extensive, repeated exposures to the stimuli from subthreshold to high levels, it is probably the treatment of choice for a small fraction of epileptics for whom seizures are initiated by external stimuli such as sounds or lights (Mostofsky & Iguchi, 1982).

Avoidant Procedures

As guile is whetted by successful cheating in an examination, so any behavior that leads to successful avoidance or escape from an aversive stimulus is reinforced. This is called "negative reinforcement," a term that is frequently misapplied to punishment. Negative reinforcement results in an *increase* in a behavior's frequency, because the behavior causes cessation of an aversive stimulus. Effective punishment, by contrast, leads to a *decrease* in the frequency of the behavior it follows. This principle has been applied in controlling a variety of behaviors.

Malament, Dunn, and Davis (1975) used negative reinforcement to help prevent pressure-related sores in five paraplegic patients. If a patient remained in the same position continuously for 10 minutes, an unpleasant tone was triggered. The tone could be stopped or avoided by the patient's lifting himself off the pressure-sensitive seat cushion for 4 seconds. A controlled, single-subject design, with unobtrusive assessment methods, indicated that subjects learned the appropriate weight-shifting behaviors, and that these were generalized and maintained in situations in which the tone was not activated.

In several case studies, patients have been enabled to control abnormal, involuntary movements by the delivery of an aversive stimulus immediately following the unwanted movements. Electric shock was used as the aversive stimulus with a cerebral palsied adult (Sachs & Mayhall, 1971), and the interruption of pleasurable music was used with a patient with multiple facial and upper-body tics (Barrett, 1962). The patients' learning to avoid or escape from the aversive stimulus served to reinforce control over the unwanted behavior. Similar procedures have been used to increase movement ability in paretic arms of hemiplegic patients (Halberstam, Zaretsky, Brucker, & Guttman, 1971; Ince, 1969).

It is noteworthy that in these cases operant training was applied to behaviors that are not usually considered *operants,* that is, to involuntary movements. This is an extension of the usual operant paradigm and presages the more radical development of biofeedback, discussed later.

Mechanisms of Change

The preceding section on operant conditioning programs and research illustrates a methodology that marks a significant departure in treatment approach for physical disorders. In the traditional treatment of decubitus ulcers, for example, it has been routine to instruct patients upon the procedures required to prevent the sores from developing (i.e., shifting weight), but other than whatever reminders might be provided by more or less insistent nursing staff, patients were left on their own, either to carry out the recommendations or not. If sores developed, they were treated as a medical problem, often requiring skin grafts. In contrast, the programs of Rottkamp (1976) and of Sand et al. (1973) conceptualize disorders that had been treated as purely medical problems in new terms: Decubitus ulcers and urinary tract infections are viewed as partly resulting from *behaviors* of the patient, which are potentially self-controllable. As the contribution of patient-controlled events to medical problems is increasingly recognized, it becomes more possible to develop less invasive, less uncomfortable, more personally satisfying, and perhaps less costly means of treating or preventing these problems. This patient-centered rather than disease-centered attitude is one of the most far-reaching contributions of psychological developments in health care.

The studies that have been described illustrate the potential benefits of innovative applications of psychological approaches, but they also evince the problems in the research to date. In neither the Sand et al. (1973) nor the Rottkamp (1976) study can it be concluded that systematic reinforcement contingencies *caused* the differences between treatment groups. Both control groups, although they consisted of the usual treatment procedures, failed to control for the additional nonspecific treatment factors present in the operant groups. Such variables as additional staff time spent with patients, introduction of a new program, and the rationale for additional treatment all are potential alternative factors that may have contributed unknown amounts to the operant programs' effectiveness.

These critical comments are not intended to diminish the potential of operant interventions. Rather, attention to such questions may enhance understanding of how programs work and thereby enable maximum benefits to be derived. If, for example, it were satisfactorily demonstrated that long-term changes in fluid intake resulted from the Sand et al. (1973) intervention, one could raise the question "What is it about the treatment that led to such changes?" Was it learning that took place at a fundamental level, similar in kind to rats learning to press a bar for a food pellet? Or are the patients' interpretations of events important? Could it be, for example, that the obvious concern demonstrated by the staff's planning, time investment, and commitment to the behavioral program serves to convince patients much more firmly than a simple instructional session can that fluid intake is indeed important? Or possibly it simply takes reiterations of the need for fluid increase in order for patients to develop their ongoing awareness of intake. Other factors also may be important, perhaps different ones for different patients.

It is characteristic of operant programs that they require careful coordination and cooperation among staff and usually considerable commitment on the part of patients. In the Rottkamp (1976) study, for example, nursing attendants were repeatedly requested to carry out 24-hour observations of patients in the study; treatment included orientation sessions for both staff and patients and 4 weeks of about 10 sessions per week, each 10 to 60 minutes long; the behaviors that were intended for change were meticulously identified and defined; and instructions and record-keeping were greatly augmented. Would such changes have a positive impact on patients' behaviors if they were instituted without the regulation of reward contingencies? The operant paradigm may have provided the framework for learning, implementing, and motivating program changes, but other approaches, such as cognitive-behavioral analysis, may serve similar functions.

In other words, successful application of an operant paradigm does not in itself result in an understanding of how changes are gained and maintained, yet such an understanding could result in increased ability to produce change. The basic "laws of learning" upon which operant interventions are based have been challenged as utterly inadequate explanatory concepts (McKeachie, 1974), yet the interventions are frequently effective. More than further and better controlled outcome studies are required; greater attention to the process of change is equally important. The substantial difficulties in carrying out well controlled treatment and process studies with the clinical population make the explanation for research results unclear, so how to maximize benefits is therefore unknown. The promise of clinically significant benefits is clear, but much work remains to be accomplished.

BIOFEEDBACK

Technological advances have made possible the monitoring of physiological systems whose processes are not normally within one's conscious awareness. Transforming the information from such monitoring to forms that are quickly and simply interpreted comprises the basis of biofeedback systems. This process, which permits conscious awareness of processes otherwise inaccessible or not readily accessible, has led to attempts to extend the operant training paradigm to physical systems that have traditionally been regarded as involuntary (smooth muscle and glandular responses). Equipment is used to detect physical signals such as brainwave patterns, heartbeat, galvanic skin response (GSR measures changes in the electrical resistance of the skin that can be caused by emotions), and blood pressure, and these signals are integrated and fed back to the subject. Feedback modalities vary from an audible tone that changes frequencies to correspond with changes in the event being monitored (e.g., a higher tone for an increase in muscle tension) to a light that varies in brightness or a series of labeled lights. Thus, physical events and states, such as blood pressure and heart rate, can be consciously monitored.

From the early learning-theory-based research (e.g., Kimmel, 1967; Miller, 1969), biofeedback has proliferated to become a mainstay of psychological treatment of physical disorders (Andrasik, Coleman, & Epstein, 1982). Applications of biofeedback range from diastolic blood pressure biofeedback to treat essential hypertension (Glasgow, Gaarder, & Engel, 1982; Goldstein, Shapiro, Thananopavarn, & Sambhi, 1982) to muscle tension or brainwave biofeedback to treat tension headache (Kohlenberg & Cohn, 1981; McKenzie, Ehrisman, Montgomery, & Barnes, 1974). But widespread use does not guarantee that the therapeutic benefits are as general as claimed, nor that the operant principles upon which the technology was based are responsible for any changes that do occur (Shapiro & Surwit, 1976). In recent years, a number of critical reviews of biofeedback have appeared, to which we refer the interested reader (Alexander & Smith, 1979; Andrasik et al., 1982; Blanchard & Epstein, 1977, 1978; Jessup, Neufeld, & Merskey, 1979; Lynn & Freedman, 1979; Miller & Dworkin, 1977; Shapiro & Surwit, 1976; Turk, Meichenbaum, & Berman, 1979; White & Tursky, 1982).

In the following section, we examine biofeedback-based interventions, using examples from treatment of several clinical disorders. Our report is necessarily abbreviated, given the voluminous literature, and it is selective, in that we have chosen examples of applications with the intention of highlighting both the potential and the limitations of such interventions.

Tension Headache

Tension headache is widely presumed to result from abnormally sustained muscle contractions in the shoulders, neck, face and scalp, often as a response to stressful situations (The Ad Hoc Committee on the

Classification of Headache, 1962; Bakal, 1975). This disorder would therefore seem to be an ideal candidate for biofeedback-based treatment. In fact, the application of frontalis muscle feedback through electromyography (EMG) for headache is probably the most widely accepted form of biofeedback treatment.

Beginning with an experiment that showed subjects could control forehead EMG activity (Budzynski & Stoyva, 1969), Budzynski and his colleagues performed several pioneering investigations of the usefulness of EMG biofeedback in headache control (Budzynski, Stoyva, & Adler, 1970; Budzynski, Stoyva, Adler, & Mullaney, 1973). In the initial study, surface electrodes attached to the forehead were used to monitor EMG activity in subjects who did not suffer headaches. The signals from the electrodes were fed back to subjects via a tone: Low tones indicated muscle relaxation; higher tones indicated progressively greater muscle tension. Subjects were instructed to try to keep the tone as low as possible, without being told how to do this. As subjects became successful at controlling the tone, the feedback was changed, so that it required progressively greater relaxation to keep the tone at the same level. Thus, subjects were exposed to an operant shaping paradigm, in which success as defined by the feedback tone served as a reward for increased relaxation of forehead muscles.

In a pilot study with five patients, Budzynski et al. (1970) found that 5- to 12-week training, with two to three 30-minute sessions per week, resulted in reduced muscle tension levels and headache levels. Upon follow-up contact, 3 months after completion of training, the results were not so uniformly positive: Two subjects were having no headaches, and one subject found them markedly reduced, but the other two subjects' headaches had returned shortly after treatment.

Budzynski et al. (1973) subsequently reported a group study that compared this biofeedback treatment with two other treatment procedures: a treatment involving only self-monitoring of headache activity and a treatment that provided inaccurate feedback (feedback actually derived from members of the true feedback group). Following training, and at a 3-month follow-up, the EMG biofeedback group was found to have significantly reduced frontalis muscle activity and headaches. No significant changes occurred in either of the other two groups. The results from this study are generally regarded as having "clearly demonstrated the specificity and efficacy of forehead muscle conditioning for tension headache" (Andrasik et al., 1982, p. 104).

Both of these conclusions, concerning *specificity* and *efficacy*, have been contested. Subjects in both Budzynski studies were required to practice their relaxation skills at home, daily. As other writers have noted

(Kondo & Canter, 1977; Turk et al., 1979), this requirement confounds the effects of biofeedback treatment per se with home practice of relaxation. Another problem with the Budzynski et al. (1973) results lies in the comparison of the true feedback and the sham feedback group. The false feedback group is commonly represented as enabling Budzynski et al. to rule out placebo or suggestion effects (Andrasik et al., 1982). But the feedback that this group received was not represented to them as from their own monitoring. Budzynski et al. pointed out that sham feedback presented as real could easily have been detected by subjects. Instead, the investigators simply presented the auditory stimulation as an aid to relaxing and keeping out intrusive thoughts. Shapiro and Surwit (1976) noted that "it seems obvious that such a procedure would have no more credibility than telling the subjects that the feedback of others was their own" (p. 92) and therefore would not assist in controlling for expectancy effects. Such problems with the Budzynski et al. (1970, 1973) studies preclude clear attribution of improvement to the biofeedback.

Additional problems arise from several reports that suggest that the EMG feedback is *not* an integral element for treatment efficacy. In one study, EMG biofeedback training was compared to a waiting-list control condition and a treatment focusing on altering maladaptive cognitions (stress-coping training) (Holroyd, Andrasik, & Westbrook, 1977). At termination of the 8-week (twice weekly) treatment and at a 15-week follow-up, *only* the stress-coping training group reported significant changes in frequency, duration, and intensity of headaches. Particularly challenging for the biofeedback approach were the findings that although the EMG feedback did significantly reduce EMG levels and increase muscle tension control, *this control was not accompanied by headache reductions.* Of the 24 subjects in this study, 19 (79 percent) were available for assessment 2 years after completion of treatment (Holroyd & Andrasik, 1982). The same pattern was evident in these results: Clients in the stress-coping training group reported continuing to use the strategies they had learned and had substantially lower duration and overall headache activity than the biofeedback group ($p < .001$ for both results). Follow-up of the same group 3 years later (71 percent of subjects) confirmed the maintenance of treatment effects and the absence of a relation between headaches and EMG levels (Andrasik & Holroyd, 1983).

A study by Andrasik and Holroyd (1980) made the EMG-headache inconsistency very clear. These investigators compared (1) an accurate frontalis EMG treatment with (2) a reversed feedback treatment (subjects received feedback encouraging greater rather than lower frontalis muscle tension), (3) a treatment that misled subjects into believing they were receiving frontalis feedback while they actually received feedback from an irrelevant muscle group (forearm flexor muscles), and (4) a headache-monitoring-only group. Upon completion of treatment and 6 weeks later, *all three biofeedback groups* were found to have significantly reduced headache activity, compared to the headache-monitoring control group; the three active treatment groups did not significantly differ from each other in headache activity. Thus, the headache reductions that occurred could not be attributed to biofeedback-mediated frontalis relaxation.

The results of several other recent outcome studies are inconsistent, but the weight of the findings provides a strong challenge to Budzynski et al.'s (1973) conclusions (Blanchard, Andrasik, Ahles, Teders, & O'Keefe, 1980; Silver & Blanchard, 1978). Findings range from the superiority of EMG biofeedback training over relaxation (Hutchings & Reinking, 1976) to the equivalence in reducing tension headache of EMG training and relaxation (Blanchard et al., 1980; Cox, Freundlich, & Meyer, 1975; Haynes, Griffin, Mooney, & Parise, 1975) to the superiority of relaxation training over EMG training (Chesney & Shelton, 1976).

Altogether, the initial findings of a close correspondence between headache and EMG activity have not been corroborated. Turk et al. (1979) proposed several possible explanations for the apparent independence of these variables: It may be that there is little generalization across muscle groups and that in some instances headaches are being caused by tension in muscle groups other than frontalis (e.g., shoulders, neck, other parts of the head); it could be that changing frontalis muscle activity is insufficient to produce change in headache; or the relationship between muscle contraction and headache may be complex and influenced by other factors. In any case, the effectiveness of EMG biofeedback in reducing tension headaches appears not to result from feedback-mediated muscular relaxation.

An important issue concerns how the gains in biofeedback training are achieved. Holroyd and Andrasik (1982) contended that the effects of biofeedback cannot be attributed simply to the subjects' beliefs that this approach will be successful, although expectancy effects may play a significant role. What do the headache reductions that occur as a result of EMG training have in common with changes achieved through other effective approaches, such as relaxation exercises or stress-coping training? Blanchard et al. (1983) found a relationship between regularity of home practice of relaxation exercises and headache reduction, and also between the regularity of successful handwarming in thermal biofeedback treatment and headache reduction. As in previous reports, these authors found no relation, however, between EMG and headache levels.

Originally, operant principles were thought to underlie the EMG feedback-related changes. More recently, attention has turned to the cognitions that may mediate both biofeedback and other treatment successes (e.g., Andrasik et al., 1982; Turk et al., 1979, 1983). Subjects frequently report using images, silent verbal strategies, and other behavioral and cognitive activities in order to produce the physiological changes required. Biofeedback may induce clients to make better use of such resources and to alter the ways in which they have attempted to cope with life's stressors.

Indirect support for this view issues from a headache treatment study by Holroyd, Andrasik, and Noble (1980). Comparing biofeedback with a pseudomeditation procedure that actively discouraged clients from altering response patterns in stressful situations, they found the biofeedback to produce superior results, even though the pseudomeditation was considered by participants to be equally credible. Holroyd et al. (1980) argued that these results were consistent with the view that the effectiveness of biofeedback interventions derives from inducing subjects to undertake new, more adaptive coping strategies under stress. More direct support is provided by Holroyd and Penzien (1982), who found that manipulating subjects' sense of control over their ability to manage stressful situations successfully affected headache activity, whereas changes in EMG levels were unrelated to such activity. If such processes are the means by which subjects come to control their responses, then more direct attention to them should be fruitful in enhancing the control processes. There may be better ways to enhance cognitive control of responses than biofeedback:

> Biofeedback may be only one technique within a multimodal treatment package. In this broad definition, biofeedback becomes merged with behavioral medicine's approach to altering medical disorders. The individual's conscious cognitive processes are presumed major vehicles for effecting change, and the specific contribution of high-density feedback to this process may be of marginal importance. (White & Tursky, 1982, p. 445)

White and Tursky's comments have struck home when we have observed the interventions of highly skilled biofeedback practitioners as compared to those of novices. Novice therapists seem to have more faith in the magic of the technology. Having attached the electrodes and calibrated the equipment, they tend to sit back and expect change. By contrast, the more practiced professional continues to act as a therapist, is more vigilant of the client's responses and behavior, almost like a hypnotherapist, and modifies the procedure and instructions to maximize desired changes. Biofeedback serves as a tool for these therapists, rather than constituting the sole agent of change.

Postural Hypotension

Spinal-cord-injured patients frequently experience hypotension (low blood pressure) that prevents them from maintaining an upright position. Such patients may become light-headed or faint from the uncontrolled pooling of blood in their lower extremities and resultant insufficient supply to the brain.

Brucker and Ince (1977) used blood pressure biofeedback to assist a spinal-cord-injured patient to achieve increased blood pressure. This patient's hypotension was severe enough to prevent standing and walking with crutches and braces even after 2 years of rehabilitation treatment. By a 1-month follow-up assessment after a biofeedback intervention, he had the ability to increase his blood pressure by 45 mm Hg, and as a result could stand and walk for up to 4 hours. The effect was voluntary, for the patient could at will return to a postural hypotensive state.

Brucker, Miller, Pickering, and Ince (reported in Brucker, 1983) followed this single-case study with a group treatment investigation. Ten complete-spinal-cord-injured patients were able to produce "significant voluntary increases in blood pressure that were not mediated by skeletal muscle or respiratory mechanisms" (Brucker, 1983, p. 306). Brucker reported that the learned blood pressure control enabled these patients, who had formerly maintained a prone posture because hypotension prevented sitting upright, to use electric wheelchairs, increase functional abilities, and interact more with the community.

Although there was no control treatment in this study, the results with a severely disabled population are sufficiently impressive to suggest that biofeedback may be useful in treating postural hypotension. Adequately controlled investigations are nevertheless warranted to replicate these results and to determine whether the biofeedback was the essential ingredient in treatment. It may be found that biofeedback is a sufficient, but not a necessary, component for accomplishing blood pressure increases. If this is the case, then the cost-effectiveness of the treatment and the means to maximize its benefits can be addressed.

Essential Hypertension

Abnormal elevation of blood pressure is estimated to affect 10 to 20 percent of the adult North American population (Epstein & Oster, 1984; Kannel & Dawber, 1973; National Center for Health Statistics, 1983). It entails considerable health risks, including a higher incidence of stroke, coronary heart disease, and kidney disease (Admire, Roccella, & Haines,

1984). The seriousness of hypertensive health problems has caused the disorder to be placed on the list of 15 top funding priorities of the U.S. Public Health Service (Department of Health and Human Services, 1980, 1983). About 5 to 15 percent of cases of hypertension are secondary to underlying organic problems, such as kidney disease or adrenal cortical tumors (Admire et al., 1984; Kaplan, 1980). Since surgery or other medical treatments are usually effective in such cases, the behavioral attempts to affect hypertension have been targeted primarily at the remaining cases, termed essential hypertension, for which no organic cause (i.e., obvious infection or physical defect) is known.

Although drug therapy has been refined to reduce the risks associated with high blood pressure by treating the disorder symptomatically, antihypertensive medication has undesirable aspects: Drugs are not effective for all patients; additional medications may be required to control complex side effects, which are frequent and include nausea, depression, drowsiness, sexual impotence, and concentration and sleep difficulties; long-term consequences have not adequately been assessed since drug treatment is relatively new; and dropout rates as high as 74 percent have been reported for drug therapy, possibly as a consequence of the unpleasant side effects (Caldwell et al., 1970; Orton, Beiman, & Ciminero, 1982; Shapiro & Goldstein, 1982). In addition, there is also evidence that reduction of blood pressure by medication does not reduce risks of associated problems to the same level as that observed in untreated patients who have the same lower levels of blood pressure (Herd & Weiss, 1984). As a result of these drawbacks and limitations to drug therapy, and also because drug-based treatment suppresses but does not cure the disorder, considerable attention has recently been given to behavioral means of altering the blood pressure of hypertensive patients (Orton et al., 1982; Shapiro & Goldstein, 1982; Shapiro, Schwartz, Redmond, Ferguson, & Weiss, 1977). Most frequently, the behavioral approach of choice has been a biofeedback technique. Biofeedback methods usually reflect blood pressure directly, although this monitoring has posed considerable technical problems (for example, noting the level at which heart sounds become audible as a blood-pressure cuff is depressurized) (Shapiro & Surwit, 1976).

Results from studies using a biofeedback approach have been inconsistent. On the one hand, significant improvements compared to control groups (greater reductions in diastolic pressure as high as 25 percent) have been reported in some group studies (e.g., Elder, Ruiz, Deabler, & Dillenkoffer, 1973; Shoemaker & Tasto, 1975) and clinical trials (e.g., Benson, Shapiro, Tursky, & Schwartz, 1971). On the other hand, there are reports of the equivalence of biofeedback and relaxation procedures (e.g., Blanchard, Miller, Abel, Haynes, & Wicker, 1979; Hager & Surwit,

1978), complete failure of blood pressure biofeedback (e.g., Frankel, Patel, Horwitz, Friedewald, & Gaarder, 1978; Surwit, Shapiro, & Good, 1978), or the superiority of biofeedback and relaxation combined, over either one alone (Glasgow et al., 1982).

Methodological differences among these studies have been invoked to account for the inconsistencies in results (Shapiro & Goldstein, 1982). The type of hypertensives studied (e.g., borderline versus established), differences in drug regimen, and length and type of feedback sessions, for example, can all have an impact on treatment results. Recent reviews of biofeedback and other behavioral treatments concluded that they demonstrate overall effectiveness, although less than pharmacotherapy (McCaffrey & Blanchard, 1985; Wadden, Luborsky, Greer, & Crits-Christoph, 1984).

More promising work in the treatment of hypertension has been reported by Patel and her associates. In a series of studies, biofeedback training of skin resistance level has been combined with relaxation training, meditation, stress management training, and other procedures (Patel, 1975, 1977; Patel, Marmot & Terry, 1981; Patel & North, 1975). Reductions in blood pressure and medication, as well as lowered responsiveness to stress tests resulted from this multifaceted treatment.

A recent report by these investigators illustrates the approach (Patel et al., 1981). Ninety-nine employees of a large industry, each of whom possessed two or more coronary risk factors (high blood pressure, excessive cigarette consumption, or high serum cholesterol levels) completed a program that included provision of health education literature concerning diet and smoking, muscular relaxation and breathing exercises, meditation, skin resistance biofeedback training, and also stress management training, during eight weekly group sessions. A comparison group of 93 subjects received only the literature, with no other direct treatment. Subjects were randomly assigned to the two groups. Both groups of subjects reduced their blood pressure significantly during the treatment period and had maintained changes at an 8-month follow-up. The follow-up assessment revealed, however, that the active treatment group had blood pressure that was significantly lower than that of the control group. The results from the Patel group bear replication by investigators in other settings. The apparent consistency of this group's findings, however, suggests that a multidimensional approach has distinct treatment advantages over biofeedback by itself. The specific contribution of biofeedback to improvement cannot be determined from these studies.

Another relatively new direction for biofeedback-assisted treatment of hypertension involves the use of thermal feedback. The procedure originally included autogenic phrases to teach hand warming, then warming of the feet, in addition to diaphragmatic breathing and regular home practice (Green & Green, 1979). Reports of success with this program (Fahrion, Norris, Green, & Green, 1984; Green & Green, 1979) suffered the same difficulties as much other research in the area in determining the specific benefits of biofeedback versus other components of the package. A study currently in progress (McCaffrey & Blanchard, 1985) shows more promise in teasing apart the essential elements. The sample is a group of 42 hypertensive patients who required two or more drugs to maintain control of blood pressure (usually a diuretic and a second-stage drug, a sympathomimetic). Over an 8-week period, 20 patients were treated with only thermal biofeedback to assist hand warming, and 20 were treated with only relaxation training. After treatment, all were gradually withdrawn from the second-stage drug. Approximately 3 months after withdrawal of the drug, 9 of the 20 biofeedback patients had successfully lowered their blood pressure, compared to only 5 of the 22 relaxation patients. Home blood pressure records similarly showed consistently significant reductions for only the biofeedback group. These preliminary results suggest that hand-warming biofeedback provides a separate, useful contribution to blood pressure control. Further details from this study and replications in other centers will be of considerable interest.

Answers to some of the questions raised by the various hypertension control studies should be available soon. In 1982, the Behavioral Medicine Branch of the National Heart, Lung, and Blood Institute began pooling data from 12 different controlled evaluations of nonpharmacological treatment of hypertension to yield sufficient aggregate data to address outstanding issues (McCaffrey & Blanchard, 1985). The total sample, consisting of over 1,100 hypertensive patients, will include over 300 treated by relaxation training alone, over 200 receiving relaxation training and other procedures, and over 80 receiving various forms of biofeedback. The results, which will emerge over the next several years, should assist in determining the separate contributions and the power of various intervention strategies.

Most recent reviews of the literature concerned with biofeedback-assisted treatment of hypertension have tended to conclude that there is currently no sound empirical evidence that biofeedback offers an advantage over relaxation training and similar procedures (Aagaard, 1983; Agras & Jacob, 1979; Andrasik et al., 1982). It is to be hoped that the conclusions from current investigations will soon permit either a more positive evaluation or a definitive statement that relaxation training is the preferred treatment modality.

Another significant problem for biofeedback-mediated blood pressure modification lies in explaining how reported changes are achieved and what they mean. The case of a patient reported by Miller (1975) illustrates the difficulty. During 3 months of training, a woman with essential hypertension acquired the ability to change her diastolic pressure from 97 to 76 mm Hg. Shortly after training, however, she lost this control and was put back on drugs. She returned for training 2½ years later and once again rapidly regained control of her blood pressure. Miller questioned the clinical significance of the changes this woman was able to produce: "Is [she] merely using her voluntary control to produce a spuriously low measure in clinical tests while failing to transfer it to crucial parts of her daily life?" (p. 362).

A group study by Goldstein et al. (1982) encountered the same issue. Although their biofeedback group was comparable to a drug-treatment group and superior to relaxation or self-monitoring control groups in blood pressure reductions according to laboratory measurements, home recordings made by subjects in the study indicated that drug therapy was markedly superior to all other procedures. It could be that blood pressure biofeedback simply teaches patients to use some temporary means of control during the actual monitoring period. The mechanisms used to lower pressure may not be amenable to continuous use or may not be generalizable to other environmental circumstances (stress-inducing situations, for example), or it may be that habitual control is not acquired without specific training in generalization and maintenance. Whatever the case, it is inadvisable to embark on large-scale biofeedback treatment for hypertensives without better means of ensuring that generalization and maintenance will occur.

Motivational issues remain to be investigated with respect to biofeedback. Some patients may be more reluctant to engage in a demanding, self-control procedure such as biofeedback-based blood pressure change than they are to adhere to a medication regimen, despite the demonstrably poor record of medication (Chobanian, 1980). For other patients, the prospect of attaining independent and drug-free control of symptoms may be particularly motivating. For still others, the biofeedback instrumentation lends credibility to the approach, giving it a face validity far surpassing that of simple relaxation exercises.

Spinal Cord Injury

Biofeedback monitoring technology has also been applied to control over muscular processes. In particular, there are some impressive reports of functional gains from the application of biofeedback to spinal-cord-injured patients (e.g., Brudny, Korein, Levidow, Grynbaum, Lieberman, & Friedmann, 1974; Middaugh & Miller, 1980; Nacht, Wolf, & Coogler, 1982; Skrotzky, Gallenstein, & Osterrig, 1978). But Brucker (1983) commented that these reports are so wanting in control over other variables that it is impossible to attribute such changes confidently to biofeedback itself.

As an example, Brucker cited a study by Brudny et al. (1974) that used visual and audio EMG feedback with two quadriplegics. Feedback was used to assist in relaxing spastic muscles and strengthening weak muscles. Both patients were reported to improve in functional arm movements as a result of training. Only one patient was described in detail; apparently his gains were maintained at a 2-year follow-up.

The absence of methodological controls and of careful assessment creates considerable difficulty in attributing the improvement to biofeedback-based training. But more significant questions about the causes of the patients' improvement are raised by an interesting and dramatic finding. The patient who was followed for 2 years also improved in the functioning of the arm *that had not been the target of treatment.* This suggests that either biofeedback effects were extremely generalizable or that the gains did not wholly result from biofeedback-mediated training. Perhaps it only required time for these changes to take place, or perhaps it was other aspects of treatment that caused improvement, such as the encouragement given to the patient or the opportunity to practice in a structured fashion.

A similar demonstration of improvement in muscle functioning is found in a case report by Nacht et al. (1982). A patient with an incomplete spinal cord injury received EMG training to enhance control over gluteus medius and gluteus maximus muscles. Eight months following training, motor neuron activity had increased impressively. There were no experimental controls in this study, once again rendering causal inferences impossible.

The Brudny et al. (1974) and Nacht et al. (1982) studies underscore both the potential for change that is offered by nonmedical treatment interventions and the need for careful investigation, with appropriate controls, in order to understand effects that are obtained. Premature crediting of the wrong causal factors will ultimately lead to discredit, just as hypnosis was long in undeserved disrepute as a result of disproof of Anton Mesmer's theory of animal magnetism.

Other Applications

Biofeedback procedures have been applied to a wide variety of medical problems: Reports of success have appeared for the treatment of irritable bowel syndrome (Harrell & Beiman, 1978), fecal incontinence (Goldenberg, Hodges, Hersh, & Jinich, 1980; Walde, 1981), digital performance of a deaf, cerebral palsied child (Sachs, Martin, & Fitch, 1972), intractable idiopathic seizures (Fried, Rubin, Carlton, & Fox, 1984; Lubar & Bahier, 1976; Mostofsky, 1981), low back pain (Nouwen & Solinger, 1979); Raynaud's syndrome (reviewed by Surwit, 1973), and dysmenorrhea and premenstrual syndrome (Calhoun & Burnette, 1984). Studies in these areas suffer, however, from the variety of problems identified in the biofeedback literature already reviewed. In general, many investigations neglect to control for extraneous variables, whether in case study or group investigations. Thus, positive outcomes are overrepresented in the literature (Whitehead & Bosmajian, 1982). In addition, scant attention has been paid by researchers to the important question of specificity of biofeedback effects.

Commenting on the current foundations of biofeedback, Lehrer (1983) warned against uncontained enthusiasm: "Taken as a whole, these conclusions strongly indicate that establishing a profession of biofeedback is, at best, premature. The odds are still too great that, within less than a generation, the whole technology may be outmoded by scientific advances. . . . Biofeedback boosters, beware" (p. 825).

COMBINED TREATMENTS

The Patel hypertension studies described earlier (Patel, 1975, 1977; Patel, Marmot, & Terry, 1981; Patel & North, 1975) introduce a different approach to psychological treatment of disease. Most of the other operant and biofeedback studies discussed focused on the use of a single treatment modality. Patel's work, however, exemplifies a recent shift toward multidimensional programs, programs incorporating elements of biofeedback, relaxation training, education, social skills training, cognitive skills training, and exercise. We shall examine how such programs have been used in attempts to provide better treatment for intractable medical problems.

Chronic Pain

A few years ago, one of the authors received a referral from a neurologist for "psychological contributions to Mrs. M's severe, tension headaches." Mrs. M epitomized the patient whose pain problems have become chronic and are resistant to the usual medical treatment and whose lives are centered around their pain. For the preceding 18 years, this 43-year-old woman had suffered increasingly severe headaches. Having exhausted most means of treatment, she sought out several neurological, ophthalmological, and dental consultations, looking for possible causes of and cures for the incapacitating pain, which had become a daily torture for her. No physical causes of the headaches had been found. Her three children and her husband organized their lives around keeping the environment as quiet and stress free as possible, and all family members felt their activities were severely curtailed as a result. Despite these efforts, Mrs. M's headaches persisted, even slowly worsened. She appeared extremely distraught and unable to function much of the time.

In recent years, Mrs. M had become increasingly depressed and withdrawn and found that she could cope only by chronic use of a variety of pain-relieving and tranquilizing medications, which her several physicians prescribed to her out of frustration at their inability to provide any other assistance. The referring neurologist was concerned about Mrs. M's addiction to these medications and about her potential for suicide. When Mrs. M was seen in the psychology department she became extremely agitated when routine questions about her medication use were posed, and she emphatically denied any psychosocial contributions to the headaches. She also was very skeptical that psychological interventions of any sort might be useful, having been reluctant to see a psychologist at all.

Mrs. M's problems illustrate the difficulties faced by many chronic pain patients. Attempts to assist such individuals have led to some of the most innovative work in the psychological treatment of medical problems. Both laboratory and clinical research have indicated promise for pain reduction and more adaptive functioning in such severely disabled patients. The literature on psychological assessment and treatment of pain has been reviewed extensively (Block, 1982; Bradley, 1983; Bradley, Prokop, Gentry, Van der Heide, & Prieto, 1981; Flor & Turk, 1984; Keefe, 1982; Keefe & Bradley, 1984; Melzack, 1983; Turk & Flor, 1984; Turk et al., 1983; Turner & Chapman, 1982; Ziesat, 1981). The following studies are illustrative of the elements of a multidimensional approach to such health problems as Mrs. M's.

Operant Emphasis

Fordyce and his colleagues (Fordyce, 1976; Fordyce, Fowler, Lehmann, DeLateur, Sand, & Trieschmann, 1973) were the first to report the application of psychological principles to the systematic treatment of chronic pain. Fordyce's approach targets the *pain behaviors* of patients, that is, the observable signs of pain, such as complaints, grimacing, and heightened inactivity, behaviors that are usually reinforced by attention from family members and nursing staff. Mrs. M's family, it will be recalled, attempted to make her environment pleasant and stress-free, in response to her complaints of headaches. Treatment in such cases consists of rewarding *well behaviors,* such as physical activity, with attention and praise and ignoring pain behaviors in order to extinguish them.

The operant approach involves a variety of additional elements: the establishment of behavioral goals, the reduction of pain medications, and physical and occupational therapy (Genest & Turk, 1979). For example, in order to alter the reward patterns for pain and well behaviors, patients and family members work with the therapist to define personal goals for treatment. Goals are based on observable behaviors, and changes in pain and other subjective experiences are deemphasized. This approach results in a change in perspective for patients, from the view that they are helpless in the face of uncontrollable pain and so might as well give up to the attitude that even though the pain may not dramatically change, their *lives* can change. The presence of pain, in other words, does not have to relegate them to complete inactivity and absence of pleasure. Patients gradually learn to function in spite of pain and may consequently be more distracted from it. A patient said to one of the authors, "I still have pain—all the time, if I think about it. But I just don't. It's a background noise. It can be distracting and bothersome if I pay attention to it. But mostly I don't anymore."

A second emphasis in Fordyce's program is on pain medications. These, also, are treated as reinforcements. They are therefore changed from the usual pain-contingent schedules to a time-contingent basis (e.g., every 4 hours). In addition, the amount of active medication, in the "pain cocktail" is gradually reduced. Additional elements in the treatment include physical and occupational therapy.

In an early evaluation of this approach, Fordyce et al. (1973) reported that 31 patients followed for an average of 76 weeks after treatment indicated significantly lowered pain, lowered interference with daily activities, reduced medication, and reduced time spent reclining because of pain. Turk et al. (1983) raised serious methodological questions about this report. Problems included the potential biases that were introduced by unspecified selection criteria for patient inclusion in the program and no indication of how many patients were excluded, the questionable reliability and validity of the retrospective data collection procedures used, and absence of control patients.

Nevertheless, Fordyce's work has stimulated several additional projects. Generally, the results, like those of Fordyce, have indicated promise for this innovative approach (Anderson, Cole, Gullickson, Hudgens, & Roberts, 1977; Cairns & Pasino, 1977; Cairns, Thomas, Mooney, & Pace, 1976; Keefe, Block, Williams, & Surwit, 1981; Painter, Seres, & Newman, 1980). Fordyce attributes the therapeutic benefits from these programs to operant principles (Fordyce, 1976). But, as noted in the description of the original model, and as is characteristic of most subsequent applications as well, contingency management was not the only element in this multidimensional therapy. Further research along these lines is necessary to establish the extent to which reward and extinction procedures are responsible for the results of these studies; other factors, such as an induced cognitive restructuring of the patient's problems, alterations in family dynamics, and learning of new social and vocational skills no doubt account for a portion of the change that takes place—how much is not yet known.

Clearly, the importance of individual elements in an operant program has not been established. Concerning the pain cocktail, for example, Block (1982) wrote,

> The pain cocktail is neither universally utilized, nor consistently necessary to achieve reduction of analgesics and narcotics. Several clinics . . . merely instruct patients to reduce medication levels. This appears to achieve good results. . . . Furthermore, there exists the possibility that the pain cocktail may actually prove to be counterproductive for long term maintenance. (p. 53)

Block pointed out that there is evidence that self-directed withdrawal of medication may increase the patient's feelings of self-control over health-related behaviors, with a consequent increase in the patient's mainte-nance of withdrawal.

A difficulty in altering medication use is illustrated by the outcome of Mrs. M's contact with a psychologist. Initial interventions focussed on relaxation training, monitoring of situational changes in headache inten-sity (she initially reported *never* being headache free), and personality and family assessment. All these steps were aimed at providing her with a decreased sense of helplessness and an increased sense of control over the pain. At the same time, preliminary arrangements were made with her family physician, who prescribed most of her medications, and with the hospital pharmacy to eventually provide a pain cocktail, which would decrease in active ingredients over time. Unfortunately, the physician prematurely discussed this plan with her before she had achieved any sense of increased control. Perceiving her medication supply to be in jeopardy, she panicked, refused to return to either physician or psycholo-gist, and found another, initially more compliant, physician. Such difficul-ties in effectively coordinating treatment efforts have led to an emphasis in some settings on an inpatient stay and detailed initial treatment con-tracts with patients. There is no doubt that Mrs. M would have refused both of these options, as do many other patients. As a result, a substantial number of chronic pain patients do not benefit from available programs because they do not choose to take part in them. In Mrs. M's case, the psychologist might have been able to avoid her premature rejection of treatment had he proceeded more cautiously and slowly, perhaps avoiding discussion of medication change with even the physician, who was eager simply to cut her off, until more groundwork had been accomplished.

In a recent review, Bradley (1983) concluded on a cautionary note concerning the contingency pain management studies:

> (a) All of the studies failed to adequately control for placebo factors; (b) it is impossible to determine what specific treatments included in the contingency management programs may have been responsible for producing the reported outcomes; and (c) the stability of reported outcomes was never adequately established. (p. 343)

Fordyce's work (Fordyce, 1976; Fordyce et al., 1973) has been seminal in leading to new conceptualizations of pain and encouraging vigorous attempts to deal with otherwise intractable conditions. But the extent to which an operant conceptualization of pain can contribute to its amelioration has not been established. Uncritical acceptance of this model might serve to limit rather than stimulate further work. In those instances in which operant programs appear to work, the reasons for success need to be examined.

Multidimensional Programs

Although we have referred to Fordyce's and his colleagues' programs as multidimensional, they are avowedly based upon an operant approach to pain management. Several other programs have been developed that have deliberately incorporated disparate elements, in an attempt to attack pain on several fronts at once.

Sternbach and his colleagues (Greenhoot & Sternbach, 1974; Sternbach, 1974; Sternbach & Rusk, 1973) developed an approach that targets the "pain games" that they believe chronic pain patients develop. Seeking attention and sympathy, avoidance of tasks, and attempts to outwit the medical establishment are viewed as preoccupations that develop from prolonged pain and tend to reinforce a life centered around pain. Therapy for these patients involves attempts to disrupt these maladaptive patterns. Sternbach assumes that patients usually can control their pain behaviors if they can be sufficiently motivated and rationally convinced to do so and if they learn how.

Beginning with a challenge to a patient's motivation, Sternbach works with the patient to develop a set of specific, realistic behavioral goals and the steps to achieve them. Individual and group therapy sessions involve monitoring of progress, planning changes in environmental contingencies, and strongly challenging failures to progress. In some respects, the public and pressured nature of group sessions resembles the passionate commitment evident at a Weight Watchers or Alcoholics Anonymous meeting. Sternbach's patient is urged "to be brave and do it, or quit and be doomed" (Sternbach & Rusk, 1973, p. 323). (Such messages leave us concerned about the self-concept of dropouts from the program.)

In an evaluation of this program, 6-month follow-up self-report data on 61 patients (67 percent of those who received treatment) indicated less pain than at admission, heightened activity levels, and lowered medication usage (Sternbach, 1974). All of these indices had relapsed somewhat from discharge to follow-up, but were still significantly improved from pretreatment. Another report indicated significant changes maintained at a 3-year follow-up (Ignelzi, Sternbach, & Timmermans, 1977). Since the pain problems treated in these programs are generally quite intractable, these results appear impressive.

Several questions remain, however. The high nonresponse rate (33 percent) at 6-month follow-up challenges the generality of the effect and the applicability of the self-control-based paradigm to all patients. More importantly, it is once again impossible to determine the specific treatment components responsible for therapeutic effects. For example, some of the other treatment modalities employed with patients were physiotherapy, biofeedback, transcutaneous electrical stimulation, vocational rehabilitation, and surgery.

Another multimodal program emphasized self-regulation in chronic pain treatment (Gottlieb et al., 1977). This program's treatment of chronic low back pain patients included biofeedback-assisted relaxation; individual, group, and family counseling to assist learning adaptive emotional expression; self-regulation of medication; physical therapy; vocational counseling; and educational components. Self-regulation was stressed in all components of the program, placing responsibility for behavioral change and maintenance with the patient.

Patients with chronic low back pain typically have a poor prognosis (Loeser, 1980), which makes the results of Gottlieb et al. (1977) encouraging. Of the 72 patients in the program, 50 completed treatment. This group was rated by clinicians as evidencing less pain behavior and increased functional activity. Unfortunately, at the 6-month follow-up, only 23 patients were evaluated; however, 82 percent of these patients were employed or in a job training program, a very high proportion for this type of patient. (Information about those who were not contacted is unavailable.) Although the results, like Sternbach's, are limited by the absence of a control group, they nevertheless are encouraging.

Several similar self-management-based programs have been evaluated (Cinciripini & Floreen, 1982; Keefe et al., 1981; Seres & Newman, 1976; Swanson, Swenson, Maruta, & McPhee, 1976). In each instance significant positive changes were reported for pain and functional behavior, for both short-term and long-term results.

Cognitive Elements in Therapy

Most of the therapeutic approaches to pain management described so far have included elements designed to alter the ways in which patients think about their pain. In Fordyce's (1976) operant treatment program, for example, part of the therapy involves communicating this outlook to the patient:

> To the extent that your pain is now controlled mainly by learning factors, we can probably help your system to unlearn it and thereby to get rid of the surplus pain. Even if your pain is not now primarily learned, these procedures can probably help you to get along with the problem and have a decrease in the amount of interference from it. (p. 153)

The intention is to alter patients' views of their problems from a hopeless, passive appraisal, such as "My pain is the result of a physical disorder over which I have no control," to a hopeful, self-efficacious view, such as "My pain is partly caused by a physical condition and partly by learned behaviors, which I can change given the right tools and effort."

In Fordyce's therapy, such cognitive reconceptualizations are treated as incidental to the therapeutic process—indeed, they are not discussed as such. Recently, there has been growing attention to the specific role that may be played by cognitive elements in therapy and an attempt to integrate cognitive and behavioral elements (Bradley, 1983; Heide & Mahoney, 1980; Turk et al., 1983). We will take a closer look at this trend, examining some of the guiding principles and the evidence for a cognitive emphasis in treatment.

THE COGNITIVE-BEHAVIORAL APPROACH

Heide and Mahoney (1980) identified four principles fundamental to a group of approaches that have been called cognitive learning therapies (Mahoney, 1977):

1. Human beings respond not to environments per se but to their cognitive representations of those environments;
2. Thinking, emotion and behavior are all causally interrelated;
3. Human learning involves the active acquisition of complex rules

and skills ("deep structural changes") rather than the passive conditioning of simple habits or responses ("surface structural manifestations");

4. The task of the clinician is to teach skills and offer experiences which replace maladaptive cognitive representations with more adaptive cognitive systems. (Heide & Mahoney, 1980, pp. 100-101)

Turk et al. (1983) described the cognitive-behavioral approach as a framework within which therapeutic programs can be structured. Therapy is proposed to consist of three primary phases: (1) a conceptualization phase, concerned with helping patients to define their problems in terms that make them amenable to change; (2) a skills training phase, in which cognitive, affective, and behavioral change is promoted (this may involve overcoming skills deficits, learning new behaviors, removing obstacles impeding adaptive functioning, rehearsal of newly learned skills, and so forth); (3) the consolidation of change, promotion of generalization, and development of the basis for maintenance. Viewing pain problems from this perspective emphasizes the patient's control and responsibility in promoting change; the patient's cognitions concerning pain powerfully affect treatment.

Pain is, in fact, one of the health problems that has been most frequently studied from the cognitive-behavioral perspective. This view suggests that any intervention for pain should begin with specific attention to the patients' own perceptions of their problems. Proceeding with intervention techniques without this awareness can lead to failure simply because the specific techniques are not seen as relevant by a patient. If, for example, it is suggested to a patient with chronic low back pain that relaxation training might be helpful, but the patient believes that his pain is a result of a physical lesion and therefore cannot be affected by anything except surgery, relaxation exercises are likely only to frustrate both patient and therapist. It is unlikely that the patient will be sufficiently motivated to attend to and frequently practice a technique he believes is totally useless. If, on the other hand, the patient's views are solicited before undertaking this therapeutic tack, it may be possible to prevent abortive training attempts (which would only serve to increase a sense of helplessness and hopelessness). For example, it may be helpful to include an educational presentation from a source credible for the particular patient, explaining how muscular tension can contribute to pain from even a clear-cut injury or lesion and how relaxation can reduce tension, thereby alleviating pain. It also may help to begin with EMG biofeedback-assisted relaxation training (e.g., Keefe et al., 1981). With this preparation, the patient may be more open to a relaxation component in therapy.

This simplified example illustrates the role of the patient's cognitions from the very beginning of therapy. The cognitive-behavioral therapist elicits from the patient not only such readily reported views about the therapy, but also basic beliefs concerning the patient's condition; its impact on himself, his family, and other areas of his life; concerns about the future; hidden agendas; and so forth. It is from the development of a shared conceptualization of the problem that treatment proceeds, along lines that make sense for both therapist and patient.

The second phase of therapy is the skills training phase, applying the treatment program that has developed from the initial conceptualization of the problem. Again, explicit attention to mental events is necessary. A physical problem may be exacerbated, for example, by an internal dialogue focusing on the patient's fears and worries about the future. These ruminative concerns may inhibit the patient from engaging in physical exercises or attempts to increase activity level. Therapy will need to provide strategies for coping with the fears, perhaps by altering the ongoing negative internal dialogue, as well as by using relaxing self-instructions and imagery during new activities (Meichenbaum, 1977).

As we have seen in the case of biofeedback, however, the cognitive elements of treatment need not always be explicit in order to have an impact. Recall Andrasik and Holroyd's (1980) finding that a reversed (i.e., muscle-tension-increasing) or a no-change biofeedback treatment was as effective as EMG-decreasing feedback in reducing headaches. Intrigued by this finding, Andrasik and Holroyd examined the headache-control strategies their subjects reported learning to use during biofeedback training. They found that subjects used a variety of strategies, but that these did not differ across treatment groups. In other words, all of the treatments led subjects to undertake new, largely cognitive strategies (e.g., attention-focusing, use of imagery, rational reevaluation, self-instructions) in response to problem situations. Subjects also seemed to see stressful situations in new terms, as challenges requiring problem-solving skills that they were learning to use. As Andrasik and Holroyd (1980) noted, biofeedback interventions may have less to do with altering levels of muscular tension than they do with teaching clients "to monitor the insidious onset of headache symptoms and engage in some sort of coping response incompatible with the further exacerbation of symptoms" (p. 584).

Although specific attention to cognitive elements of the pain problem plays a role in cognitive-behavioral treatment, other aspects, such as physical therapy, drugs, and social and vocational rehabilitation, are incorporated within the framework. Self-control is emphasized (e.g.,

Keefe et al., 1981) in keeping with evidence that the feeling that one is directing one's own responses enhances treatment effectiveness (Avia & Kanfer, 1980; Kanfer & Seidner, 1973). In a program at the Miller-Owan Hospital in Duluth, Minnesota, for example, patients take part in behavioral group therapy sessions that develop coping skills and foster a self-directive attitude (Cinciripini & Floreen, 1982). Patients are themselves led to note antecedents and consequences of their pain behaviors, which are viewed as social and cognitive cues that elicit changes in others' behavior and discourage wellness. Changes are based on self-initiated alternative patterns of response, such as using appropriate assertive behaviors in place of pain behaviors, or increased use of well behaviors such as visiting friends and seeking other pleasant activities.

Finally, the likelihood that changes will generalize and be maintained is partly a function of the extent to which the patient acquires tools for generalization and maintenance during therapy (Davidson, 1976). Rehearsal of acquired physical and mental skills in a variety of real and imagined situations and the patient's assumption of increasing responsibility for the course of treatment are some of the means used. Planning for the inevitable relapses and highly probable impediments to continued improvement can help to reduce the element of surprise and assist a quick return to active coping.

Efficacy of a Cognitive-Behavioral Approach for Pain

Several reviews of laboratory and clinical studies involving cognitive-behavioral pain treatments have appeared (Bradley, 1983; Tan, 1982; Turk & Flor, 1984; Turk & Genest, 1979; Turk et al., 1983; Turner & Chapman, 1982). Convincing data concerning the clinical utility of a cognitive approach to pain treatment are provided in a study by Rybstein-Blinchik (1979). Forty-four rehabilitation patients received one of four treatments: (1) therapy focusing on training the reinterpretation of sensations (e.g., replacing "I feel pain" with "I feel numb" or "I feel aroused," as appropriate); (2) therapy focusing on use of attention-diversion strategies in response to pain; (3) therapy that led clients to focus on their physical sensations (somatization); or (4) an attention-placebo control treatment. Patients' expectancies of change did not differ across the four treatment conditions, thus discounting an expectancy-based explanation of any group differences. Patients were seen for four 1-hour sessions over 3 weeks. Following completion of treatment, the patients who had received the reinterpretation-based therapy used significantly fewer and milder verbal descriptors of pain and evidenced fewer pain behaviors than did patients in the other three conditions. Unfortunately, the study included no follow-up assessment. Nevertheless, the results are important because, as Bradley (1983) noted, this is the only such clinical investigation to use an adequate attention-placebo treatment to control for nonspecific treatment effects and expectancy for change and to include reliable, direct observations of patients' pain behaviors in addition to self-reports of pain as outcome measures.

An investigation by Rybstein-Blinchik and Grzesiak (1979) provided similar treatment for similar patients and reported improvement maintained 1 month following therapy. For such chronic problems as those treated, however, this is an inadequate follow-up period. In addition, this study included no control groups.

The Holroyd and Andrasik (1982) follow-up of a cognitive-behavioral treatment for tension headaches (described in the discussion of biofeedback) provides evidence for the durability of such treatment effects. Two years after treatment the benefits of the cognitive-behavioral treatment over a biofeedback treatment were still evident, and clients reported that they were continuing to use the coping skills they had developed in therapy.

Numerous other interventions with chronic pain have incorporated cognitive-behavioral elements in therapy. An increased sense of self-control is generally the goal, with components that include cognitive reconstruction, suggestion, distraction, anxiety reduction, and self-paced mastery exercises frequently used to contribute to that goal. The enthusiasm for incorporating cognitive elements in therapy has, however, outstripped the evidence for their efficacy. Following a 340-page review and description of a cognitive-behavioral perspective of pain and behavioral medicine, Turk, Meichenbaum, and Genest (1983) recently concluded, "Although we have reviewed a host of studies providing encouraging clinical data with a wide variety of behavioral medicine problems, a convincing set of data has not been forthcoming. . . . For 'convincing data,' we require the inclusion of adequate control groups matched for credibility . . . and adequate follow-up assessments of clinical populations" (p. 345). These authors went on to note that the same conclusion could nevertheless be drawn concerning almost all other treatment approaches. In attempts to provide whatever benefits are possible for patients in dire need and to justify research expenditures from tight budgets, a popular approach has been to throw everything possible at patients—drugs, operant programs, biofeedback, social support, etc.—in the hope of having some impact. Although such shotgun therapy is an understandable response to pressing clinical needs, advancing our understanding of how treatment works and thereby how to maximize benefits and minimize costs requires restrained, systematic investigation, which may not always provide the most short-term benefit.

One approach that may assist in the development of programs for pain treatment is to contrast those who benefit and fail to benefit from therapy. Keefe et al. (1981), for example, compared the 28 best- and worst-outcome patients of a group of 111 consecutive chronic low back pain referrals to the Behavioral Physiology Laboratory at Duke University Medical Center. They found that patients who benefited most from a behavioral treatment had had fewer surgeries, shorter periods of continuous pain, *higher* initial levels of pain, and were not on disability payments. Some of these results conflict with those from other outcome prediction studies. Swanson, Maruta, and Swenson (1979) found that treatment failures had higher initial pain levels than treatment successes. Swanson et al. (1979) and Roberts and Reinhardt (1980) also reported that a shorter history of pain was associated with better outcome; Painter et al. (1980) reported the opposite; and Keefe et al. (1981) found no relationship.

Some findings are relatively consistent in this literature. It is a common finding that being dependent upon disability payments or having a claim pending is associated with a poorer outcome (Block, Kremer, & Gaylor, 1980; Keefe et al., 1981; Newman, Seres, Yospe, & Garlington, 1978). Multiple surgeries have also been linked with poorer treatment response (Keefe et al., 1981). Moderate elevations on the Minnesota Multiphasic Personality Inventory (MMPI) Hypochondriasis and Hysteria scales, on the other hand, have been suggested to result from chronic illness, rather than to indicate a treatment-resistant, somatizing pattern (Keefe et al., 1981; Painter et al., 1980).

SUMMARY

The growing body of literature concerned with treatment of chronic illness reflects the prevalence of chronic disorders in Western society. Previous chapters have emphasized the increasing problems caused by extended illness. In 1968 the U.S. rate of long-term disability was 250 per 10,000 people; by 1980 it had climbed to over 400 per 10,000 (Burish & Bradley, 1983).

Spurred by interactional theories of stress and coping, research has attended to the multiple factors affecting adjustment, including personal, social, physical, and environmental factors (Genest, 1983). Cognitive factors have been central in much of this work (Bradley & Burish, 1983). Despite an expanding literature (Burish & Bradley, 1983; Moos, 1977), there is a paucity of well-controlled investigations. Watson and Kendall (1983) have provided a helpful summary of methodological issues—and potential solutions—facing researchers in this area. Their remarks underscore what we have discussed in this chapter. Briefly, Watson and Kendall suggest the following:

1. Long-term, longitudinal designs are desirable and sometimes necessary. Early assessments and then repeated periodic follow-up assessments are needed to understand changes that occur with chronic disease.

2. Simple comparisons of research groups should be supplemented by attempts to predict the course and outcome of various groups. In other words, instead of simply investigating whether a given intervention is helpful, research also needs to find means of identifying patients who are more and less likely to be helped by treatment, so as to maximize treatment benefits.

3. Appropriate control groups must be used. This point seems elementary, but our review of the research illustrated that it is not. Many of the studies in this area have used no controls or have used inadequate ones. Although the sacrifice of research requirements to the immediate demands of clinical treatment is often understandable, it must be recognized that in the long run, treatment improvements depend upon finding ways of reconciling these sometimes divergent goals.

4. Assessment requires reliable and valid measures. Once again, this point seems so obvious as to need no repeating. But Watson and Kendall found evidence that research was proceeding without attention to this need.

5. Finally, the measures used should not overtax the subjects. As Watson and Kendall noted, this need places further emphasis on the quality of measures. If the measures used are reliable, valid, and nonredundant, their number can be reduced and both practical and statistical aspects of research will be facilitated.

It is evident that Watson and Kendall are calling for extensive and expensive work. Unfortunately, the basic developmental work—construction, validation, and psychometric analysis of tests; longitudinal descriptive and process studies; use of multiple groups; etc.—is often sacrificed to a need for a quick fix. Less than 30 percent of psychological research can be called "basic"; the remainder constitutes investigations or demonstrations of specific applications or program evaluations (Nelson & Stapp, 1983). This distribution of efforts is supported by many of the researchers themselves. Ed Blanchard (1985), a prominent leader in health psychology and president of the Division of Health Psychology within the American Psychological Association, remarked, "I believe that applied research and outcome research have a stronger or perhaps more legitimate call upon public resources [than does basic research]" (p. 1).

This chapter has touched on many innovative psychological treatment programs for physical disorders. The development in this area has proceeded to a great extent in the order in which the material was presented: Classical conditioning approaches have been used to alter rather limited targets such as bladder control; more extensive operant programs have been developed, with generally more complex goals, such as increased muscular coordination; biofeedback has grown from early attempts at limited control over a single modality such as finger temperature or heart rate to sophisticated treatment programs with significant health-related goals, such as reduction of hypertension; and, multidimensional treatment programs have attacked such intractible and complex problems as chronic pain, generally employing a cognitive-behavioral framework, while making use of the full range of psychological techniques. The cognitive-behavioral approach involves both explicit attention to the patients' inner processes (their appraisals, beliefs, images, and thoughts concerning the problem, the impact it has on their lives, and the treatment) as well as conceptualizing therapy as multidimensional and multi-phased. All therapeutic interventions are treated as having separate, though overlapping, components concerned with (1) altering the patient's view of the problem in order to encourage change, (2) training the patient in skills, including whatever active change methods are taught and rehearsed, and (3) encouraging generalization and maintenance of the changes that have been achieved.

This development of approaches has been accompanied by greater involvement of psychologists in the direct treatment of health problems. With appropriate attention to systematic research of new methods, more gains are certain. A caveat often recited by Miller (1986) is worth repeating: "We must be bold in what we attempt, and cautious in what we claim."

Chapter Four

Stress

STRESS. The word assails us forcefully. It flashes across magazine headlines and newspaper captions. It occupies the concerned hosts of television talk shows and radio phone-in programs. Feeding on our firm belief that things could and should be better than they are, "stress" peddles self-help books and vitamins by the millions. It worries us because we "know" stress can make us sick, and we've been told to reduce stress in our lives.

In medicine, it has long been assumed that stress causes and worsens many diseases, from heart disease to allergic responses (Dohrenwend & Dohrenwend, 1978). In 1910, Sir William Osler wrote of the angina pectoris that he commonly found among Jewish businessmen:

> Living an intense life, absorbed in his work, devoted to his pleasures, passionately devoted to his home, the nervous energy of the Jew is taxed to the uttermost, and his system is subjected to that stress and strain which seems to be a basic factor in so many cases of angina pectoris. (Osler, 1910, quoted by Hinkle, 1973/1977, p. 30)

It is commonly believed that attention to stress is an important facet of prevention and treatment of illness. This leads to actions ranging from a physician's, ordering a hypertensive patient to "take it easy" to elaborate multidimensional interventions designed to alter Type A behavior in cardiac patients (e.g., Roskies et al., 1979). A closer examination of this popular but often vaguely defined concept is in order before we consider the preventive approaches to health promotion that have focused on stress reduction.

DEVELOPMENT OF THE CONCEPT OF STRESS

Selye's General Adaptation Syndrome

The predominant view of stress in the health disciplines was shaped largely by Hans Selye's work on the general adaptation syndrome (Selye, 1936). Selye's theory of stress originated with a serendipitous observation during an attempt to isolate a new sex hormone: Rats that were injected with an ovarian extract displayed a reaction that did not correspond to any known hormone (Selye, 1982). He noted that their adrenal gland secreted corticoid hormones, their thymus and lymph nodes shrank, and they developed stomach ulcers. The less pure the injection, the stronger the physiological reaction. Selye later found that events as diverse as cold, heat, infection, trauma, hemorrhage, fear, pain, and loss of blood led to a similar physiological response. This led him to hypothesize that the pattern was a general reaction of the body to demands placed upon it. Selye called this reaction the general adaptation syndrome (GAS).

Alarm reaction. The first stage in the GAS Selye termed an alarm reaction. It is a response to a disruption in the organism's homeostasis, led by an excitation of the hypothalamus, the "bridge" between the brain and the endocrine system. The pituitary is caused to discharge into general circulation the adrenocorticotrophic hormone (ACTH), which has consequently been called the "stress hormone" and is frequently used to assess stress. As ACTH reaches the adrenal cortex, the cortex becomes enlarged and hyperactive, secreting corticoids, which supply a ready source of energy for the adaptive demands being made on the organism and initiate other self-protective reactions. Other hormones such as adrenaline are secreted to aid in the response to the stressor. The thymus, spleen, lymph nodes, and other lymphatic structures shrink; blood volume decreases and the blood experiences degenerative changes in its constituents; and, eventually, ulcers in the stomach develop.

Resistance. With continued exposure to the noxious agent that elicited this reaction, the organism passes to a stage Selye termed resistance. In this stage the changes that occurred during the alarm reaction cease, and often the opposite of those occur, such as hemodilution, hyperchloremia, and anabolism. The organism may appear quite well adapted to the stressor, but there is a toll being exacted for the continued depletion of adaptational energy. This toll becomes evident when the reaction passes to the third and final stage.

Exhaustion. Prolonged exposure finally induces the third phase, the stage of exhaustion. Although recovery may still follow termination of the noxious event, Selye believed that exhausting adaptive capacities frequently results in permanent, if slight, damage to the system. If the stressor is not terminated, death follows.

Selye's theory has three central aspects: (1) It defines stress by virtue of the organism's response (if the GAS is elicited, the organism is said to be experiencing stress). (2) The theory presumes that adaptive resources are genetically determined and finite. Selye (1982) wrote, for example, of one's being "born with . . . [a particular] amount of adaptation energy" (p. 16). (3) The theory deemphasizes differences among stimuli and among organisms. During the same period as Selye developed his GAS theory, Wolff wrote about stress similarly, describing it as "a dynamic state within the organism; it is not a stimulus, assault, load, symbol, burden, or any aspect of environment, internal, external, social or otherwise" (cited in Hinkle, 1973/ 1977, p. 31).

Life Events

In contrast to Selye's and Wolff's assessment of stress based on the *response,* the work of another group of researchers has focused on the occurrence of stressful *events.* Hypothesizing that change requires adaptation, which itself is stressful, Holmes and Rahe (1967) constructed a Social Readjustment Rating Scale (SRRS) to assess the amount of stress to which an individual has been exposed. The experience of significant recent life change is considered to cause stress and to require adaptational energy and resources to cope.

Although the focus of the life events work is environmental events, compared to Selye's emphasis on the organism's response, the two views share other core assumptions. Leventhal and Nerenz (1983) noted that Selye's model

> forms the intellectual substrate for students of life events who relate illness to the total number of life changes and the total amount of behavioral adaptation they demand and not the unpleasant character of these events or their association with anger, fear, disgust, etc. (p. 6)

In addition, the life-events approach, like Selye's, assumes that organisms have a finite capacity to tolerate stress (Bakal, 1979); if this capacity is exceeded, the organism, like an overloaded bridge, collapses. It comes as no surprise to find that both the engineer's description of the overloaded bridge and the psychologist's description of the overtaxed individual as "stressed" derive from the same Latin root *strictus* denoting stretched out or drawn tight. The common usage actually has older roots than the technical one, originating in the 17th century's indication of hardship, straits, adversity, or affliction (Onions, cited by Hinkle, 1973/1977).

The scale developed by Holmes and Rahe (1967) assesses stress by applying weighted *life change units* to the events in a person's life. These weights are based on the estimated amount of change or readjustment required for each event on the part of the individual experiencing it. Estimates were derived from ratings obtained from a normative sample of primarily white, middle-class adults. The total life stress experienced during a period of time is assessed by summing the weights, or life change units, of the 42 events represented on the SRRS. Events such as death of a spouse, divorce, marriage, pregnancy, change in financial state, and change in sleeping habits are included.

Since the development of the SRRS, a variety of similar instruments have been investigated, some for particular populations, others with the intention of improving upon the original; some examples are the Recent Life Changes Questionnaire (RLCQ) (Rahe, 1974) and the PERI Life Events Scale (Dohrenwend, Krasnoff, Askenasy, & Dohrenwend, 1978). During the 1970s, the life events conception of stress stimulated so much research that Holmes (1979) estimated that over 1,000 publications appeared based on the SRRS alone.

Problems with Event-Based and Response-Based Conceptualizations

Relevance of Context

Many studies have demonstrated an association between life events change units and the development of health problems from heart disease to childhood leukemia to diabetes (Holmes & Masuda, 1974; McLanahan & Sørensen, 1984; Rahe & Arthur, 1978). Indeed, the breadth of phenomena correlated with life stress measures is so great as to raise questions about artifacts of measurement and the confounding of criterion and predictor variables (Perkins, 1982). That is, some of the items in the life events scales, such as changes in eating or sleeping habits, may occur *because* one is ill, rather than prior to the stress-related illness (Hudgens, 1974). Furthermore, commonly used measures of illness, such as self-reports of ill-health or self-referrals to physicians, have been criticized as reflecting variables other than the actual presence of illness (Mechanic, 1974). The question raised here is whether the evidence indicates that stress tends to *cause* illness.

Even if we accept the validity of the results, the stress-illness relationship seems equivocal. The size of the correlations between stress and illness that have been found has typically been low. Usually, less than 10 percent of the variance in health variables is accounted for by the life stress measures (Perkins, 1982). Negative results have also been reported, for example, in the absence of the expected epidemics of illness during or following the London blitz in the 1940s (see reviews and critiques by Dohrenwend & Dohrenwend, 1974, 1978; Hinkle, 1973/1977; Holmes & Masuda, 1974; Perkins, 1982; Rabkin & Struening, 1976). Similarly, the Israeli sociologist Antonovsky (1979) found that over 25 percent of the survivors of German concentration camps emerged without physical or emotional impairment. These settings are universally regarded as some of the worst living conditions imaginable, yet they were not, as one might expect, uniformly destructive in their impact.

After a 33-year follow-up study of 52 survivors of concentration camps or other stressful living conditions in World War II (e.g., some had hidden under extremely adverse conditions in ghettos), Leon, Butcher, Kleinman, Goldberg, and Almagor (1981) concluded:

Concentration camp and other survivors of World War II and their children as a group do not manifest serious psychological impairment. This finding does not minimize the horrendous experiences these survivors endured and the residual effect of these experiences on mood states, memories, attitudes toward others, and past and present medical problems. However . . . these individuals have been able to cope with the terrible experiences they lived through and the residue of these experiences. They truly are survivors, who have been able to work, lead productive lives, and raise psychologically healthy children despite their ordeals. (p. 514)

Although some relationship between significant life events and health seems to have been established, the early expectations of the research have not been borne out by empirical data. As Rabkin and Struening (1976) concluded, "In practical terms . . . life event scores have not been shown to be predictors of the probability of future illness" (p. 1015). It would seem that the association of events and illness does not provide strong support for the conceptions of stress based on significant life events or on nonspecific responses to events. Holroyd (1979) argued that "a strong relationship between life events and illness is unlikely to be found if the way the individual interprets and copes with events is ignored" (p. 193).

Concerning response-based definitions of stress, Mason (1975a) argued that the stress responses observed by Selye are mediated by psychological variables. He pointed out that despite Selye's use of various agents to produce a stress response, these diverse stimuli shared the property of being novel, strange, or unfamiliar. The GAS, Mason argued, is not a direct consequence of the physical agents, but of the psychological response, the evaluation of the event. Support for the central role of appraisal is provided by a study of adrenal cortical responses during stress (Symington, Currie, Curran, & Davidson, 1955, cited by Lazarus, 1975). Animals who were injured while unconscious did not respond with the GAS response. Symington et al. also noted that patients dying of a fatal disease evidence adrenal cortical changes characteristic of the GAS only if they are conscious at the time of death. If they are comatose during final stages, the adrenals appear normal upon autopsy. It has also been noted that many situations involving stress are characterized by the organism's lack of control (Frankenhaeuser, 1980). And a stress response may occur without the occurrence of either an antecedent stimulus or the phenomenological experience of distress (e.g., anxiously awaiting to be awarded an Oscar). Hinkle (1973/1977) wrote:

> It is difficult to accept the hypothesis that certain kinds of situations or relationships are inherently stressful and certain others are not. The likelihood is that the consistencies that appear in the findings of Holmes and others are based upon certain consistencies in the social relationships of many people in many societies. . . . One can accept that events and situations can be grouped into those that are more likely to be meaningful and those that are less likely to be meaningful, especially if one is dealing with people from the same level of the same society; but it is difficult to assume that one sort of event is intrinsically more "stressful" than another. (pp. 46-47)

It would seem, then, that the critical element in the development of stress is not any property of the *stressor* nor of the *physical response,* but is the individual's appraisal of the event and of her own ability to meet the demands presented by the event. The impact of events upon the individual is in large part a function of the way the individual interprets and copes with those events. Indeed, in his later work, Selye introduced a modification to his theory. He proposed two kinds of stress: "the pleasant stress of fulfillment (known technically as *eustress*—from the Greek *eu* meaning good, as in euphemia and euphoria) without the harmful consequences of damaging stress, that is *distress*" (1982, p. 16). Thus, the primary criticism that has been leveled at both the life events work and the response-based conception of stress is that they neglect the situational and individual contexts in which stress occurs.

Specificity

The response- or stimulus-based models of stress are further challenged by data concerning the specificity of responses to stressors. Stress reactions have been found to differ as a function of (1) neurophysiological level of response, (2) qualities of the stressor, and (3) differences among individuals.

First, we shall examine the finding that stressors do not affect all neurophysiological .response systems equally. Leventhal and Nerenz (1983) summarized:

> Many investigators have made clear the need to differentiate among verbal, expressive motor, and autonomic response (Graham, 1972; Lacey, 1967; Lang, 1977; Leventhal, 1970). A stressor may initiate change at only one, at any two, or at all three levels of response, and the change may occur in different components at a level (heart, kidney, etc.). (p. 7)

The second issue, that of the qualities of the stressors, has its roots in early work by Alexander and colleagues at the Chicago Psychoanalytic Institute (Alexander, 1950; Alexander, French, & Pollock, 1968). Alexander postulated that different stressors, along with different physical and psychological predispositions, tend to lead to different types of physical problems. Although systematic evidence for this position is lacking, data from various sources provide hints of intriguingly specific responses.

In laboratory investigations, Schwartz and Weinberger (1980) found that having undergraduates imagine particular situations consistently led the students to report emotional experiences that were specific to the scenes. Graham's clinical studies also suggested that particular thoughts tended to lead to specific physiological reactions (Graham 1972; Graham et al., 1962).

Finally, Lacey and his colleagues have demonstrated specificity in responses as a function of individuals, rather than stressors (Lacey, Bateman, & Van Lehn, 1953). About one-third of subjects who were exposed to several stressors responded with the same physiological changes to all stimuli; but the pattern of changes differed among subjects. Additional clinical studies provide support for this *individual response stereotypy*, with findings, for example, of a tendency for hypertensives to respond with a rise in blood pressure and ulcer patients with a change in gastric secretions or motility to all stressors (Whitehead, Fedoravicius, Blackwell, & Wooley, 1979).

Findings of the specificity of the stress reaction based on physiological levels, stressors, or individuals have been interpreted in correspondingly diverse ways. Some authors view these data as at best weak evidence for specificity, consider that a clear relationship between life events and illness has been demonstrated, and propose that several illnesses are a result of *general* reactions to stress (e.g., Whitehead et al., 1979). Others instead reject as weakly founded the proposal that the association of life events and illness is unmediated by cognitions and propose that the individual's responses to events hold the key to the relationship (e.g., Hinkle, 1973/1977). Yet another view accepts as well established the evidence in favor of specificity of events and levels of response, while similarly arguing that the individual's self-regulatory behaviors and cognitions play a central role in determining the type of response (e.g., Leventhal & Nerenz, 1983).

Despite many areas of disagreement, there is general insistence among writers in this area that the concept of stress must be heavily weighted by the individual's appraisals of events and available resources (e.g., Lazarus & Folkman, 1984). Since the 1970s, a view of stress that attempts to incorporate elements of the event, the situation surrounding it, and the individual experiencing it has become more predominant among theorists and researchers.

INTERACTIONAL VIEWS OF STRESS

Views of stress as consisting of an interaction between the person and environment have been extensively developed (e.g., Cameron & Meichenbaum, 1982; Coyne & Lazarus, 1980; Lazarus, 1966; Lazarus & Folkman, 1984; Lazarus & Launier, 1978; Leventhal, 1970; Leventhal & Everhart, 1979; Leventhal & Nerenz, 1983; Pearlin, Lieberman, Menaghan, & Mullan, 1981). From this view, physical, emotional, or even imagined events may constitute stressors, that is, stimuli that make demands upon the individual. There is an arbitrariness to distinctions among types of stressors, since the perception of the stressor is the most important factor. The degree to which the individual is stressed by such events varies according to a complex interaction of factors, including the assessment of the event, the resources that are judged to be available to deal with it, and the coping attempts that are undertaken.

Lazarus identified three stages in the process determining the degree of stress experienced. The first stage involves the *primary appraisal* of the event: Based upon knowledge of himself and of the event and upon prior learning (including conditioned emotional responses), the individual decides whether he is in jeopardy. If the stressor is perceived to be imminently threatening or already to have caused some harm or loss, the *secondary appraisal* takes place. If, on the other hand, the event is judged to be irrelevant to well being, benign, or even positive in its potential, no further development of the stress transaction takes place, that is, no state of stress exists.

If the individual progresses to the second phase, he assesses resources to deal with the threat: What behavioral and emotional resources are available to respond to the stressor? Holroyd and Lazarus (1982) noted that this decision is influenced by "previous experiences in similar situations, generalized beliefs about the self and the environment, and the availability of personal (e.g., physical strength or problem-solving skills) and environmental (e.g., social support or money) resources" (p. 23).

This secondary appraisal is akin to a judgment of how much *control* the individual has over the situation. Mason and his colleagues have reported that predictability versus unpredictability lead to different patterns of catecholamine and corticosteroid excretion (Mason, 1975b; Mason, Sachar, Fishman, Hamburg, & Handlon, 1965). Similarly, workers' control over the pace of their jobs (e.g., machine-paced or not) has been related to excretion of catecholamines and self-reports of distress (Frankenhaeuser, 1978).

The decision-making concerning what means of control are available determines the third phase, *coping*. The actions that are determined to be available and most suited to the stressor are then taken.

To pose a simple example, if one notices that a mole has increased in size and appears darker, one might think about the possible implications, try to remember when one last noticed the mole and whether it really had changed, and decide to monitor it more closely in case it were cancerous. One is appraising the stimulus as potentially, but not certainly, threatening. If one's concern remained (i.e., the appraisal led to increasing certainty of a threat), the next step might involve a visit to a physician (taking action to cope with the stressor), who, let us suppose, provides reassurance that the mole is not malignant, but says to keep an eye on it in any case.

Following the coping effort, the individual *reappraises* the original stressor to determine whether its threat value has been diminished, or if another cycle through the secondary appraisal and coping are necessary. To continue our example, it might be that one is alarmed to find that the mole continues to grow and becomes raised—that is, the threat is not appraised as having diminished, but as having increased. A second evaluation of options may lead to the determination to consult the physician again and to seek a second opinion.

Holroyd and Lazarus (1982) described the model simply as a two-stage question sequence: "Am I okay or in trouble?" constitutes the initial appraisal problem and "What can be done about the situation?" constitutes the secondary appraisal, which precedes coping attempts. From the interactional viewpoint, stress occurs in the face of demands that tax or exceed the resources of the system, or, to put it in a slightly different way, "demands to which there are no readily available or automatic adaptive responses" (Lazarus & Cohen, 1977, p. 109). Even the determination to take effective action (such as to see the physician again about the mole) frequently reduces stress somewhat because it is accompanied by a reappraisal that the situation can and will be handled. The situation is under control.

This sequence of appraisal of the stressor and resources available to deal with it are deemed to be only partly conscious and intentional (Leventhal & Nerenz, 1983). Just as one does not go through a prolonged consideration of data and careful weighing of alternatives in deciding to flee from a truck in full career, the experience of great threat may abbreviate rational processes, causing biased and emotionally based decisions (Janis & Mann, 1977). Even in less extreme situations, much of the interaction between the individual and the environment probably takes place automatically, without conscious recognition (Lazarus & Folkman, 1984; Meichenbaum & Gilmore, 1984).

IMPLICATIONS OF AN
INTERACTIONAL MODEL OF STRESS

Proponents of an interactional view of stress do not deny that stress plays a role in the etiology of illness. The primary impact of this view of stress on theory and research in the area is to change the focus from the assumption of a general, nonspecific, and event-determined physical response to a search for specific cognitive and dispositional variables that mediate the differential responses across individuals (Gentry & Kobasa, 1984). Lazarus and Folkman (1984) recently summarized:

> It is widely assumed that stress, emotion, and coping are causal factors in *somatic illness*. The major controversy is not whether this assumption is true, but whether there is generality or specificity in the relationship between stress, emotion, and somatic illness. Generality theories, for which Selye's General Adaptation Syndrome provided the impetus, hold that all demands are more or less qualitatively equivalent in producing physiological mobilization and that the mobilization increases general susceptibility to all diseases. An epidemiological version of the generality theory is the concept of "host resistance." Generality models cannot easily explain individual differences in physiological response patterns and disease outcomes, however, and specificity models, some of which incorporate cognitive appraisal and coping, are gaining prominence. Appraisal processes provide a common

pathway through which person and environment variables modify psychological response, and hence emotions and their biological concomitants. (p. 224)

It is no longer assumed that identifying the stressors present for an individual or group assists in determining the risk for illness. Ostensibly stressful events do not have an invariant impact across or within individuals. Events interact with mediating variables, which interact among themselves (Pearlin et al., 1981). An intriguing example of an interaction's determining the impact of stress on health is provided in the longitudinal study of an Italian-American community in Pennsylvania. Between 1955 and 1961, it was found that the town of Roseto had an unusually low death rate from heart disease (Stout, Morrow, Brandt, & Wolf, 1964). Roseto had less than half the rate of myocardial-infarction-related (MI) deaths of nearby communities. Further studies confirmed this unusual finding (Bruhn, Philips, & Wolf, 1972, 1982; Bruhn & Wolf, 1978). The most interesting aspect of the low MI rate was that it occurred in a population that appeared similar to the other samples studied and to American norms on conventional risk factors such as cholesterol levels and smoking. In fact in some respects the Italian culture supported practices that elevated risk, with a generous caloric diet, high levels of fat and wine, and lack of exercise. Yet these factors appeared to be unrelated to risk in this community. The neighboring comparison communities were also of similar genetic background, having been settled primarily by Italian immigrants at the same time as was Roseto.

The investigators singled out close family ties and strong social support systems as the difference that buffered the deleterious effects of stressors for Rosetans (Bruhn, Philips, & Wolf, 1982). Most Rosetans were related to one another, and families rallied to the aid of members in distress. Membership in strong social clubs and organizations was universal, religion important, and work regular, comfortable, and sociable. Comparison communities had become much more assimilated with mainstream American culture, and differed from Roseto in these characteristics. Support for this interpretation of the Rosetan pattern was provided in the unfortunate increase of MI rates that was recorded as the community became more assimilated into American ways. Evidence of loosening family and community ties was available in 1965, and "by 1970 materialistic and individualistic values had displaced much of the cohesive group concern of Roseto" (Bruhn & Wolf, 1978). By 1975 the MI death rate had reached that of the neighboring communities, which was comparable to U.S. norms.

Roseto illustrates the complexities of interaction effects in mediating the impact of stress. Searching for other mediating variables and detailing their roles may be a fruitful means of identifying protective mechanisms, which may eventually be useful in both treatment and primary prevention.

The potential connection nodes between aspects of the stress process and physical health are numerous. Zegans (1982) noted some of the hypotheses concerning the ways in which the experience of stress may lead to pathology of tissues and organs:

1. The acute body response itself may cause damage, particularly if an already compromised organ is involved.

2. The acute response may cause transient insult to a tissue, but repeated occurrence of the stress may cause permanent tissue damage.

3. The acute physiological reaction can become chronic if it becomes conditioned to a benign stimulus resembling the stressor. Such a benign stimulus may be a more regular part of the individual's environment and provoke an unnecessary coping response.

4. A coping strategy may be used successfully but the physiological component is not terminated when the challenge is mastered. A *reverberating circuit* is established, which puts unusual strain on the body.

5. A minor stress provocation releases an inappropriately severe physiological response. Modulation is lacking that grades the body's reaction according to the nature of the threat. When all stresses are responded to as major assaults, abnormal physiological reactions are possible.

6. A physiological response appropriate and adequate to cope with a given threat may result in damage to some other aspect of the body through inhibiting a benign but vital body process or stimulating an irritating one.

7. Coping strategies can misfire when the behavioral component is inhibited but the physiological aspect is expressed (fight behavior inhibited but not its physiological component). The physiological aspects of a blocked action can be continuously repeated since no appropriate cutoff signal is received. (p. 146)

Zegans goes on to note that current knowledge is extremely limited concerning how these interactions between cognitive-affective and physiological aspects of stress effect tissue damage.

The hypothesized mechanisms influencing disease processes differ from one disease to another disease. In diabetes mellitus, for example, elevated stress levels are thought to exacerbate hyperglycemia by the autonomic nervous system's impact on secretion of insulin by the pancreas and by sympathetic regulation of glycogen to glucose conversion in the liver, fat to free fatty acid change in adipose tissue, and cortisol production in the adrenal cortex, which alters glucose tolerance (Surwit & Feinglos, 1984).

The mechanisms by which stress may affect cancer have been extensively studied by experimental studies in animals and correlational ones with human beings (Cunningham, 1985). Hypothesized mechanisms of effect are extremely varied, as would be expected in this complex disease process. As an example, Newberry, Liebelt, and Boyle (1984) pointed to the broad impact of stress-related catecholamine changes on the immune system, on blood flow rates through smooth muscle contraction in blood vessel walls, on reduced inflammation, and on changes in clotting mechanisms.

An example of the impact on health of sustained levels of stress is provided by events at the Kennedy Space Center during the mid-1960s. During this period, the sudden death rate among men working at the Center was almost 50 percent higher than that of control groups matched for age and sex. In addition, this population showed the highest level of consumption of alcohol in the United States, the divorce rate was three out of four marriages, and the incidence of general neurotic symptoms, anxiety, and depression was extremely high. It is not difficult to pose hypotheses for the occurrence of these negative events. Consider the exigency of their situation. There was extreme pressure to put a man on the moon by the end of 1969. International attention focused on their efforts and therefore on any potential failure. Their work was exceedingly complex, requiring coordination of thousands of individuals and hundreds of organizations. Yet they were working within a shrinking budget and the near-certainty that most workers would lose their jobs upon attainment of the objective. Indeed, as the project neared its goal, layoffs accelerated, leaving overspecialized, once highly valued workers with poor prospects for future employment.

Another indication of the impact of prolonged stress elevation on health is provided by Pennebaker's work (Pennebaker, 1982, 1985). In a series of correlational, laboratory experimental, and retrospective studies, Pennebaker has advanced the idea that the experience of a traumatic event can have long-term consequences on health. The relationship is hypothesized to result from attempts to suppress recall of or thoughts about the trauma. Such attempts are actually associated with increased and aversive thoughts about the event, which in turn lead to increased autonomic activity. Pennebaker (1985) found that people who discussed traumatic events such as parental divorce or death prior to age 17, suffered no apparent long-term health consequences, whereas those who avoided talking about the events were experiencing significantly more days ill or in the hospital and more visits to physicians an average of more than 19 years later.

Many current preventive programs target stress as a contributor to illness. Other programs treat stress as an undesirable potential consequence of illness, which can in turn exacerbate problems or cause additional physical or psychological difficulties. Chapter 5 examines the acute stress that can accompany medical procedures and surgery. Chapter 6 will look at the chronic stress that underlies many diseases and health problems.

SUMMARY

Physiological reactions to stress, from an interactional perspective, are hypothesized as being mediated by cognitive variables—the individual's appraisal of the threat presented by a particular situation. Much of this appraisal occurs automatically and unconsciously, although this is not always the case. Because stressful events do not have an invariant impact across or within individuals, identifying common stressors does not in itself indicate the risk posed by any one of those stressors to a particular individual. Further, the mechanisms by which stress effects tissue damage vary among diseases. Although much work remains to be accomplished to unravel the connections among stressors, mediating variables, and physiological effects, the available information already underscores the potential importance of cognitions in ameliorating the impact of stress.

Chapter Five

Acute Stress

Treatment or diagnosis of illness is often unpleasant. Some procedures, such as surgery, cardiac catheterization, sigmoidoscopy, or chemotherapy, cause both physical and mental distress. Various means to diminish the stress of these events have been attempted in order to ameliorate suffering, reduce complications, and speed recovery. One of the simplest of preventive interventions has been extensively studied in this context: the provision of information.

STRESS AND APPRAISAL

An interactional model of stress suggests that the appraisal of the event and of one's resources for dealing with it are important in determining the level of stress experienced. Most patients know little about what to expect during major medical interventions except from dramatizations and accounts of other patients, which tend to emphasize fearful aspects of the experience. One of the reasons medical procedures induce high levels of stress is because this lack of accurate information affects the appraisal process and leads the patient to view the impending assault as more threatening and frightening than it need be. Work by Janis (1958), which predated this model, provided support for an appraisal-based interpretation of stress in patients undergoing surgery.

Interviews with patients before they had major surgery led Janis to identify three groups of patients according to their levels of anticipatory fear. Janis found that patients tended (1) to be very fearful, giving ready expression to worries and anxiety, (2) to express a moderate level of fear, tending to seek out information from hospital staff to allay their concerns, or (3) to show little or no fear before surgery. Following surgery, Janis found that the group that had shown moderate fear preoperatively showed less emotional disturbance.

Janis hypothesized that moderate fear is optimal for preparing for the stressful event. The fear produced motivation to develop adaptive coping strategies, which in this instance seemed primarily to consist of obtaining information about the impending surgery.

Janis's findings of a curvilinear relationship between level of fear and postsurgical outcome have been disconfirmed by later studies, although the importance of fear has been underscored (Anderson & Masur, 1983; Reading, 1979). Sime (1976), for example, found a linear relationship: the higher the fear, the slower and more difficult the recovery. In addition, various factors, such as internal versus external locus of control (whether individuals felt in control of the situation or felt it was out of their hands) or an information-seeking versus avoiding disposition in the patient, have been suggested to influence the impact of information (Gil, 1984; Scott & Clum, 1984). In a recent systematic review of this literature, Gil (1984) proposed an interactional model that resembles the cognitive-coping model previously described (Lazarus & Folkman, 1984). Despite the current absence of a clear understanding of how fear, information, and other variables interact, there is a general consensus that provision of information has a positive effect (Anderson & Masur, 1983; Reading, 1979).

The information-gathering of medical patients can be understood in terms of appraisal processes. These processes assist patients in modifying the unknown aspects of the procedure or surgery, making it seem more manageable, and therefore heightening the sense that they have the resources necessary to handle it.

Since Janis's work, numerous studies have evaluated the stress-reducing potential of provision of preparatory information for medical patients. Three types of information have been compared: information concerning *sensory* aspects of the experience, *procedures* to be used, and ways of *coping* with the experience and its aftereffects.

Sensory information provides patients with accurate expectations concerning the types of sensations that they are likely to experience as a result of the procedures. Surgical patients, for example, can be told about the type, intensity, and duration of discomfort that is usual for the type of operation they will have. Such information can reduce the likelihood that patients will engage in catastrophic thinking about their surgery when they experience discomfort. As one of Janis's subjects reported, "I knew there might be some bad pains, so when my side started to ache, I told myself that this didn't mean anything had gone wrong" (Janis, 1969, p. 98). This patient can be seen to be appraising the situation in a relatively nonthreatened manner, and therefore avoiding the stress that he would experience if, for example, he began to worry that the "bad pains" he experienced meant something had gone wrong.

Evidence for the value of sensory information is provided by a study reported by Johnson and Leventhal (1974). An endoscopic examination requires the patient to swallow a fiberoptic tube and remain still, with the tube extending into the gastrointestinal tract for up to half an hour. This procedure is considered a sufficiently unpleasant procedure that patients are routinely assisted to relax by injections of Valium. When Johnson and Leventhal's study was carried out, endoscopy was generally much more aversive, since fiberoptic tubes were not in general use, and a more rigid tube, with a diameter similar to that of a thumb, was the rule. Gagging, coughing, and difficulty in breathing were common, all of which make the experience more unpleasant and sometimes painful. Patients who were provided with information about the sensations likely to be experienced (e.g., prick of the needle, drowsiness, feeling of fullness in the stomach, a gagging sensation) were less distressed and more cooperative during the examination than subjects provided with only information about the medical procedures to be used.

Procedural information itself can, nevertheless, assist patients in attaining a sense of self-control over their experience. Unpredictable events are appraised as uncontrollable. Provision of details concerning the procedure per se enables patients to view events as less unknown and therefore less threatening, and to maintain a greater sense of control (Thompson, 1981).

Animal studies have suggested that predictability in a stressful situation results in having cues available that enable one to predict "safety." That is, because one knows more about the stressor and the situation in which it is embedded, the surrounding events are less fear-arousing, and consequently the experience of stress is more limited to discrete events (Weiss, 1970). The cues for safety become more salient with increased procedural knowledge.

Providing patients with *information on ways to cope* should have an impact on the secondary appraisal process, their evaluation of the resources they have available to deal with the stressful event. It should also alter the actual coping behaviors, enabling patients to make better use of active strategies that are likely to alter the situation itself.

Coping instructions, such as those on how to breathe to reduce pain, have been found to induce more rapid recovery from surgery (Lindeman & Van Aernam, 1971) and to lead to lower use of analgesic drugs (Healey, 1968).

These three types of information have been compared in studies preparing patients for surgery and other aversive medical procedures, such as an endoscopic examination (e.g., Johnson & Leventhal, 1974) or a cardiac catheterization procedure (Kendall et al., 1979). In general, it has been found that both sensory and procedural information are effective in reducing patients' distress and that coping information may be useful over a wider range of circumstances. In the Johnson and Leventhal (1974) endoscopy study, those subjects who received both coping and sensory information were better off than those receiving only procedural or sensory information.

Kaplan, Atkins, and Lenhard (1982) examined the contribution of the patient's sense of self-control to the coping effort. They investigated means of assisting patients to deal with sigmoidoscopy (a 2- to 3-minute examination, requiring insertion of a scope in the anal cavity, which most patients find physically uncomfortable and embarrassing, though not painful). All patients in the study were provided with sensory information concerning the examination. In addition, some subjects were taught to use self-instructions to reduce emotional arousal and increase coping attempts during the procedure. Half of these were provided with self-control-based self-statements (e.g., "I can control my reactions; I'll just stay calm and the exam will go easier"), whereas half were given external-control-based statements to repeat (e.g., "I can really trust the doctor because he knows exactly what he is doing. Leave the worrying to the doctor—he is the specialist in this area"). One-third of the subjects received an attention-placebo program. Training in relaxation was also systematically manipulated across groups. It was found that self-instructional training led to lower anxiety ratings and fewer verbal and behavioral indications of distress. There were few differences between the self- versus external-control conditions, suggesting that under some circumstances or for some individuals—perhaps different ones in each instance—either type of stratagem may be effective. Relaxation training also lowered self-rated anxiety.

TARGETING APPRAISALS TO REDUCE STRESS

If information-based interventions are helpful because they alter the appraisal processes and the coping responses undertaken to reduce stress, then perhaps directly targeting appraisals and coping for change can result in enhanced effects. Langer, Janis, and Wolfer (1975) did this in a study of patients who were to undergo a variety of elective surgical procedures, from hysterectomies and cholecystectomies (gall bladder removal) to tubal ligations. A group of patients was prepared for surgery by training in reappraisal of anxiety-provoking cues in less stress-producing ways. Negative internal dialogues that tended to lead to negative appraisals were identified and altered. New coping strategies, such as attention-diversion and cognitive-coping strategies (e.g., considering the positive outcomes of the surgery), were introduced and rehearsed. Patients in the first group received appraisal and coping information; patients in the second group received procedural and sensory information; patients in the third group received appraisal, coping, procedural, and sensory information; and patients in the fourth group received only a general interview with a psychologist. Both before and after surgery, nurses rated the amount of stress experienced by the patients, and records of their requests for analgesics and sedatives were kept. Both groups who received the appraisal and coping training (alone, or with the preparatory information) demonstrated significantly less preoperative and postoperative distress and requested fewer analgesic and sedative medications.

A similar attempt to alter the stressfulness of surgery was reported by Fortin and Kirouac (1976). These researchers provided herniorraphy, hysterectomy, and cholecystectomy patients with (1) an orientation to the surgical experience and hospital, including what to expect after surgery (e.g., the possibility of nausea, pain, and weakness), (2) elementary biological facts related to their surgery and suggestions concerning self-care, (3) an explanation of the purpose and techniques of respiratory and muscular exercises, with routines to follow postsurgically, (4) techniques for changing position in order to minimize postsurgical discomfort, and (5) techniques, such as slow, deep breathing, to cope with postsurgical nausea, vomiting, pain, dizziness, and weakness. This information was provided by nurses as part of preadmission procedures, 15 to 20 days before surgery. Patients in the treatment group were compared to matched control subjects who were also preadmitted but did not receive the specific elements of the program outlined above. It was found that the experimental preparation program led to significantly accelerated resumption of physical capacities (e.g., at 33 days postsurgery, 86 percent of experimental subjects, compared to 53 percent of controls, had unimpaired physical function), lower use of analgesics, and higher ratings of comfort during the recovery period.

INTERVENTIONS WITH CHILDREN

A similar approach has proven effective in reducing the distress experienced by children undergoing surgery. Visintainer and Wolfer (1975) provided 3- to 12-year-old children admitted to the hospital for tonsillectomies with a cognitive-behavioral program that included provision of procedural and sensory information, encouragement of expression of feelings, identification of goals and strategies for the child (e.g., holding an arm still in order to shorten the blood test), support, and rehearsal. The intervention, which differed in format according to the children's ages, occurred at six stress points during hospitalization: (1) admission, (2) shortly before the blood test, (3) late in the day before surgery, (4) just prior to preoperative medications, (5) before transport to surgery, and (6) upon return from recovery. An intervention at the same times and along similar lines was provided for a parent (generally the mother). This experimental intervention was compared with (1) a single-session preparation, which included the same elements but was conducted in one 45-minute period shortly after ward admission; (2) supportive nursing care without specific provision of information, guidance, or rehearsal, but also provided at the six "stress points," and (3) routine hospital procedures. Approximately 20 children were randomly assigned to each condition.

The design of this study is exemplary: (1) It carefully controlled for the *content* and *contact* elements of the intervention through separate treatments with random assignment; (2) it enhanced external validity by tailoring treatments to individuals and constructing the intervention around naturally occurring events in hospitalization; and (3) it utilized parental questionnaire and open-ended inquiry, as well as blind assessment of a variety of dependent variables, from ratings of behavioral upset and cooperation during several stages of the hospitalization (e.g., blood test, transport to surgery) to recovery room medications, pulse rate, and time to first voiding.

The results from this study are sufficiently illuminating that we will discuss them in some detail. First of all, there was a clear superiority of the cognitive-behavioral, six-point intervention over the supportive care and routine treatments on almost all measures. In comparing this intervention with the benefits from the traditional, ideally supportive nursing role, the author's comments are challenging:

> Evidently consistent supportive care at critical points during hospitalization without factual and sensory information and opportunity for rehearsal through plan or practice is not as effective a stress-reducing practice as the combination of information

and support. . . . Consistent supportive contact from the same nurse alone is not enough, even for younger children. (p. 199)

Visintainer and Wolfer also compared the results for the six stress-point preparation and the single-session preparation. They hypothesized that the multiple-point intervention would be more effective because it would allow a better relationship between child (and parent) and nurse, repeatedly reinforce desirable coping responses, thus aiding in generalization, and be easier for the child to assimilate, facing one task at a time. These hypotheses were generally borne out, with the multiple intervention being superior on almost all relevant comparisons.

In yet another area, Visintainer and Wolfer's results challenge the popular mythology. Even casual observation of the treatment of children in medical settings (and other institutions) indicates a fairly pervasive bias of adults to assume that the younger the child, the less important it is to provide information and the more important to provide warm and consistent, reassuring support. Drawing on this bias, Visintainer and Wolfer had anticipated that the youngest children (3 to 6 years old) would require less information and benefit more from consistent, supportive care. The data failed to support this relationship on any outcome measure: Even the single-session preparation benefited the younger group more than just supportive care. As the authors noted,

> this suggests that even for younger children, the need for information and the desire to maintain control over the environment are factors in reaction to stress. It further supports the speculation that parents who are prepared and understand the environment and their role in it are more effective caretakers for their children than parents who are faced with an unknown situation. (p. 200)

Other investigators have provided extensive support of the beneficial impact of providing children with information concerning procedures and strategies through the use of films (e.g., Faust & Melamed, 1984; Melamed, 1977).

A similar study by Wolfer and Visintainer (1979) involved a larger sample (163 children) and the addition of a home-care preparation booklet that provided sensory and procedural information. Provision of the booklet in itself was found to improve children's adjustment and coping with the stresses of hospitalization and minor surgery. But 19 percent of those who were provided with the booklet did not make use of it. This points to an important consideration, which we raised in the chapter on adherence: It is insufficient simply to provide services without regard to their acceptability to or use by the targeted population. Wolfer and Visintainer also found that parental satisfaction was improved and parental anxiety lowered when the use of the preparation booklet was followed by systematic preparation in the hospital.

PREPARED CHILDBIRTH

Childbirth does not deserve to be called an "aversive medical procedure," but it *is* normally a stressful event. The psychoprophylactic programs for childbirth that have become popular in recent years are primarily information-based preventive interventions that have gained widespread acceptance.

Following the lead of a few enthusiastic professionals such as Dick-Read (1953), Velvovski (Velvovski, Platonov, Plotitcher, & Chougom, 1960), Lamaze (1958), and Bing (1969), a strong popular movement for prepared childbirth led first to independent programs and eventually to classes integrated within about one-third of U.S. hospitals (Wideman & Singer, 1984). We will not describe these programs here (see Bing, 1969; Karmel, 1965; Lamaze, 1958). They are generally well known, and several reviews are available (Beck & Hall, 1978; Beck & Siegel, 1980; Genest, 1981; Wideman & Singer, 1984). Instead, we would like to explore briefly how it is that they have come to exist in the system. The mushrooming of childbirth preparation programs is an interesting phenomenon, for it seems to contradict what we have said about the system's lack of support for preventive efforts. A closer look is illuminating.

We described the important contribution of research evidence that supports the efficacy of trial interventions and provides information concerning the mechanisms of action of interventions. This work, we said, could provide the basis for undertaking large-scale preventive efforts. Yet childbirth preparation programs have not been established because of this work. Very little research has been done: Wideman and Singer's (1984) search revealed 13 articles in *Index Medicus* from 1960 to 1980, and most of these were "how to" accounts rather than research papers. The work that has been carried out often yielded inconclusive or inconsistent results (Beck & Siegel, 1980; Genest, 1981; Wideman & Singer, 1984). Although there have been reports of reduced labor pain, reduced medication usage, and fewer complications among prepared mothers, there have also been reports of null findings. Furthermore, most studies have been poorly controlled and random assignment has been virtually nonexistent.

The increased availability of psychoprophylactic programs for childbirth has not resulted from scientific evidence for their efficacy, but from a strong consumer demand. This demand is both based on and reflected in one of the literature's most constant findings: that both mothers and fathers who participate in classes are more satisfied with their experiences than those who do not (e.g., Cogan, Henneborn, & Klopfer, 1976; Henneborn & Cogan, 1975). The strong motivation of parents-to-be led to fee-for-service programs often run by individuals in their own homes or sponsored by community agencies on a break-even basis. Proliferation of private programs has spawned more widespread attempts to provide similar services by hospitals and community clinics, under various cost-sharing arrangements. Thus, the institutionalization of this preventive program can be traced not to natural developments in the health-care system (that is, not as an outgrowth of scientific findings), but rather to high consumer demand, which funded private service, leading to pressure to incorporate these health-related programs under the aegis of the formal system.

PREVENTION OF CHEMOTHERAPY COMPLICATIONS

A clear need for assistance in the reactions to chemotherapy in cancer treatment has spurred recent interest, and programs in this area are beginning to appear.

Nausea and vomiting are frequent accompaniments to the chemotherapy treatment of cancer. These side effects are not only pharmacologically induced; they appear also to become conditioned, so that they occur in anticipation of as well as following treatment in proportions of patients that have varied among studies from 18 percent to 65 percent (Ahles et al., 1984; Burish & Redd, 1983). Burish and Redd (1983) noted that following two or three treatments, some patients begin vomiting as the drugs are injected, while the skin is cleaned in preparation, or even simply upon approaching the hospital, talking to an oncology nurse, or thinking about treatment. This conditioned emesis is more than unpleasant; it frequently affects the willingness of patients to undergo chemotherapy (Nerenz, Leventhal, & Love, 1982). In addition, it contributes to premature termination of therapy. Early termination of chemotherapy because of severe nausea and vomiting occurs in 33 percent of children and 59 percent of adolescents (Smith, Rosen, Trueworthy, & Lowman, 1979).

Burish and Redd (1983) found that five controlled studies had been conducted evaluating the value of three types of techniques to treat these conditioned side effects: progressive muscle relaxation training, hypnosis, and systematic desensitization. Each of the five studies had found strong evidence supporting the usefulness of its treatments in alleviating the conditioned nausea or vomiting or both. By contrast, control treatments such as Rogerian counseling and attention-control, and unstructured contact with a therapist had no impact.

LeBaron and Zeltzer (1984a; Zeltzer & LeBaron, 1983) reported on their own and others' controlled investigations, case reports, and experimental case studies concerning the use of hypnotherapy and relaxation to ameliorate pain and anxiety in children and adolescents receiving cancer treatment. They noted that hypnotic techniques have proven particularly effective with this population in reducing the distress experienced during such procedures as bone marrow aspiration and lumbar punctures.

LeBaron and Zeltzer (1984b) noted that the needs of patients vary and it is important to tailor such treatments to suit the individuals. They found, for example, that despite the investigators' expectation that adolescents would evince a need for mastery and independence, the adolescent patients, on the contrary, wanted the therapist present. They seemed to rely on the therapist's being active and directive, and they rejected the majority of the self-guided techniques used in studies with adults. Because these therapists sensitively offered their patients a variety of attention-diverting techniques (including playing games, telling stories, providing reassurance and information, teaching muscular relaxation, and helping focus attention on objects in the treatment room), the therapy was able to be guided by the preferences and needs of the patients. The authors noted that this temporary dependence of the adolescents did not prevent them from quickly resuming control once they had experienced a reduction of symptoms.

IMPLEMENTATION OF PROGRAMS

In all, preparatory interventions for potentially stressful medical events have clearly proven their usefulness. Besides the humane benefit of reducing anxiety and providing comfort to patients, Wolfer and Visintainer (1979) noted that such preparation may have other long-term benefits: It may lead to a positive introduction to hospitalization, fostering positive attitudes toward health care, and may enhance understanding and the sense of personal control over one's well-being, which may in turn positively influence health-seeking behaviors. Finally, any intervention that speeds recovery lowers costs of medical care.

Yet, the use of preparatory programs is by no means universal:

> Given that potential preparation benefits include the improved well-being of the patient, reduced medical costs, and the fulfillment of legal-ethical requirements, it is surprising that health-care providers are still debating whether such preparation is neccessary (Rayder, 1979). Although many hospitals have devel-

oped programs for children, they have not provided similar treatments for adults. (Anderson & Masur, 1983, p. 35)

Despite the established usefulness of preparatory programs and patients' preferences for their availability (Messerli, Garamendi, & Romano, 1980), attempts by progressive professionals to introduce appropriate preparatory interventions may be met with rebuff (Rayder, 1979). This results partly from the manner in which established medical and nursing routines resist the anticipated emotionality of communications concerning patients' concerns and fears (Levine, 1979). Most medical professionals receive little formal preparation in dealing with those issues that may surface while discussing impending medical procedures, especially when the outcome of the procedures will not be benign. In fact, however, the emotional discharge that is anxiously anticipated occurs rarely. But the impersonality of medical routines partly functions to keep a "professional" distance from emotional involvement, that is, to maintain personal equilibrium in the face of the patient's distress. It is not disputed that such equilibrium is needed to reduce the stress that health professionals experience. But introducing programs that systematically provide preparatory contact for patients need not sacrifice the professional's well-being. Use of psychological resources—from psychology departments, private consultants, or other sources—could assist direct service personnel to develop programs that would be appropriate to their patients' needs and their own skills, while offering training in dealing with aspects of interpersonal contact that may be viewed with apprehension. In addition, access to appropriate referral contacts for problems that are not readily dealt with on the front lines can alleviate the health professionals' anxiety of being faced with situations out of their depth.

It is important to note that initiation of preparatory programs requires careful planning, piloting, and assessment of the programs' impact. For example, simply providing procedural information to patients before surgery is seldom sufficient (Scott & Clum, 1984). Since little is known about which patients benefit most from which types of preparation, ongoing systematic study of a program's impact can be expected to be useful.

Putting the positive findings into practice obviously requires more than publishing the results. It will take integrated attempts on the part of invested professionals to tailor interventions to the practical considerations of treatment settings, with particular attention to the needs of staff members as well as patients. Especially in view of the extreme and sustained levels of distress associated with some medical procedures (e.g., Anderson, Karlsson, Anderson, & Tewfik, 1984), increasing the availability of the documented, successful programs would seem to demand a high priority. Unfortunately, although some professionals, including nurses, psychologists, and physicians, have recognized the need and established programs, these efforts are successful in spite of a nonsupportive system rather than because of it.

SUMMARY

Patients about to undergo an aversive medical procedure are likely to experience stress that lasts from a few hours to a few weeks, depending upon the nature of the surgery and recovery period. In such circumstances, interventions are generally aimed at reducing the psychological distress itself and aiding the procedure or recovery process, or both. The health-care system lacks systematic development of and support for these preventive programs, which would parallel, for example, the research on and implementation of new treatment approaches for leukemia, heart disease, or diabetes. Nevertheless, because they are short-term programs and do show benefits in standard medical treatment (e.g., increased adherence rates, more willing patients, and reduced complications) and because of consumer demand, brief stress-reducing preventive programs have found a place in the health-care system and are likely to evolve as part of regular procedures. More extended programs, such as those for cancer patients, are less well-developed and such interventions will require more extensive adjustments in the system or intentional policy decisions for substantial growth.

Chapter
Six

Chronic Stress

Short-term stress is generally not viewed as having long-term impact on a person. Extended elevation of stress levels, however, may lead to severe or permanent physical harm (Selye, 1982). One major direction of recent stress and illness research has been to examine the contribution of continuing minor daily stressors and how they are handled, rather than focusing on major traumatic events (Kanner, Coyne, Schaefer, & Lazarus, 1981). Early reports indicate that daily hassles may be as significant in potential for harm as less frequent, major life events (DeLongis, Coyne, Dakof, Folkman, & Lazarus, 1982; Kanner et al., 1981; Lazarus & DeLongis, 1983; Zarsky, 1984).

The development or exacerbation of illnesses such as peptic ulcer, diabetes mellitus, cardiovascular disease, and cancer have been linked to chronic or severe stress. Work in this area has unfortunately been quite fragmented, frequently focusing on specific diseases to the exclusion of commonalities. We will discuss the issues raised in research on and treatment of chronic-stress-related illness by reference to these separate literatures, noting common themes.

PEPTIC ULCER

Although the etiology of duodenal ulcers is complex, they frequently have been found to be associated with abnormally high levels of gastric

113

secretion of hydrochloric acid and pepsinogen and with a lowered resistance of the mucous lining of the duodenum to these digestive agents (Baron, 1962; Weiner, Thaler, Reiser, & Mirsky, 1957). Stress is frequently accompanied by higher stomach-acid levels (Selye, 1982), and it is thought that extended and repeated stress plays a role in the development of some types of duodenal ulcers. Gastric ulcers are not as strongly associated with higher acid levels and are less strongly linked with stress (Ackerman & Weiner, 1976).

A series of animal-behavioral studies of the relationship of stress to peptic ulcers has been carried out by Weiss (1970, 1984). In Weiss's paradigm, rats were shocked under conditions that either enabled avoidance and/or prediction of the shock, or did not. Pairs of rats were yoked so that those without the ability to avoid shocks received the same number of shocks as those who could avoid. Weiss found that ulcer formation was predictable from the number of avoidant responses required (i.e., the number of shock threats) and the level of control available: The more shock threats and the less control, the greater the lesion formation.

Evidence linking stress and peptic ulcers in human beings is inconsistent. There have been several studies that reported an association, in some instances using careful controls for potentially confounding variables (Cobb & Rose, 1973; House, McMichael, Wells, Kaplan, & Landerman, 1979). On the other hand, some investigations have failed to find evidence for a correlation (see Holt, 1982). But anyone who has had an ulcer can testify to the strong links that remain in the minds of most medical practitioners as well as lay people. One of the first questions asked by general physicians and specialists alike invariably seems to be a probe into the level of stress in one's life. This general belief in a stress-ulcer relationship has led to interventions aimed at moderating the stress in order to prevent the occurrence or recurrence of ulcers.

A study undertaken in 1936 compared a group of peptic ulcer patients who received a psychotherapeutic intervention with a comparable group who received no treatment (Chappell, Stefano, Rogerson, & Pike, 1936). The therapy was multidimensional, focusing on stress-reduction by such techniques as redirecting thoughts to pleasant images to control worry and reducing the hard-driving effort and demands patients tended to place on themselves. After 6 weeks of daily therapeutic sessions, 30 of the 32 treated subjects (15 others had dropped out early in treatment), compared to 2 of the 20 controls, were symptom-free. Follow-up showed these effects were largely maintained after 3 years. Although the absence of an attention-control treatment is problematic, this early intervention promised an interesting avenue for future study.

A recent intervention along the same lines achieved comparable changes in considerably less treatment time. Brooks and Richardson (1980) compared 11 patients who were provided "emotional skills training" with 11 assessment control patients. Both groups continued to receive their individual medical therapies. The emotional skills group received information about the role of anxiety in their symptoms and were taught a variety of self-control strategies, including identification and change of self-defeating thoughts, deep muscle relaxation, and assertiveness skills. Following eight treatment sessions, the patients in the treated group were less anxious, experienced less pain, reported fewer ulcer symptoms, and used less antacid medication than the control group. At a 42-month follow-up, data were available for 8 control and 9 treated subjects. Five of the 8 control patients had experienced a recurrence or had surgery for their ulcers, compared to only 1 of the 9 treated patients.

The reader may have noted that the behaviors of ulcer patients that are targeted for treatment are similar to those identified as comprising the Type A behavioral risk pattern for coronary heart disease. Weiss (1984) suggested that what has been identified as a susceptibility to gastrointestinal pathology is really a behavioral manifestation of vulnerability to a variety of diseases. Attempts to prevent heart-disease-related deaths have received much attention in recent years and they represent one of the most extensive applications of psychological principles to a medical problem.

CARDIOVASCULAR DISEASE

We noted that the behavioral targets for change in ulcer treatment programs are similar to those in the familiar Type A pattern, which is associated with risk for coronary heart disease (CHD). The rationale for intervention with both populations is based on an assumption that high levels of stress over prolonged periods lead to physical pathology. Yet, as Roskies and her colleagues noted, "It is far from obvious why . . . [the Type A behavior pattern] should be classified as a stress disorder" (Roskies et al., in press, p. 5). Views of stress as originating in the environment would find that Type As have little exposure to the severe stresses that produce posttraumatic stress disorders, nor is there evidence of extreme occupational stress. Although the relationships among primary and moderating variables are complex, in general the professional and managerial jobs of most Type As have been found less stressful than those of blue-collar workers (Holt, 1982). Further, Roskies et al. (in press) noted that Type As do not suffer from obvious deficiencies in coping resources and strategies. "On the contrary, the Type A managers with whom we work are so full of energy and activity that they give the impression of being super-healthy. . . . Their ability to fulfill valued social roles is also noteworthy" (pp. 6-7).

In order to appreciate the stress experienced by Type A individuals, one has to turn to an interactional theory. It is the appraisals of these individuals and interactions among events, appraisals, and coping attempts that point to stress among Type As: the tendency of Type As to *perceive* threat or challenge where others do not; to overreact with hostility and intense attempts at mastery (accompanied by heightened physiological activity); to be unconvinced of their own ability to achieve control over events; and to become extremely anxious about alternative courses and despondent if unable to master a situation. These characteristics, and others indicated in the discussion that follows, are indicative of stress-inducing processes within the interactional model offered by Lazarus and others. Before considering the programs that have attempted to alter such maladaptive transactions with the environment, we will briefly examine the development of and evidence for the Type A classification.

Psychological Components of Cardiovascular Disease

As the quotation from Sir William Osler in Chapter 4 illustrated, it has long been believed that there is a strong link between psychological events and the development of coronary heart disease (CHD). The National Heart, Lung, and Blood Institute recently endorsed this link when it accepted the available evidence as demonstrating that Type A behavior is associated with increased risk of coronary heart disease (The Review Panel on Coronary-Prone Behavior and Coronary Heart Disease, 1981). Widespread acceptance of this view has led to what Powell (1984) has called the heyday of Type A research.

Specification of the Type A behavior pattern was an attempt to systematize such observations as Osler's. Friedman and Rosenman (1959) introduced the classification for individuals "aggressively involved in a chronic, incessant struggle to achieve more and more in less and less time" (Friedman & Rosenman, 1974, p. 67). The specification of this description enabled the role of personality factors in heart disease to be studied prospectively, rather than in the traditional post hoc fashion, for the first time (Roskies, 1983).

The Type A pattern has been viewed by these authors as a personality characteristic, that is, a relatively enduring disposition to behave in such ways across a wide variety of situations. Type A individuals have been characterized as engaging in a "chronic and excessive struggle to obtain an unlimited number of things from the environment in the shortest period of time and/or against the opposing efforts of other persons or things" (Syme, 1984, p. 21). At work, they are likely to take on more tasks than necessary, without realistically assessing time and other constraints, and in leisure time, they continue to display a pervasive inability to relax, competitive striving, and a low sense of security (Glass, 1977; Glass, Snyder, & Hollis, 1974; Suinn, 1982).

Price (1982) suggested that the Type A person's struggles are fueled by a set of beliefs and fears. For example, a fear of insufficient worth or of being considered unsuccessful leads to cognitions concerning the need to constantly prove by accomplishments that "I am successful" or worthy of esteem, love, or approval, which in turn leads to constant striving for material success, accomplishments, and status. Similarly, the fear of an insufficient supply of life's necessities (e.g., time, achievements, recognition) is the source of thoughts such as "All resources are scarce, so I must beat others to get what I need," which lead to hard-driving and competitive attempts to achieve more and more. A Type B pattern has been defined as the relative absence of the Type A attributes and is generally compared to Type A in research on cardiovascular risk.

Evidence relating Type A behavior to heart disease has been provided most convincingly by the Western Collaborative Group Study (WCGS), an outgrowth of the work of Rosenman and Friedman (Rosenman et al., 1975). In an 8½-year follow-up of 3,524 men in the WCGS study, it was found that men with the Type A behavior pattern experienced twice as much coronary heart disease (either with or without myocardial infarction) as those without this pattern (Table 2). This relationship existed even though the influence of the other risk factors was taken into account. The known risk factors of elevated cholesterol and blood pressure levels, cigarette smoking, positive family history, physical inactivity, and obesity accounted for only one-third of the disease incidence in the total group (Chesney, 1984.) Several studies have also documented increased coronary arteriosclerosis in Type A individuals (e.g., Frank, Heller, Kornfeld, Sporn, & Weiss, 1978; Williams, Haney, Lee, Kong, Blumenthal, & Whalen, 1980). In other words, the predictability of coronary heart disease increases substantially when Type A behavior pattern is considered as well as physical and other risk factors (Rosenman, Brand, Sholtz, & Friedman, 1976). Another large-scale longitudinal study, known as the Framingham study, found a relationship between Type A behavior and CHD, also independent from other standard coronary risk factors (Haynes, Feinleib, Levine, Scotch, & Kannel, 1978; Haynes, Levine, Scotch, Feinleib, & Kannel, 1978).

**Table 2.   Coronary Heart Disease (CHD) and
Myocardial Infarction (MI) for Type A and
Type B Men over a Period of 8½ Years**

	Intake Age: 39-49		Intake Age: 50-59	
	Type A	Type B	Type A	Type B
Number of subjects	1,067	1,182	522	383
Number with CHD	95	50	83	29
Incidence of CHD per 1,000	10.5	5.0**	18.7	8.9**
Number with MI	79	41	62	24
Incidence of MI per 1,000	8.7	4.1**	14.0	7.3*

Note. Table is adapted with permission from "Coronary Heart Disease in the Western Collaborative Group Study: Final Follow-up Experience 8½ Years" by R.H. Rosenman, R.J. Brand, C.D. Jenkins, M. Friedman, R. Straus, & M. Wurm, 1975, *Journal of the American Medical Association, 233*, p. 875. Copyright 1975 American Medical Association.

*$p < .01$

**$p < .001$

The significance of the problem of CHD is readily apparent: It is the leading cause of death in the United States, accounting for more than one-third of all deaths (National Center for Health Statistics, 1983). Its economic cost is upwards of 60 billion dollars, or over one-fifth of the total cost of illness in the United States, and it accounts for over 11 million visits to physicians annually (Levy & Moskowitz, 1982; Rowland, Fulwood, & Kleinman, 1983). Despite a decline in rates of coronary heart disease since the mid-1960s (e.g., from 1973 to 1978 age-adjusted CHD mortality rates declined by 17.5 percent among whites and 20 percent among blacks in the United States [Rowland et al., 1983]), 35 percent of CHD deaths are considered premature, that is, occur in persons under the age of 65 (Fishman, 1982).

Assessment of Type A Behavior

Although the objectivity of the assessment tools used for the Type A pattern has been debated, the structured interview developed by Rosenman and Friedman, the Jenkins Activity Survey for Health Prediction, and the Framingham Type A Scale all have been found to have predictive validity for coronary heart disease (Haynes, Feinleib, & Kannel, 1980; Haynes, Levine, Scotch, Feinleib, & Kannel, 1978; Jenkins, Rosenman, & Zyzanski, 1974; Rosenman et al., 1975). The structured interview, which heavily weights the interviewer's judgments of speech stylistics and behavioral mannerisms, is considered to be a more valid instrument than the questionnaires (Blumenthal, O'Toole, & Haney, 1984; Krantz & Deckel, 1983; The Review Panel on Coronary-Prone Behavior and Coronary Heart Disease, 1981). Trained interviewer reliability ranges from .74 to .84 (Caffrey, 1968; Jenkins, Rosenman, & Friedman, 1968) and test-retest reliability over 1½ years is .80 (Rosenman et al., 1964). Friedman and Powell (1984) have also introduced a videotaped version of the interview for more general use. The ability of newly trained interviewers to render appropriate judgments for the interview-based classification has been questioned, however (Powell, 1984), in light of recent negative findings from a large-scale study (The Multiple Risk Factor Intervention Trial Group, 1979). The issue of how best to assess Type A behavior remains unresolved. Assessment procedures are likely to continue to evolve, because the construct itself is continuing to develop.

In particular, there have recently been attempts to refine the Type A construct in order to account for the finding that not all Type A individuals develop CHD, and not all studies have obtained a relationship between overall Type A and CHD (Case, Heller, Case, & Moss, 1985; Dembroski & MacDougall, in press). An intriguing relationship was recently reported by Williams's group at Duke University Medical Center (Williams, 1984a). Among 2,100 patients who underwent coronary angiography over a 10-year period, there was an interaction between Type A and age in predicting coronary arteriosclerosis: With patients younger than 45, Type As had more severe arteriosclerosis than Type Bs; between 45 and 54 the two groups' occlusions were about equal; surprisingly, among the oldest group, over 54 years of age, the Type Bs were found to have more severe disease than the Type As. Williams (1984a) suggested that those Type As who survive to later years may be especially hardy, thus eventually doing better than the type Bs. It is also possible that personality characteristics may be overshadowed by long-term exposure to environmental hazards and that genetic predisposition may play more of a role with advancing years.

Although the Type A pattern appears as an interrelated set of dispositions, it may be that particular aspects of the behavior are more malignant than others. These distinguishable elements may vary across Type A individuals, resulting in differing risk levels. Kahn et al. (cited by Chesney, 1984), for example, found that aggressiveness and rigorous speech characteristics among Type A individuals correlated with the disease, whereas the time urgency component did not. Matthews, Glass, Rosenman, and Bortner (1977), reanalyzing some of the WCGS data, found that only the Type A assessment items concerned with time urgency (e.g., "irritation at waiting in lines"), hostility (e.g., "potential for hostility"), anger (e.g., "angry more than once a week"), and vigorous speech characteristics (e.g.,"explosive voice modulation") were relevant in disease prediction. Factor analyses led Matthews et al. to conclude that competitive drive and impatience were the crucial components being assessed by such items. Cooney and Zeichner (1985) found that despite comparable levels of performance, Type As spent more time attending to negative and less to positive feedback about themselves than did Type Bs.

These and other findings are now pointing research toward hostility and anger (particularly unexpressed anger) as forming the core of Type A risk (Blumenthal et al., 1984; Chesney, 1984; Dembroski, MacDougall, Williams, Haney, & Blumenthal, 1985; Krantz & Glass, 1984; Shekelle, Gayle, Ostfeld, & Paul, 1983; Williams, 1984a, 1984b; Williams et al., 1980). This enables the reassessment of the risk of some persons who might, for example, exhibit Type A characteristics such as verbal pressure and high activity levels, but in whom these behaviors reflect more benign attributes, such as enthusiasm. It is certain that a redefinition of Type A so that it exempted those of us who see ourselves as exhibiting such "benign" activity patterns would be welcome. Based on factor analyses of the MMPI-based Ho (hostility) scale (Cook & Medley, 1954), Costa, Zonderman, McCrae, and Williams (in press) suggested that "cynicism" best captures the critical combination of items that hostility indices measure. Williams (1984b) offered the Webster's definition: a contemptuous distrust of human nature and motives.

As Powell (1984) pointed out, it is tempting to try to reduce the critical elements of the Type A construct to a single unifying trait. Such a unidimensional conceptualization "would be convenient because it would clarify an elusive construct and provide a clear direction for interventions aimed at reducing CHD risk" (pp. 7-8). But currently the data do not permit this simplification:

> A closer fit, given our current level of understanding, is to assume that Type A behavior is a multidimensional phenomenon, including an array of overt behaviors, cognitive styles, behaviors in response to environmental demands, and physiological concomitants. Under this conceptualization, the Type A perception of others may be "hostility" and the Type A perception of self may be "low self-esteem." What produces the Type A reactivity may be "need for control," but a summary for it may be "struggle." (Powell, 1984, p. 8)

Dynamics of Type A Behavior

It is not yet clear how Type A acts as a risk factor or *how* it facilitates the progression of heart disease (Eliot & Buell, 1981; Krantz & Glass, 1984). David Glass and his colleagues have provided an analysis of the dynamics of the behavioral pattern that has proven useful in guiding intervention (Glass, 1977; Glass & Carver, 1980; Glass et al., 1980). Laboratory studies summarized by Glass in his 1977 volume, *Behavior Patterns, Stress, and Coronary Disease,* suggest that Type A behavior is a style of coping with events that threaten the person's sense of control over the environment. The approach to dealing with such events is to wrestle them to the ground, thus asserting control and maintaining it in the face of extreme pressure and adverse circumstances. It is no accident that this self-enhancing competitive pattern is so frequently found among executives (Howard, Cunningham, & Rechnitzer, 1976). It often seems that this is the only way to survive in competitive fields. As a middle-aged owner of a small business who was seeing one of the authors for therapy complained, "If I don't keep pushing myself all the time, all I can see ahead of me is ruin."

Roskies (1983) noted, "In contrast to individuals who are unable or unwilling to adapt to social norms, Type A individuals have internalized thoroughly Western society's emphasis on the ability to control one's environment" (p. 268). This assertive, hard-driving, competitive, and time urgent life may lead to substantial financial rewards, which reinforce the pattern. Even if the pattern does not clearly lead to pecuniary advantage, it is a self-reinforcing pattern. The sense of control that is achieved is rewarding because it enhances self-esteem and the regard of others. Such rewards lead to habitual patterns that become internalized means of reducing anxiety (e.g., "If I could only put in an hour more each day, I'd be able to clear my desk") and as such are extremely resistant to change. More insidiously, the *avoidance* of demotion or job loss—threats that are frequently in the minds of workers, whether or not they are real—can be attributed to maintenance of these behaviors. This is a kind of superstitious behavior (i.e., "If I don't change anything I'm doing, maybe things will be OK").

The consequence of these obvious and subtle reinforcers is that Type A behaviors are rigid and pervasive. The response to *un*controllable environmental events is the same as to controllable ones: increased effort, pace, assertiveness, to the level that an observer would call frantic. This hyperresponsiveness passes to hyporesponsiveness when it becomes clear that control has not been achieved. Hostile competition gives way to depressed helplessness (Glass, 1977). Appels and Mulder (1984) reported a 22-fold increase in risk of an imminent myocardial infarction in patients with a syndrome of exhausted depression.

Although the links between behavioral and physiological mechanisms in coronary heart disease are tentative (Krantz & Manuck, 1984), the alternation of behavioral hyper- and hyporesponsiveness seems to be accompanied by disease-relevant physiological changes. Under certain conditions, such as a harassing, competitive task, physiological responses of Type A individuals are distinguishable from those of non-Type A individuals (Glass et al., 1980). Changes such as high levels of cortisol and catecholamines increase "the wear and tear on . . . coronary arteries" (Roskies, 1983, p. 269). The increased attempts at control on the part of the Type A patient have been associated with elevations in serum cholesterol, neuropeptides, systolic blood pressure, and catecholamine levels (Dembroski, MacDougall, & Shields, 1977; Goldband, Katkin, & Morrell, 1979; Herd, 1984; Krantz & Deckel, 1983).

But, as Krantz and Glass (1984) noted, "All of the evidence bearing on physiological mechanisms underlying a Type A-CHD relationship is as yet preliminary. Conclusive results must await future research" (p. 56).

Despite the incompleteness of information concerning the mechanisms of association between Type A behaviors and heart disease, the evidence linking the two is strong:

> Unlike any other individual-difference variable studied in conjunction with illness, Type A behavior meets most of the stringent criteria used by epidemiologists to establish a cause-effect relationship. . . . Among these criteria are the strength of association of Type A with clinical CHD; the consistency, persistence, and reproducibility of findings; the fact that Type A precedes CHD, rather than being caused by it; and the fact that the Type A-CHD link is plausible in light of biomedical knowledge of how CHD develops. (Krantz & Glass, 1984, p. 53)

Interventions

As Suinn (1982) noted, research concerning ways to intervene with the Type A pattern has been "slow, tentative, and cautious" (p. 935). This may have resulted partly from the skepticism concerning susceptibility of the style to change (The Review Panel on Coronary-Prone Behavior and Coronary Heart Disease, 1981; Rosenman & Friedman, 1977) and partly from a lack of firm knowledge of the mechanisms involved. Nevertheless, there have been a handful of attempts to modify the Type A pattern, some of them involving extensive treatment procedures. Roskies identified some of the factors in treating Type As that create an appeal for psychologists working in health settings, despite the difficulties involved:

> Eager to prove to our medical colleagues that the new behavioral technology can be of practical value in the prevention and treat-

ment of disease, we are in search of medical problems responsive to behavioral input. The type A pattern is not only an unusually clear demonstration of the etiological importance of behavior, successfully and independently predicting the future emergence of a major somatic disease, but is also an excellent example of the type of medical problem for which traditional pharmaceutical and surgical remedies have little relevance. (1983, p. 265)

It is interesting to note that nonmedical intervention (diet, exercise, and other therapies) is now standard treatment for CHD patients as a result of the recognition that clinical medicine clearly does not have the tools for the task. Increasingly, these methods are recommended for the entire population as preventive measures.

A problem faced in attempting to modify the Type A pattern is *what to change*. The pattern is multidimensional, involving an interaction between a demanding environment and a response style. Cross-cultural studies suggest that significant changes in environmental demands can alter the extent of Type A behavior. Whereas 75 percent of a Canadian managerial sample was found to evidence the Type A pattern (Howard et al., 1976), the incidence was found to be only 15 percent among a sample of Japanese-Americans living in Hawaii (Cohen, Syme, Jenkins, Kagan, & Zyzanski, 1979). Laboratory studies also attest to the importance of environment. Type As and Bs show similar baseline values in resting physiological and endocrine reactivity. It is only when experimental challenges are introduced that the Type As show greater sympathetic system arousal (Dembroski et al., 1977; Glass et al., 1980). Making significant changes in the appropriate aspects of an individual's natural environment, however, may cause more problems than it solves. As The Review Panel on Coronary-Prone Behavior and Coronary Heart Disease (1981) noted, "The type A behavior pattern is closely related to a work pattern and way of life esteemed in our society. Thus, a side effect of intervention could be loss or impairment of skills that contribute to a person's success or sense of well-being" (pp. 12-13). Meagher (1982) suggested that the results of such interventions could themselves lead to additional stress.

Anxiety Management Training

Most interventions have, instead, focused on the individual's *reactions* to environmentally based challenges. A program developed by Suinn and his colleagues illustrates the approach (Suinn, 1975; Suinn & Bloom, 1978; Suinn & Richardson, 1971). Based upon a general method for controlling anxiety, called *anxiety management training* (Suinn & Richardson, 1971), Suinn and Bloom's intervention for Type A individuals focused on (1) learning deep muscle relaxation; (2) using imagery to induce anxiety in order to identify the muscular or other physiological cues accompanying arousal of anxiety; and (3) rehearsing in imaginal situations the use of physiological cues to initiate relaxation as an alternative coping response to the usual Type A behaviors.

Over 3 weeks of twice weekly sessions, seven experimental and seven waiting-list control subjects participated in the study. Apparently, subjects were volunteers who self-selected as fitting the Type A pattern. Suinn and Bloom (1978) reported a significant reduction for experimental over control subjects in the Hard-Driving subscale of the Jenkins Activity Survey (JAS), but in none of the other three subscores, nor on blood pressure or lipid levels. Anxiety levels were lower for the treated than untreated subjects.

Although the results from anxiety scales and the one subscale of the JAS suggest that there might be some potential for a more extensive stress-management-oriented intervention, the use of only a waiting-list group as a control renders the modest findings difficult to interpret. They may have been merely expectancy-related and may have even disappeared over a lengthier trial.

A Cognitive-Behavioral Approach

Some of the most extensive investigations of modifying Type A behavior have been carried out in Montreal by Roskies and her associates (Roskies, 1983; Roskies & Avard, 1982; Roskies et al., 1979; Roskies et al., in press). Roskies' points of intervention were derived from the interactional view of stress, discussed in Chapter 4. First of all, *appraisals of potential stressors* were targeted. If, for example, the minor irritations of daily life, the daily hassles (Kanner et al., 1981), are treated as major events, every stolen cab, every curt telephone operator becomes a stimulus to make the blood boil. Learning to view events from a more balanced perspective or to minimize instead of maximize threat can reduce overall stress levels. Second, *appraisal of resources* to cope with stressors was also considered important. Uncertainty about one's ability to handle challenges transforms relatively mild demands into major threats to well-being or even to survival. Type A individuals tend to appraise minor events as almost out-of-control and therefore requiring intense coping efforts. Learning to have more confidence in lower levels of response can break the cycle of overreaction. Finally, developing more confidence partly results from having a varied repertoire of *coping responses* available, and making use of the whole range. Thus, another goal of intervention was to train and rehearse coping skills in response to different types of situations.

Roskies' experimental interventions have attempted to alter the behavior and cognitions of participants in all of these areas. Treatment has included between 13 and 20 weekly or twice weekly group sessions during which participants were led to acquire new habitual appraisal and coping methods. The group interaction was utilized to facilitate reconceptualization of stressors and approaches to them. A full range of cognitive-behavioral clinical intervention skills was utilized with this group, including the presentation of information, teaching and modeling of skills, role playing, assignment of homework, rehearsal of new behaviors, ongoing collection of data, use of data to have participants challenge their own maladaptive patterns and beliefs, and use of feedback from personal interventions to refine the changes (Roskies, 1983; Roskies & Avard, 1982). The goals were to have participants (1) become more aware of their patterns of indiscriminate hyperresponsiveness, (2) acquire a variety of new ways of evaluating and responding to stressors, and (3) practice these in diverse situations until they were habitual.

The Roskies study is particularly interesting because it included both Type A and non-Type-A men. Participants were middle managers in three large Canadian companies. They volunteered to take part in a research stress management program, and their training was paid for by their companies.

Another interesting aspect of the program was its explicit attention to *marketing* (Frederiksen, Solomon, & Brehony, 1984). Since the Type A pattern is positively valued in many ways, attempts to alter it are obviously susceptible to considerable adherence problems, particularly if change is seen as likely to reduce productivity or occupational success. In contrast to many treatment programs, which simply offer services without attending to the factors that may impede utilization of those services, Roskies and her colleagues recognized and dealt with these obstacles as part of their approach. In advertising their program, they emphasized the wasted energy and unnecessary tension of Type A individuals and held out the promise of increased efficiency by reducing unnecessary energy and discomfort. This message was reinforced throughout the program, through selective use of such information as the laboratory findings that Type Bs do not perform more poorly on stress tasks, despite their more relaxed approach (e.g., Cooney & Zeichner, 1985; Dembroski, MacDougall, Shields, Petitto, & Lushene, 1978), and the fact that not all successful coworkers were Type As. In terms of dropout rates, this approach seems to have been effective. Roskies et al. (in press) reported that of the 118 men enrolled in one program, 107 completed it, attending 90 percent of the sessions. The cognitive-behavioral intervention was reported to reduce behavioral reactivity significantly and substantially compared to careful control interventions that emphasized aerobic fitness training or progressive weight training (Roskies et al., in press). Follow-up results for these interventions have yet to be reported and will be important in evaluating their clinical utility.

A Multidimensional Intervention

The longest intervention period to date is that of the Recurrent Coronary Prevention Project (Friedman et al., 1982), a 4½-year clinical trial with postcoronary infarct patients, begun in 1978. The experimental treatment in this project is multidimensional, including cardiac counseling provided by cardiologists and a cognitive-behavioral component, including teaching participants to identify exaggerated physiological, cognitive, and behavioral reactions that constitute overt manifestations of Type A behavior (e.g., arguing tenaciously about minor issues) and training in physical and mental relaxation as alternative responses. In addition, cognitive restructuring was employed to alter perceptions concerning the causes and significance of daily events. As in the Roskies intervention, the group itself was used for therapeutic purposes to motivate change and promote nonadversarial peer interactions. Subjects randomly assigned to a control group received the cardiac counseling only. The cognitive-behavioral plus cardiac counseling group was scheduled to meet for a total of 44 sessions over 3 years; the cardiac-counseling-only group, for 24 sessions over the same period.

Powell, Friedman, Thoresen, Gill, and Ulmer (1984) reported that after 2 years the experimental treatment group demonstrated reductions in Type A behavior as reported by self, spouse, coworkers, and independent observers of a videotaped interview. These reductions were significantly greater than those of the control subjects. The authors also reported, however, that a significant proportion of subjects dropped out of treatment (26.5 percent) or failed to change (21.5 percent) over the first 2 years of the study. Over 3 years, the proportion of dropouts increased to 34 percent and treatment failures increased to 22 percent for a total of 56 percent of the treatment sample classified as nonresponders (Friedman & Powell, 1984). These proportions indicate that even very successful outcomes for those who are treated do not constitute complete success from such a program and reinforce the Roskies group's emphasis on marketing as an essential component.

A report of results from 592 patients over the first 3 years of the project found a significant difference in recurrence of coronary infarct between the two groups: The experimental treatment group had a recurrence rate of 7.2 percent, compared to 13.2 percent in the control

(cardiac-counseling-only) subjects (Friedman et al., 1984). A similar difference was found in incidence of angina between the two groups, but not in arrhythmias, congestive heart failure, and hypertension. These arrhythmia and hypertension results were clouded, however, by active drug treatments. The relatively promising results of this study await confirmation in long-term behavioral and cardiac data from the patients after completion of the study. The group reports that they are collecting this information (Friedman et al., 1984).

Although results have been obtained from only a few well-designed studies, the research to date indicates that broad-spectrum treatments emphasizing behavioral and cognitive components can alter Type A behaviors. Further, the changes that occur seem to influence the course of CHD, though longer term follow-up is needed before the full impact on disease outcome can be established.

CANCER

In many ways, the development of psychological work with cancer parallels that in CHD, although it lags behind. Historically, the hypothesized influence of psychological factors reaches back centuries (Kowal, 1955; LeShan, 1959). Whereas cardiovascular vulnerability was thought to be related to a hard-driving, aggressive pattern, cancer was linked to depression and loss.

In recent years, there have been attempts to define objectively and study individual differences and experiences that may predispose one to malignancy, as well as to determine the psychophysiology of such influences (Levy, 1985). But this work has not yet achieved the legitimacy conferred by the Type A-heart disease link (Cunningham, 1985). Despite the growing activity in the area, the status quo is still sufficiently antithetical to the idea of significant psychological influences on cancer to lead one recent reviewer to accuse the biomedical community of "committing a 'Type II error' [dismissing as unfounded what may in fact be true] by continuing largely to ignore the possible influence of mind on cancer" (Cunningham, 1985, p. 24). He wondered aloud "why this resistance occurs and what is needed to convince the skeptical that this subject deserves further investigation" (p. 24). Our brief examination of this intriguing area will indicate ways in which health psychologists have contributed and directions that may be fruitful for future preventive work.

Stress as a Causal Factor

The potential links between stress and changes that can influence the pathology of cancer are diverse. Numerous effects have been established in experimental studies with laboratory animals. These effects are dependent upon such complex interactions that slight changes in the conditions of the experiment can alter or even reverse the results (Newberry et al., 1984). Interestingly, Sklar and Anisman (1981) concluded that the primary negative impact comes from acute, not chronic stress. Acute stress, they found in an extensive review, has been found to favor cancer growth in laboratory animals. Depletion of catecholamines, increases in acetylcholine, and increased levels of several hormones tend to depress the immune response. By comparison, chronic stress tends to lead to adaptation of the hormonal and immune system and is found to decrease tumor growth.

Results from animal studies in this area are consistent with an interactional model of stress, in that they have provided evidence for the role of coping responses. Several investigators have found that the availability of a coping response (experimentally represented by having a shock stressor made behaviorally escapable or by enabling escape from social stress by fighting) neutralizes the stressor's influence on neoplastic development. In the same experimental paradigm as Weiss (1984) used to study stress and stomach ulcers, it has been found that if animals are placed in a two-chambered cage and allowed to escape a shock on the grid floor of one chamber by moving to the other chamber, growth of tumors that have been implanted does not differ from tumor growth in animals receiving no shock. By contrast, another group of animals can be yoked to the first group so that they receive exactly the same number and duration of shocks, but with their behavior having no impact on shocks; that is, this group cannot escape by moving to the other chamber. Shock for them is turned off only when the other, yoked, animals move. This group, receiving inescapable shock, shows about a 60 percent enhancement of tumor growth compared to the other two groups (Sklar & Anisman, 1980).

It has also been found that the effects of aversive stimuli vary with the organism's prior stress history (i.e., adaptation may occur, and therefore less reactivity, with repeated exposures to stress), as well as with environmental conditions. A change from social isolation to communal housing, for example, promotes tumor growth (Sklar & Anisman, 1981).

The work in this area is limited primarily by the difficulty of generalizing across species. Sklar and Anisman (1981) cautioned against facile generalization to human cancer from the findings of animal adaptation to chronic stress:

> In humans the possibility certainly exists that chronic stress may have variable effects on cancer development, depending on the

effectiveness of adaptive systems. Indeed, the relative effectiveness of these systems could account for the variable effects on cancer development seen among individuals exposed to comparable amounts of carcinogen. (p. 395)

Despite such limitations of animal models, it is clearly impossible to carry out the same kind of experimental investigations with human beings, and the animal work is useful in pointing to leads that can be investigated using naturalistic methods among human beings.

The Immune System

Additional work bearing on psychological contributions to the etiology of cancer is available in the burgeoning literature on experimental animal and human behavioral immunology. It is interesting that there is more evidence showing that psychological factors influence the immune system than there is that the immune system plays a crucial role in naturally occurring cancer, although such a role is generally assumed and represents one of the main thrusts of current biological research on cancer (Bowers & Kelly, 1979; Cunningham, 1985; Jemmott & Locke, 1984; Locke & Hornig-Rohan, 1983; Pettingale, 1985). Particular emphasis has been placed on the activity of immunological cells called natural killer cells (Levy, 1984).

Jemmott and Locke (1984) reviewed evidence establishing that experimental stress increases susceptibility to infectious agents and incidence and growth rate of some experimentally induced tumors. They noted that, despite methodological shortcomings of the research, the evidence that stress impairs the functioning of the immune system is sufficiently strong to warrant considerable expansion of work in this area:

> Even though we can choose particular studies and criticize them methodologically, when we consider the literature as a whole, we cannot resist the conclusion that stress is a potent factor in the etiology of immune-relevant disease and can affect parameters of immunologic functioning. A major strength of this research is its diversity. A variety of illnesses have been examined as well as a variety of immunological parameters.... One comes away with the sense that the basic hypothesis has survived this onslaught. (pp. 102-103)

Correlational Evidence for a Psychological Process-Cancer Link

We have noted two lines of research that indirectly support a connection between psychological parameters and the development of cancer: animal studies that have established a stress-cancer link and human and animal research strongly suggesting that stress suppresses immunological responses, thus enhancing susceptibility to tumor growth. A third type of research has used correlational designs to examine factors that may be related to the natural occurrence of cancer.

In a review of these studies, Cunningham (1985) separated the research into three groups: (1) *retrospective* studies, in which psychological assessment of cancer patients is simply compared with the same assessment of controls without disease—a relatively confounded design, with difficulty in making causal connections; (2) *progress* studies, in which psychological assessment occurs after development of disease and is then correlated with progress of disease—a shorter longitudinal design with some methodological confounds; and (3) *prospective* studies, in which psychological assessment precedes development of disease in a general sample, and a cohort is followed longitudinally—these are clearly the most methodologically sound.

Retrospective Studies

Some of the earliest retrospective work has remained the most influential. LeShan and Worthington (1956) found that 77 percent of a sample of cancer patients reported suffering loss of a major relationship 6 months to 8 years before diagnosis, compared to 14 percent of a control sample. This loss, it was hypothesized, led to despair or hopelessness, which created a vulnerability to cancer (LeShan, 1959). The vulnerable despair pattern has been reported by other investigators. Becker (1979), for example, found that 72 percent of women developing breast cancer before age 48 reported loss of an important person in early childhood. Yet, as Cunningham (1985) noted, there are numerous studies that have looked for a correlation between loss and cancer and failed to find it. The evidence is sufficiently divided to make conclusions from this literature tentative at best.

A second major thesis in this work has been that cancer patients are emotionally more inhibited or repressed. This hypothesis seems to have more consistent support (Kissen, 1966; Cunningham, 1985). Some studies have attempted to minimize the potential confounding of the impact of a cancer diagnosis on psychological factors being assessed. Greer (1979), for example, assessed patients prior to biopsy for breast tumor diagnosis. The women who were found to have malignancies differed significantly from those with benign breast disease in evidencing greater suppression of anger and other feelings. Diagnostic predictions made solely from psychological variables were as accurate (72 percent) as those based on clinical medical variables. Watson, Pettingale, and Greer

(1985) found that breast cancer patients reacted similarly to healthy controls on a physiological level (heart rate and skin resistance changes were similar) when they were exposed to the same stressors (films depicting unpleasant events, such as industrial accidents); but the patient group attempted to control their emotional reactions more than the control group, reporting, for example, that they tried to hide their feelings rather than show them.

In general, the inhibited expression finding seems to have moderate support, but no studies of this type permit clear causal connections to be made. In some instances, other possible contributing factors, such as hospital admission or smoking history, which might affect either psychological test results or cancer or both, have been overlooked or are otherwise unable to be ruled out as causal agents. In most retrospective studies, the biggest confound is the possible impact that receiving the diagnosis of cancer or having cancer may have on psychological factors and self-report measures. Connections between the two may result from cancer's alteration of the patients' functioning. It is possible, for example, that the cancer patients' views of their past life may be colored by their current illness (Anisman & Zacharko, 1983). Similarly, Watson et al.'s findings of greater attempts at emotional control in cancer patients could result from a fear of loss of control that resulted from the diagnosis. In addition, studies assessing the history of stress during the year or so preceding diagnosis overlook the fact that most cancers are not clinically observable until several years following the appearance of the first malignancies (Anisman & Zacharko, 1983).

Progress Studies

There are few reports of this type available, though some of the research that has occurred has been quite carefully carried out. Once again the results are inconsistent. Weisman and Worden (1975) found that longer survival was correlated with closer interpersonal relationships, less emotional distress, good acceptance of attempts of others to provide support, and better coping with illness-related problems. In contrast, Derogatis, Abeloff, and Melisaratos (1979) discovered longer term survival to be associated with *higher* levels of distress, higher anxiety, depression, guilt, and hostility.

Greer (1979) has reported evidence from several sources studying breast cancer and malignant melanoma that converge on the suggestion that a positive, though frequently angry, determination to beat the disease is associated with a better prognosis than a helpless apathy or resignation. Denial seems to lie between the other two patterns in its impact, though denial is seldom complete and is frequently associated with some anger.

A recent, 10-year follow-up of the patients originally assessed by Greer and his colleagues reported maintenance of the findings (Pettingale, 1984). Of those breast cancer patients categorized as having a "fighting spirit," 55 percent had a favorable outcome (recurrence-free survival) 10 years later, compared to 22 percent of those showing either "stoic acceptance" or a "helpless and hopeless" response pattern. The same group is currently studying a larger population (170) of breast cancer and lymphoma patients, using more advanced methods of both physical and psychological assessment (Morris, Buckley, & Blake, 1984).

Several studies have noted a trend of greater psychological influence on the disease in younger patients (e.g., Becker, 1979; Greer, 1979). This tends to confirm the validity of the findings, for it would be expected that advancing age would bring more long-term environmental and biological mechanisms to contribute to the disease etiology. An interaction of psychological effects with age could also account for the null finding in some studies that have included older subjects (e.g., Watson & Schuld, 1977).

Some studies of cancer progression provide convincing evidence for, if not understanding of, a powerful role of psychological factors in tumor development. Investigations have found evidence that psychological factors may affect tumor growth primarily by altering the activity of natural killer (NK) cells (Levy, 1984; Locke et al., 1984). In an investigation of subjects with breast cancer, it was found that there was a relationship between low NK activity and being rated as "well-adjusted" (which was considered to reflect some difficulty in expressing emotions, common among such patients), having poor social support systems, and experiencing depressive-like fatigue symptoms (e.g., lack of vigor, apathy, listlessness). Levy (1984) pointed to endogenous opioids as a potential link between behavior and NK activity. She noted that there is evidence that these substances, including those associated with stress, perform a mediating role in suppressed NK activity.

A case reported by Klopfer (1957) is noteworthy as a demonstration of the potential impact of psychological processes on neoplasms. A patient who had a generalized, advanced malignancy with huge tumor masses read in the newspaper of a new drug called "Krebiozen." He insisted upon being treated with the drug and was given one injection on a Friday. He was so ill, described as "gasping his last breath through an oxygen mask" (p. 338), that his physician expected his death over the weekend. The following Monday, when the physician visited the ward, he found the patient up and around and chatting happily. The condition of all the other patients treated with the drug, however, was the same as or worse than pretreatment condition. Within a few days, with no treatment of any kind other than the single injection of the drug, the patient's tumor masses had become half their original size, "melted away like snow balls on a hot stove" (p. 338). Treatment was continued as planned with injections 3 times weekly, and within 10 days he was discharged with almost all signs of the disease absent. The patient and physician were unaware at the time of treatment that Krebiozen in fact had no tumor-reducing properties.

Subsequently the media increasingly carried reports of the failure of Krebiozen, and the patient's faith in its curative powers began to wane. He became depressed and ill after 2 months of practically perfect health. His physician told him not to believe the reports, that the drug really did have promise, that his relapse had been caused by the fact that the drug deteriorates on standing, and that he would be treated with a better, stronger version. The patient once again became ecstatic; when he was given an injection that contained nothing more than fresh water, recovery from his near-terminal state was more dramatic than the first time. The water injections continued and he remained symptom-free for over 2 months. Then the AMA published an announcement that Krebiozen was worthless as a treatment for cancer. Within a few days of the report's publication, the patient was readmitted to the hospital, his faith gone, and he died in less than 2 days.

How tumor growth in this and other patients is affected by psychological states is unknown, but these reports encourage a closer look. In summarizing the progress literature, Cunningham (1985) noted that there has been little consistency in the variables assessed in different studies and some contradictions among results obtained when the same variables have been assessed. Nevertheless, the evidence is accumulating that psychological characteristics can influence the course of the disease. Further progress studies may be one of the most fruitful avenues of research, since they can control for some of the confounds inherent in retrospective studies, yet do not demand the numbers of subjects required by extensive follow-up or longitudinal designs.

Prospective Studies

Data from prospective investigations bear out several of the hypotheses suggested by the retrospective and progress reports. Much of the interest in a psychological process-cancer link in human beings was stimulated by a recent examination of cancer incidence in a sample originally assessed for a longitudinal study of heart disease (Shekelle et al., 1981). The incidence of cancer death in this sample was found to be over twice as high among men who had been assessed as depressed by the MMPI D scale 17 years previously. The study, involving over 2,000 men, found no association between depression and any other causes of death, nor could the depression-cancer association be accounted for by any third risk variable, such as age, smoking, or family history. Similar prospective designs have provided support for a finding that was reported earlier in several retrospective studies: greater repressive tendencies among those who develop cancer (e.g., Dattore, Shontz, & Coyne, 1980; Graves & Thomas, 1981).

Information originating primarily from one source, a longitudinal study of 1,100 Johns Hopkins medical students graduating between 1948 and 1964, has implicated lack of familial closeness as a precursor of cancer (Thomas & Duszynski, 1974). Although the study's assessment of familial closeness has been questioned and the possibility raised that the correlation was simply a design artifact, recent reexamination of long-term data for 913 men in the study confirmed the original findings (Shaffer, Duszynski, & Thomas, 1982). Higher risk of cancer was found to be significantly associated with poorer father-son relationships and this risk persisted even after the influence of other possibly confounding variables was taken into account. Cunningham (1985) concluded:

> Overall, although results are variable, this prospective research suggests that people contracting cancer are not a psychologically random sample of the population. The nature of the predisposing personality structure is not yet very clear, although some possibly interrelated features have been described: lack of emotional closeness . . . and a tendency to depression, dependency, and repression of affect. (p. 18)

Bieliauskas (1983) believes that it is not depression per se that predisposes one to cancer. "Rather, a state of chronic distress might be a more accurate label for findings implicating depression as a contributor to such risk" (p. 25). In support, he noted that the MMPI D scale, which has been the main source of data linking the two, is in fact a general index of psychic distress rather than depression and may reflect an inefficient coping style. It may be the presence of this coping style, along with severe stressors, that increases the risk for cancer. This sort of causal path, Bieliauskas has contended, would provide the link between the findings of prospective studies of depression and cancer and results from studies of coping in animal and human psychoneuroimmunology.

Overall Results from Naturalistic Studies

As Cunningham (1985) noted, "It is probably impossible to design a completely unambiguous study in this difficult field: Critics can always claim that uncontrolled factors other than the personality variables under study were responsible for the differential growth of cancer" (p. 22).

Indeed there are significant methodological problems in this literature, which render interpretation and conclusions difficult (Fox, 1978). But the various studies do seem to converge on (1) establishing a potentially important role for psychological factors in the etiology and course of cancer, (2) pointing to tendencies toward depression and repression as possible foci, and (3) implicating the immune system as a critical component (Scurry & Levin, 1978-1979; Stoll, 1985). Nevertheless, it is important to note that the predictive power of emotional factors is still quite low compared to variables such as smoking (which is, however, a *behavioral* factor and therefore a legitimate subject of psychological inquiry, to which we shall return). Though elevation in depression can double cancer risk, smoking cigarettes, in comparison, results in about a ninefold increase in risk of lung cancer alone (Lubin, Richter, & Blot, 1984), and an equatorial habitat is associated with a tenfold increase in melanomas over the northern latitudes (Fears, Scotto, & Schneiderman, 1976). Although there is sufficient evidence to warrant further investigation of psychological variables in cancer risk and of their mechanisms of influence, the particular role of such factors is likely to remain enigmatic for some time. Better assessment methods and more careful, multifactorial studies may increment the predictive power of psychological variables.

Behavioral Risk Factors

Whereas we have been describing emotional and physiological parameters implicated with cancer risk, a psychological view also includes the risk conferred by virtue of habitual behaviors, such as smoking, alcohol consumption, or other established risk factors. For the most part, such habits have received attention not in programs targeted at cancer alone, but as part of broader, lifestyle interventions aimed at altering risk of several chronic conditions. Before discussing (in Chapter 8) these general interventions, which constitute the most far-reaching of all preventive programs, we will mention some treatment approaches that have specifically targeted the psychological factors that predispose to cancer.

Psychological Treatment Approaches

Despite accumulating evidence for the role of psychological factors in cancer, few preventive or treatment attempts have yet been made. "Psychotherapy aimed at affecting the physical disease itself is a distinctly unorthodox . . . practice that has, as yet, little explicit theoretical or research basis" (Cunningham, 1985, p. 23). There are, however, some rationales put forward for such preventive or treatment intervention. In particular, it is noted that there is considerable evidence for psychological control of immune-based responses, such as have resulted in cure of warts and changes in allergic responses through hypnosis (Bowers & Kelly, 1979).

The best known and earliest work in this area is that of Carl and Stephanie Simonton (1975; Simonton, Matthews-Simonton, & Sparks, 1980). They and their colleagues train their patients in extensive use of meditative visualization imagery to supplement conventional medical treatments in combating already established cancers. Patients are trained, for example, to imagine their immunological defenses battling and destroying cancerous cells. Individuals are encouraged to develop their own involving symbolic images to depict this conflict. Some, for example, have used the image of a white knight on a horse riding up to and spearing the cancer, which may be represented as a small, ugly animal. Others have seen the cancer as foul, shapeless meat, and the immunological defenses as a swarm of attacking sharks. The Simontons have noted that the images chosen may provide important information about patients' sometimes unconscious views of their disease, as was evident in one patient's seeing his cancer as a wall of granite that he chipped at futilely.

The Simontons report the mean survival time of their patients to be about twice that of the average for comparable disease conditions. Of a sample of 159 patients originally diagnosed as having medically incurable cancer, 14 were said to show no evidence of the disease following treatment, 12 to show tumor regression, and 17 to have stabilized (Simonton, Matthews-Simonton, & Creighton, 1978). But, as the Simontons and their colleagues note, they have a highly selected sample—95 percent of the patients in their private oncology practice choose not to participate in this program (Sparks, cited in Bowers & Kelly, 1979)—and these uncontrolled results are by no means conclusive.

The therapists credit the success of their approach to enhancement of the effectiveness of the immune system (Simonton et al., 1978). Bowers and Kelly (1979) noted that although this may be a plausible therapeutic rationale to provide for patients, it may not be the actual means of effectiveness.

> Host defenses are capable of destroying small numbers of tumor cells (1-10 million), but 100 million tumor cells almost always result in tumor progression. Since a neoplasm only 1 cm in diameter contains approximately 1 billion cells, most tumors have already overcome immune defenses by the time they are clinically detectable. Therefore, it is unlikely that immunotherapy alone will ever bolster host defenses sufficiently to reverse tumor growth in patients with advance disease. (Carter, 1976, p. 422)

The immune-based rationale for undertaking this type of treatment, then, may be specious, but this does not consitute evidence against the approach's effectiveness.

Several other authors report case studies or uncontrolled group results that are similarly inconclusive (e.g., Mahrer, 1980; Newton, 1982-1983; Weinstock, 1977). Levy (1986) reported work in progress, with Judy Rodin and Martin Seligman, in which the apathy, stoicism, and help-lessness that are thought to be prognostically most negative for cancer patients are receiving a frontal assault. These investigators are carrying out psychotherapy with cancer patients, based on Beck's well-established model for treating depression (Beck, Rush, Shaw, & Emery, 1979). The ongoing negative thoughts, such as "I'm helpless and can't do anything about my fate," which contribute to depression are identified and patients are assisted in countering these. In addition, underlying maladap-tive beliefs and assumptions that promote an inactive stance are ferreted out and subjected to reality testing. For example, the patient may believe—although it is not usually immediately obvious to him that he has this belief—that one gets what one deserves in this world, and so if he has cancer there must be some reason for it and he should accept it as just. Attacking this belief promotes other changes and a more active, problem-solving stance.

This work is intriguing, but it has yet to bear fruit. What has had a much greater impact on public opinion and policy and people's daily activities is the evidence that has linked environmental and behavioral events with tumerogenesis. The data from this area and from the work on correlates of cardiovascular disease have influenced the development of large-scale health-promoting interventions.

SUMMARY

Although to an observer the contributions of psychological investiga-tors concerned with stress and illness currently appear more fragmented than they used to, this fragmentation reflects the recognition that "stress" and "illness" are insufficiently precise constructs to represent the reality of human functioning. As a result, investigations have become much more specific in attempting to define links between psychological functioning and disease.

The work reviewed in this chapter indicates promise in many areas of investigation. Laboratory research has linked stress and ulcer formation, although the mechanisms are as yet unclear. There has been, however, some indication that psychological treatment may assist in avoiding re-currence, a problem for most ulcer patients.

The primary construct linking psychological variables and heart disease has been the notion of a Type A personality. Recently, this construct has been undergoing refinement, and it now appears that anger (especially unexpressed) and hostility may be the main components responsible for elevating risk. This is currently a very active area of research, with intervention studies underway. Preliminary results from these are promising, though concern with dropouts indicates that attention to motivation and adherence are major issues.

Interest is rapidly growing in the potential links of psychology and cancer. It appears from animal studies that the primary connection is through acute stress, though this is unconfirmed from human research. Also in laboratory animals, it has been found that tumor growth is affected by an interaction of stress and coping responses—an exciting finding since it meshes well with currently popular interactional theories of human stress. The relationship of psychological variables and cancer has been proposed to exist by virtue of immune-system links. The human retrospective, progress, and prospective studies all have serious methodological limits, but jointly point to depression and repression as possibly important variables. Despite the excitement surrounding developments in this area, it is important to recognize that physical factors are still of overriding importance. Recent uncontrolled attempts at treatment, while encouraging, need to be followed up with more controlled studies. There are indications that this type of work is already underway.

Chapter Seven

Social and
Cultural Issues
Relevant to Change

In previous chapters, we have contended that collectively Western society would be served better by more serious large-scale efforts to prevent diseases than by accelerating expenditures to treat them. Such efforts are dependent upon health-related policies, which both influence and are influenced by public attitudes. In this chapter, we will consider both pressures for change and obstacles to implementing prevention-oriented policies. Financial, political, ethical, and logistical problems arise within the health-care system itself, from vested interests outside the system, and from the general public itself.

INDIVIDUAL RIGHTS AND THE COMMON GOOD

The health of Canadians has improved greatly in the last century; but the progress has never been smooth, never uniform, never achieved without some public hostility and opposition. Time and time again, science raced ahead, and the public lagged behind, refusing to accept help with the diseases and conditions that were killing it. Nor has that situation entirely changed. (Canada's Amazing Health History, 1984, p. 344)

The above telling quotation is from an edited text of a film shown at the 75th Annual Conference of the Canadian Public Health Association,

Calgary, June 1984. Several historical examples of public opposition to actions that the medical profession considered were in the public's best interest are cited in the text: Quebec's refusal to allow smallpox vaccination until 1885 when a major epidemic killed hundreds of unprotected Quebecers, while in Ontario, where the population had been vaccinated, only 21 people died; and the situation in Montreal where a 1914 study concluded that 90 percent of Montreal's milk was unfit for human consumption, yet compulsory pasteurization was not allowed by the public until 1925. The message of the film is clearly that physicians have always known what is best for the health of the public and the problem has been in getting the public to act on physicians' good advice. This paternalistic attitude in medicine has historically failed to motivate people toward health promoting behaviors.

Another example cited, this time to demonstrate current opposition to physicians, is that of communities refusing to allow fluoridation of drinking water despite proven effectiveness against tooth decay. The topic of fluoridation raises at least three interesting areas for discussion. Those communities fighting against fluoridation apparently do so largely on the basis that long-term usage of fluoride might, in and of itself, prove hazardous. Their challenging claim, that physicians may not really know best, has considerable justification (though that is not to say the public always knows best). Even though fluoridation is generally regarded to be safe, little is known concerning the interaction between various chemicals and human health that would provide absolute reassurance that long-term exposure to fluoride is not hazardous. A second issue is the physicians' complaint, explicit in the movie, that people are not motivated to act in their own best interests, even when physicians tell them what to do. These two issues of (a) unestablished causality and risk of disease (i.e., Will fluoridation damage long-term health?) and (b) motivating behavior change to alter risk are discussed in other chapters. The third issue which arises when a community attempts to make a decision affecting everyone is the broad cultural issue of individual rights and freedom of choice.

The personal freedom cherished in Western cultures functions as a basis for American medicine (Callahan, 1977): Though there are some practical limitations on the exercise of freedom, physicians basically are free to specialize in whatever line of medicine interests them, patients are free to choose whatever care they wish, and, above all, everyone is free to live the kind of life he chooses, whatever the cost to the individual or society of hazardous living habits.

Advances in the various sciences have raised ethical problems concerning rights and freedoms: Forestalling death in various circumstances, establishing limits to rehabilitative efforts, providing or proscribing abortions, deciding when to use organ transplants in light of limited organ availability, and controlling human behavior are some of the extremely complex problems now facing us. Biomedical and behavioral engineering technology have moved ahead faster than society has been able to develop an ethical code to handle these questions. In dealing with these ethical issues, society as a whole must make decisions which will ultimately affect most, if not all, of its members. Our values require constant examination because medical treatment demands decision-making concerning happiness, a good life, and a good death. The challenge is, as it has always been, for policymakers to reconcile individual freedoms with the rights of others.

Sapolsky (1980) humorously extrapolated the idea of banning cigarette smoking (which seems reasonable to a great many people) to include United States Health, Education, and Welfare officials in armbands hauling away not only smokers, but the consumers of sugar-coated cereals and alcoholic beverages. The absurdity of this proposal is intended to provoke serious thought about individual freedoms that may interfere with the rights of others (for instance, the smoker who pollutes the air of a nonsmoking coworker) and that also may cost society as a whole a great deal of money (lung cancer treatment is expensive).

Since healthy lifestyles and environments promise to have a greater impact on future health and longevity than clinical medicine, cultural and social issues concerning *health promotion* are coming to the fore. But principles and planning for health promotion are hampered by attitudes that lead to resistance to change. Beliefs and attitudes such as these are widespread in Western culture: "They will soon have a cure for everything so why should I worry?" "I have a right to smoke (or drink or not wear a seatbelt); it's a free country" or "I've got to die sometime so I may as well have a good time while I'm here." Education about influences on health is needed for the enactment of wise policy decisions. Further difficulties will exist in motivating people to adhere to health-promoting lifestyles and/or regulations until research advances in the behavioral sciences make it possible to encourage and improve adherence to health regimens. Policy issues of when and how to use this developing behavioral technology must also be addressed. Policy discussions must also deal with the roles of the media and of public education in influencing attitudes and beliefs in a culture.

VESTED INTERESTS

Major impediments both to establishing health-promoting government policies and instituting changes in society are those organizations that have vested interests in maintaining things as they are. Thus, for example, the tobacco lobby is not eager to see a ban on smoking in the workplace, and the petroleum industry angrily counters suggestions that air pollution from their plants increases rates of cancer in nearby populations. Even the health-care system has some self-interest in controlling any changes made, and thus we see physicians resisting midwifery, psychology, and other health-care professions in the medical establishment.

The tobacco industry lends itself well to a discussion of vested interests versus health-promoting activities of governments and other agencies. The United States is a leading producer of tobacco and through price control supports tobacco growers. Several states are themselves producers of tobacco, while others benefit from excise taxes on cigarettes (Sapolsky, 1980). An estimated 54 million Americans smoke. Of these, 340,000 die *each year* from diseases caused by smoking, the same number as the combined total of U.S. dead during WWII and the Vietnam War (Mervis, 1984).

Mervis discussed some of the effects of the tobacco lobby on the U.S. federal government: Legislation to strengthen the warning that appears on cigarettes was delayed in 1984 by the tobacco lobby, which managed to have the proposal tied to a requirement that cigarette companies purchase more U.S.-grown tobacco. In addition, a plan passed in 1984 to reduce the federal deficit contained a rider cutting in half the federal excise tax on cigarettes, which resulted in an annual reduction in federal income of over 2 billion dollars. In the light of Warner's (cited by Mervis, 1984) demonstration that the 1983 doubling of the excise tax on cigarettes caused a drop of 4 percent in adult consumption and a 13 percent drop in teenage consumption of cigarettes, it seems clear that the tobacco lobby's interest often prevails over preventive health in U.S. governmental policy.

Sapolsky (1980) cites an example to ilustrate the power and determination of the tobacco lobby: When California voters were considering whether to restrict smoking in indoor work areas and public places, the tobacco lobby spent 6 million dollars in advertising against the proposal. The basis for their advertising was that such a proposal violated personal freedom. The restrictions nevertheless passed, part of a rising general reaction against the right of smokers to pollute the environment of nonsmokers.

Like others invested in promoting behavior that many view as a risk to health, the tobacco industry falls back on the claim that there is no conclusive proof linking cigarette smoking and danger to health. The industry in the United States supports the Council for Tobacco Research, which constantly attempts to counter studies on tobacco and health risk with the claim that causality has not been conclusively established. In contrast, the major groups opposed to smoking, the Cancer Societies, Heart Associations, and Lung Associations in both Canada and the United States, designate funding largely for biomedical research into cures, which is noncontroversial. These organizations have not formed an effective political lobby against the tobacco industry (Sapolsky, 1980). More important to change is the social pressure against smoking which is growing, despite the tobacco industry's advertising of smoking as socially desirable and benign. For growing numbers of people, it is unfashionable to smoke. As the risk to health of others' smoking is becoming more widely acknowledged, more people feel and say that their rights are being infringed upon by smokers. More and more municipalities have imposed or are considering imposing restrictions on smoking in the workplace and in public areas. Airlines and bus companies have begun to designate some flights and buses as nonsmoking, and there are indications that some airlines may become entirely nonsmoking. In a rather futile attempt to retaliate, one tobacco company has instructed its employees not to fly via an offending airline.

Society increasingly shows resentment of the powerful vested interests in our culture—the tobacco, alcohol, automobile, and petroleum industries, to name a few—as people become more aware of the risks to their health posed by these industries. Whether it is possible to channel this resentment toward open policy discussion is not clear. Instead, some health educators have proposed fighting fire with fire. Edwards (1963), for example, advocated this in his paper "Indoctrination: A Respectable Technique in Health Education"—respectable because it involved turning the legitimized weapons of advertisers against their own messages.

The role of the media in shaping the public's attitudes toward health also needs exploration. The portrayal of hazardous health activities, such as drinking, on television shows or in advertisements creates an aura of respectability for these behaviors; conversely, the presentation of role models engaging in health-promoting activities or encouraging, through public service ads, the avoidance of health-threatening behaviors has powerful potential for shaping the attitudes at least of younger viewers. Further, informational news specials related to health disorders can be expanded to include information about preventive, health-promoting activities as well as about the status of medical treatment for the problems. An informed public, willing to support health-promoting proposals with votes, is one possible way of counterbalancing the effect of lobbies on legislators.

It is important that we realize, however, that public education campaigns themselves constitute attempts at persuasion. They are undertaken not just to provide unbiased, value-free information, but to lead their recipients to view things differently, and, as a result, to be more likely to engage in or refrain from certain targeted behaviors. One can, in fact, argue that if an educational campaign is highly successful in producing change, it must be coercive in that its message is difficult to resist (Faden & Faden, 1978). Most people might judge it to be reasonable to try, for example, to persuade parents of infants to use infant safety seats in their cars by presenting information on the substantial reductions in injury that result from this precaution. But this agreement does not alter the fact that a campaign of this sort is as much an attempt to influence behavior as are cigarette advertisements. Its interference with voluntary behavior must in each instance be judged ethically by balancing coerciveness and potential harms and benefits.

THE HEALTH-CARE SYSTEM

Though few are likely to view the medical establishment itself as an interest vested in maintaining poor health, and no doubt medical care-givers themselves would hotly deny such a charge, there are some parallels with industry. Physicians have power, status, and high incomes, and medicine is big business and can be an end in itself, apart from improving health (Callahan, 1977). There is a history of considerable resistance to changing this situation, as Norton (1982) summarized in his discussion concerning the history of prepayment for medical care:

> Organized medicine has consistently opposed prepayment plans, as well as all other types of health insurance, at least initially: "The AMA has opposed every change in health-care service, dating back to the formation of the Mayo Clinic in the 1870's when the Mayo doctors were not allowed to join the AMA because they dared to practice as a group" (Gumbiner, 1975: 19). Rosser and Mossberg noted that "for many years the AMA actively subverted Blue Cross by expelling doctors hired under group health plans and threatening to stop intern-training programs in associated hospitals, thus pressuring hospitals to turn away patients referred from physicians in group plans" (1977: 64). This policy led to indictment of the AMA on criminal charges of conspiracy in 1938. More recently, lobbying by the AMA led to the passage of laws preventing the founding of prepayment plans without the support of 51% of the practicing physicians in the state. (pp. 30-31)

Failures in the health-care system, however, may be rooted more in the effects of tradition, organizational problems, and the massiveness of its responsibilities than in vested self-interest. The system is a fragmented, unwieldy mammoth, sometimes resistant to change, but at other times, because of its size and lack of functional unity, unable to respond quickly and with flexibility to changes seen by the profession as desirable. Above all, since it operates on a fee-for-service basis, the idea of promoting preventive activities (i.e., prevention of the need for services) is difficult to implement. Scrutiny of the effectiveness of the current system for provision of medical care and promoting health reveals that it is costly, outmoded, and inadequate in its response to many health-care needs.

Health-Services Research

An American Psychological Association (APA) Task Force on Health Research (1976) described the health industry as an unmanaged system. The Task Force stated that health is one of the most crucial social problems facing the nation because conventional methods of providing and financing health services are nearly exhausted.

The Task Force criticized the American health-care delivery system because the term *system* implies organization and dynamic interaction of functional units; such organization and relationship are found only in limited degree in health services today. The lack of coordination of services that characterizes clinical medicine, general hospitals, optometrists, pharmacies, podiatrists, long-term care facilities, drug manufacturers, and the myriad other parts of our health goods-and-services grab bag is difficult to overstate. There is little evidence of an overall plan (APA Task Force on Health Research, 1976, p. 264).

Lewis (1974) identified health services research as the study of preventive, environmental, and other types of services that are not necessarily intended to cure disease or illness (for example, research concerning what things motivate people to seek care), involving independent disciplines whose practitioners not only don't talk to each other, but who sometimes don't even like each other. The areas of investigation include (1) the workings of a system and the subsystems through which people both identify the need for care and attempt to provide care; (2) subsequent interactions between patient and caregiver; (3) utilization of goods, commodities, and facilities; and (4) the costs involved. Lewis noted, "Health services research is value laden. It asks questions and may provide information that not everyone is prepared to accept" (pp. 84-85).

The APA Task Force on Health Research (1976) argued that psychologists are particularly well-suited to analyze issues related to the health-care system, such as adherence and motivation, denial and delay when symptoms present, constitutional factors that predispose to illness, somatotypical factors, assessment of lifestyles and risk of illness, attitude determinants and change, and program evaluation. The extensiveness of the Task Force proposals for further study reflects the absence of internal self-monitoring of the system and the dearth of preventive efforts.

Inadequate Self-Evaluation

Not only has the health-care system itself not been adequately monitored, but individual elements of health care have not, as a rule, been subjected to critical examination. Eisenberg (1977) used the example of tonsillectomies and adenoidectomies to illustrate that research concerning the efficacy of medical treatments often lags far behind practice. According to Eisenberg, about 1 million of these combined surgeries are done every year in the United States—30 percent of all surgery on children—at a cost of about 500 million dollars. During the 1950s this surgery resulted in some 200 to 300 deaths per year, and current mortality is estimated at 1 death per 16,000 operations. Yet at the time of his examination of the area, there had been no research done by biomedical researchers to address effectiveness on health of these surgeries. Eisenberg's point is emphasized by the fact that the current rate of 647 hysterectomies per 100,000 women can be extrapolated to show that half of all women in the United States will have had their uterus removed by the time they reach the age of 65. By 1977 there had been no research conducted to address the effectiveness of this procedure on the health of women. The temptation is to believe that many surgeons are not highly invested in determining effectiveness. Eisenberg compared the medical practice of prescribing treatment on the belief that it will do some good, despite lack of real evidence, to the widespread practice of bloodletting during the 18th and 19th centuries and called for controlled clinical trials to separate effective remedies from the harmful ones, careful delineation of disease patterns to establish underlying pathophysiology, basic biological research, and investigation into the identification and modification of cultural patterns, social forces, and idiosyncratic personal behaviors that have effects on health.

Insufficient Informational Efforts

Despite increasing public interest in health-related matters, the public remains exceedingly ignorant. Burnham (1984) traced historical trends in the popularization of health in the United States and found a contemporary appetite for facts and an aversion to context. Accustomed to news packaged in 10-second bits by television reports and grocery check-out magazines, modern health consumers have little time for, or even interest in, the coherent rationale behind new developments, without which there is no framework to organize knowledge and action. Burnham (1984) wrote of this trend:

> In journalism . . . discrete facts were welcome, but not long, involved series or matrices. Not only was a scientific fact complete in itself but a scientific discovery had to be a media event—again, complete in and of itself. While political columnists did spring up to interpret politics, health columnists, by contrast, continued to be confined to specifics, as if they were still part of objective news. (p. 196)

The public's lack of an organized body of knowledge about health and health promotion constitutes a further impediment to a progressive health policy and system.

Economic Problems and Inequity

Government policy development for health care is hampered in part by the underdevelopment of conceptualization and measurement of health. Callahan (1977) claimed that the definition of medical goals requires a definition of health, but concluded that the World Health Organization's definition of health as "a state of complete physical, mental, and social well-being and not merely the absence of disease or infirmity" (p. 26) places society in the position of seeking unattainable goals because of the implicit assumption that medicine is responsible for the creation of happiness. This broad definition makes specification of the limits of the health enterprise impossible. There is a resulting limitless economic burden on society.

Defining health seems to demand the asking of unpleasant questions relating to priorities. Not only do cost-benefit issues have to be addressed, but the differences between needs and desires must be differentiated. In a growth-based economy, people are encouraged to view needs and desires as the same, to feel optimistic that their desires can be fulfilled, and to view a life with unfulfilled desires as less than optimal (Callahan, 1977). Thomas (1977) noted that awareness of risk of disease, an associated apprehension that minor illness may turn into a killing disease, and the expectation that all kinds of disease can be effectively treated have changed the public perception of health. Unhappiness, discontent, fear, anxiety, and other personal maladjustments are inappropriately seen as areas for medical attention. Further, since Western society views happiness almost as a right and since health (considered in the minds of most people to equate with availability of medical care) is generally thought of as fundamental to happiness, then everyone, regardless of financial means, should have the right to the medical care she feels is necessary.

Western nations have therefore attempted to alter the social order with respect to provision of medical care. The various methods of creating universal access to medical care are having a positive effect, if success is measured by the fact that the poor, who cannot pay, are some of the largest users of medical facilities (Matthews, 1984). This high usage, however, cannot be taken as a measurement of improved health. Since the poor very often live without adequate food and shelter, often without clean water, and sometimes with a lack of social support, it is likely that many of the problems they present to medical professionals stem from these factors. It is clear that assuring access to medical services for the poor does not *prevent* or truly cure the health problems created by poverty.

The established idea of "right to health care" as a principle of social policy can be construed in two different ways, with considerably different social, economic, and political implications (Callahan, 1977). This "right" can mean either that everyone should have a fair portion of whatever resources are available, or it can mean that each person can claim whatever resources are needed, and, by implication, that there is a social obligation to provide additional resources if current levels are insufficient to meet this open-ended demand. In the latter case, the right to health care has to compete for funding with other rights such as those to nourishment, education, and housing.

Wildavsky (1977) discussed the social principles operating in the equitable provision of medical care. Although governments have tried to make medical care equally available to rich and poor, there is always rationing because of limited time of medical professionals, limited space in medical facilities, distance from medical centers, and because the complexities involved in using the medical facilities mean greater accessibility for some than others. Callahan (1977) defined equity as requiring that whatever a person needed to save his life would be made available to him. But he was quick to outline the problems of inequality inherent in this definition: (1) Some people require few resources while others require a great deal to save their lives. (2) Even using the greatest-good-for-the-greatest-number criterion results in injustices to those with rarer conditions. (3) How would limits be set if it is decided they are needed? (4) Should medical care be denied or limited for illnesses resulting from hazardous lifestyles, such as drug addiction? Can we blame anyone for such diseases, given the influence of environment on health? Further, how could we prove culpability when sometimes diseases, such as lung cancer, develop in individuals who have tried to live healthy lives?

Even when governments attempt to provide more money for health care, there are still inequalities in the system. Wealthier, better educated people receive better care because they are better able to negotiate the system. However, the wealthier also end up paying twice, first, in taxes, and, second, for their own health costs because they get less subsidized care. Other people, those just above the "cut-off" point for subsidy, carry costs disproportionate to their income. Additionally, with the provision of greater access to the system comes crowding and greater demands for more facilities (Wildavsky, 1977). Though the need for a totally equitable system may be a problem without a solution, the presence of so many obvious flaws calls for continuous examination and change. In a later section in this chapter, we will discuss some of the options for balancing the needs and limits on resources.

Demand for Services

Because of the prevalent cultural belief that greater access to medical care means greater health, the public demands as much medical care as it is possible to get. Wildavsky (1977) explored the resultant interplay in the health-care system. Since medicine and health do not correlate exactly, there is uncertainty in treatment, which physicians attempt to resolve by providing as much treatment as the patient can afford in order to reduce the likelihood of malpractice suits. Patients, who are anxious for treatment, demand more medical personnel and facilities, and medical personnel are disposed to use as many resources—diagnostic tools or treatment technology—as are available.

Although people may demand that some of the funds now being spent to increase medical accessibility be directed toward other social benefits, they are rarely prepared to sacrifice satisfaction of their own health-care needs for greater social benefits. Medical costs rise equal to the sum of private insurance and government subsidy because patients demand everything possible be done and care providers fear being faulted for doing less than they might. Insurance companies and government subsidies provide the money for all of it with little cost to the patient himself beyond the high insurance costs, which are deducted from paychecks or paid for by income tax, thereby seeming largely outside the patient's personal responsibility. Hospitals make enough profit to expand, serving patients more extensively; concurrently, physicians' incomes rise. The insurance companies are an integral part of the process; when more money is needed, they raise their rates. The ultimate limit to this escalation is the amount of money individuals and governments are willing to put into the system.

Since funds for health care are not unlimited, Western countries have struggled with various methods to provide equitable distribution of health care resources. In Canada and Great Britain, medical costs are under almost total control of the governments. Almost everyone is insured for almost everything, as far as treatment for illness is concerned. In the United States a mixture of government subsidies and aid to the elderly and poor combine with private insurance companies to cover the preponderance of medical costs. Few individuals are fully satisfied with any of the systems.

Contradictory attitudes are exemplified by the situation wherein doctors are urged to treat more and more patients, yet criticized for making more money as a result. Along the same lines, hospitals are criticized for exploiting workers if they pay low wages, yet criticized for taking advantage of insurance by paying higher wages.

> If money is a barrier to medicine, the system is discriminatory. If money is no barrier, the system gets overcrowded. If everyone is insured, costs rise to the level of the insurance. If many remain underinsured, their income drops to the level of whatever medical disaster befalls them. Inability to break out of this bind has made the politics of health policy pathological. (Wildavsky, 1977, p. 111)

SYSTEMS FOR PROVISION OF CARE

There are three basic systems that have been considered in Western nations for providing and paying for health care: (1) a system with health insurance for emergencies, with payment graded according to income; (2) a mixed public and private system; and (3) total coverage through a public system (Wildavsky, 1977).

The "catastrophic insurance" system requires individuals to pay medical costs up to a specified proportion of their incomes. Above that, the general insurance takes over, funded by public revenues. This results in a relative equivalence of ability to pay for treatment across economic levels, and therefore leaves each individual fairly free to determine how much he can use medical services. Such schemes are geared, however, toward treatment rather than prevention, since individuals are reluctant to spend for preventive efforts. A further drawback is that once the individual has contributed his maximum toward costs, then there is no incentive to contain additional costs, encouraging a "sky's-the-limit" attitude toward large expenditures. A correction is possible to this system, however: If overutilization were to occur, the government could simply adjust the percentage limits for each level of income. In our view, the main drawback of this approach is its deemphasis of prevention.

There are more serious problems with the mixed public and private system, currently in place in the United States. In 1983, 80 percent of U.S.

citizens had private (or employment-related) health insurance, which covered part and often nearly all of their health expenditures and allowed them to choose among the treatment facilities available. This private coverage is concentrated among those in higher income brackets: 94 percent of those whose annual incomes exceeded 10,000 dollars had medical insurance of some kind, compared to 70 percent of those earning under 7,000 dollars (National Center for Health Statistics, 1983). Poorer people also have subsidized public facilities available, but these limit their decision-making concerning their own care and often do not include the best resources, particularly for specialized treatment. Subsidized care may also have a significant negative impact on motivation and adherence. The APA Task Force on Health Research (1976) noted that many people who do not have the personal resources for health insurance and do not meet the criteria for medical subsidy do not receive health services of any kind on a consistent basis. In short, as is widely recognized, the mixed public and private system results in two unequal levels of health care, with those who can afford it getting the best.

A completely public system requires more physicians than would private practice, wherein physicians are encouraged by monetary gain to work longer hours. This places more demands on funding sources and institutions to train additional professionals. In a public system, with universal access to care and generally lower fee rates, physicians are likely to spend less time with patients. The British experience has confirmed these problems and demonstrated a number of others as well: Central governmental control has not been able to distribute physicians evenly across the country, nor to encourage growth in the numbers of general practitioners in relation to the elite specialists; there is no evidence to suggest that preventive medicine is more prevalent under this system; and demands on the system have increased under the public system. Canada's universal-access, publicly funded system has overcome some of the disadvantages of the British system by (1) placing no ceiling on physicians' incomes, and (2) covering the cost of each medical service at an amount predetermined by a regulatory body, while permitting physicians to bill for more than this amount. Thus, every individual has most services paid, though a minority of practitioners charge more than the insurance-reimbursed amount. Access to these few physicians has, as a result, been more limited by income; but in exchange, physicians have felt more in control of their practices, even if they do not elect to bill extra amounts. The federal government has recently moved to force termination of the practice of extra-billing, attempting to completely equalize availability of services, which would create a system much more like that of Britain. In some provinces, the outrage and organized protest from physicians has been unprecedented, whereas in others there has been little resistance.

Two developments in the U.S. system have shown promise for helping to contain costs and, in one instance, to place more emphasis on prevention. Preferred provider schemes involve contractual agreements among consumers, caregivers, insurance companies, and—often, though not necessarily—employers. Typically, in a preferred provider scheme, an insurance company contracts with one or more health-care facilities (which may include hospitals, clinics, mental-health services, etc.) to pay for services at a reduced rate in exchange for sending all its customers to these facilities. In turn, the employer is offered reduced premiums for health insurance, as are employees for their portion (if any) of the premiums, as long as employees use the contracted facilities. If employees elect not to use these facilities they may be covered for some portion of the costs or none at all, depending upon the plan. These plans have become popular with employers because they lower insurance costs, with providers because they ensure steady referrals in a competitive market, and with insurance companies because they reduce costs. Consumers, on the other hand, have shown some disfavor because of the limitations placed on their choices (Allen, 1984).

A second notable development in the system is the growing popularity of the Health Maintenance Organization (HMO). The HMO is an organization that serves both as insurer and care provider. Individuals voluntarily subscribe to or join the HMO by prepaying fees at fixed rates for complete or nearly complete coverage of all health-care needs. Subscribers receive outpatient medical care, usually at a clinic operated by the HMO, by physicians and other professionals who are salaried employees of the HMO, and inpatient care in either a hospital owned and operated by the organization or one with contractual arrangements with the HMO. HMOs tend to stress preventive health care more than many facilities because it is in their self-interest to take steps that will result in long-term financial savings at the expense of the short-term, lesser costs of preventive efforts. Tulkin and Frank (1985) described how the HMO at the Kaiser-Permanente Medical Center in Hayward, California, has been led to increasing emphasis on behavioral programs engineered by psychologists in order both to treat disorders such as alcoholism and to prevent secondary problems by reducing smoking, encouraging weight loss, and assisting in the development of strategies for coping with stress.

HMOs have been found to result in more economical health-care delivery, primarily as a result of fewer annual days of hospital utilization as compared to traditional insurance plans (Luft, 1978). Roemer (1974) also reported a lower frequency of elective surgeries and generally high patient satisfaction.

Both of these newer developments—preferred provider schemes and HMOs—offer advantages over the existing dual system in the U.S., with the HMOs having the advantage of more attention to preventive health care. Nevertheless, as Norton (1982) noted, their advantages should not be oversold. The type of medical care they provide is primarily remedial, and it needs to be balanced with public policy efforts toward more general preventive measures (e.g., fluoridation, seat-belt legislation), which cannot be handled at this level.

COST EFFECTIVENESS

Before changes can be demanded by a health-conscious public, the cost effectiveness of planned measures needs to be addressed. That is not to say that cost effectiveness of any measure must be demonstrated before it is undertaken, but only that decisions should be made on the basis of an understanding of the issues involved. For example, chronic diseases, which affect an increasing proportion of the population (Burish & Bradley, 1983), usually advance through acute episodes that leave the patient in a somewhat worsened state of health and/or functioning; treatment, which includes rehabilitation to improve or maintain level of functioning, extends over many years at great economic cost. AIDS is an example of a disease for which treatment is very expensive and currently does not seem curative. AIDS patients are treated primarily to prolong their lives, sometimes for a short time, at great cost.

Computing the costs of prolonging or saving lives is sometimes considered an outrageous dehumanizing of human suffering. We have heard, for example, neonatal specialists declare that there is no cost too great to save the life of even one infant. Although in a specific instance deciding to withhold medical care because it is too costly is the sort of decision none of us would like to make, it is nevertheless a simple fact that the economic resources of a country are limited whereas the potential for medical costs is virtually limitless. If, for example, artificial hearts should be determined to be generally acceptable treatment for those with incurable heart disease, it would be financially impossible to provide them. It is similarly not possible to provide donor organs for all people eligible to receive them—even though not receiving them results in death in many cases. The funds to solicit organs systematically and to match donors and recipients efficiently are not available.

Estimating economic costs of illness has been accomplished through cost effectiveness analysis to determine the most efficient treatments and to justify expenditures or to make comparative cost-benefit analyses across diseases (Cooper & Rice, 1976). Economic costs of illnesses are measured as (1) outlays for prevention, detection, and treatment, and (2) costs or loss in output due to disability and early death (Cooper & Rice, 1976). It is estimated that by 1990 the economic cost of illness will reach 12 percent of the U.S. GNP (National Center for Health Statistics, 1983).

Such analysis of the cost of health care for illness in the present system strongly suggests the need for change—change not only in the provision of curative medicine, but change also in the approach to health. Wildavsky (1977) suggested that since maintenance of health is only minimally related to medical care, less expertise may be as good as more professional training, and he recommended the use of more economical approaches to care, such as an increased role for nurse-practitioners. He suggested that physicians' traditional opposition to this infringement on their territory could be circumvented by elevating their status so that they would deal with only more complicated matters. He cautioned, however, that physicians are likely to use assistants as additions to the medical establishment rather than as the antidote to increasing numbers of physicians.

Among Eisenberg's (1977) suggestions for improvements in the system were more comprehensive insurance coverage for outpatient care to diminish unnecessary hospitalization; reimbursement schedules that would bear a closer relationship to the time spent with the patient and less to the medical specialty of the diagnostic or treatment procedures; malpractice insurance revised to allow for compensation without physician culpability, negligence to be dealt with separately; and peer evaluation to improve physicians' performance.

It is frequently noted that the majority of visits to physicians are for nonmedical problems such as alcohol abuse, depression, or anxiety (Yates, 1984). It might be reasonable, then, to expect that psychological interventions could reduce medical care overutilization and unnecessary expenditures by offering more appropriate assessment and treatment options for such patients. Cummings and Follette (1976) reported a follow-up study of 85 patients who had been seen in an HMO for psychotherapy seeking help for a medical problem (e.g., headaches) 8 years previously. At the time of follow-up, these patients were asked what was the original reason for their seeking help. Seventy-eight of them (92 percent) gave as the reason the problem discussed with the psychotherapist (e.g., marital, familial, job-related) rather than the presenting symptom. When these 78 patients were asked directly about the symptom that had been recorded as the reason for referral on their medical records (e.g., "Did you ever have severe headaches?"), all but 5 denied ever having consulted a doctor for the complaint. "Thus the patient seems to have understood that the [psycho-social] problem was more 'real' than the symptom" (Cummings & Follette, 1976, p. 172).

A case-history reported by Cummings and Follette is illuminating:

> Mrs. W., age thirty-nine, married sixteen years, with three children, was referred by her internist for severe headaches that had become less and less responsive to medication for the past ten months. She was seen by a psychologist three times, during which time her anger at her husband (whom she reluctantly said was seeing his secretary) was discussed, along with her feelings of being old at thirty-nine and unattractive. Between the second and third sessions she blew up at her husband, put her foot down regarding his staying out at night, and was surprised to find he was remorseful and eager to make amends. On telephone interview eight years later she denied ever having suffered from severe headaches, and recalled clearly that she consulted a psychotherapist for a marital problem. She did not find the sessions helpful, and stated flatly that she and [her] husband worked it all out and they had been happier than ever. (pp. 172- 173)

The benefits of psychotherapy do not have to be recognized by the patient to be real.

Von Baeyer (1986) summarized the findings from an extensive literature on brief psychological interventions with medical patients thus:

> The finding that is clearly evident in the great majority of studies is that *medical patients who are given brief psychological treatment reduce their utilization of medical services following the treatment.* This has been shown to be true for a wide range of services, including length of hospital stays, number of visits to a physician, use of laboratory and X-ray procedures and use of medication. Medical service utilization dropped for patients receiving outpatient as well as inpatient psychological services. The kinds of psychological services for which a benefit was found included psychological assessment, individual and group psychotherapy, preparation for surgery or other invasive procedures, and behavior therapy. In some studies, reductions in medical utilization were realized following even a single evaluative session with a psychologist. In most cases, regardless of duration of treatment, these effects were maintained long after the patients had completed therapy. . . . By the early 1980's, more than a score of carefully executed studies using randomly assigned control groups had been published, almost all showing the same effect. It is now possible to state with considerable

confidence that psychological treatment causes the well-known reductions in medical utilization. (pp. 9-10)

Although the economic impact of these interventions has not been nailed down as firmly by controlled studies as has their impact on use of medical services (von Baeyer, 1986), there are numerous studies providing strong support for the view that psychological interventions are cost effective. Cummings (1977), in a review of data from the Kaiser-Permanente health insurance plan, concluded that just one to four sessions of psychotherapy resulted in a savings of 2.59 dollars in medical expenses for every dollar invested in therapy. In other studies, Cummings and Follette (1976) reported a 75 percent reduction in medical utilization over a 5-year period in patients initially receiving two to eight psychotherapy sessions (considered brief therapy), and a 60 percent 5-year reduction in medical utilization after one psychological session only.

Yates (1980) has suggested that ongoing cost-effectiveness data collection be incorporated into institutional programs to build a database and enable more empirically guided policy decisions. Despite many thoughtful and excellent suggestions for more economical and improved quality of patient care in the literature, the strongest case to be made is, in our view, for emphasis on a preventive approach.

TOWARD CHANGE

The health-care system lacks unified goals applicable to the system as a whole. The general focus on treatment of disease instead of health-promoting activity, that is, primary prevention of disease, is the most outstanding, illogical, and largely unrecognized gap in the system. The current health-care system has, of course, evolved out of the cultural beliefs and social principles operative in our society. Changes in the system will stem naturally from changes in the culture as a product of social forces dominated, it is to be hoped, by a growth in education and awareness. A study of psychological literature concerning the health-care system calls for multidisciplinary development of policy to lead the way toward a structure that would function as a true system, adequately responding to the health-care needs of the population.

Governments and other large institutions are notoriously slow to respond with appropriate action even when established policy has led the way. An excellent Canadian federal document (Lalonde, 1974), one also well-known and widely cited in the United States, gave high priority to prevention efforts more than 10 years ago. To date, the funds for the recommendations have not been made available at any level of government (Matthews, 1984). Instead, Canadian health services have been governed by an earlier Canada Health Act, which attempted to guarantee universality of rights to hospital services and medical care. This document made no provision for preventive medical services and, most importantly, did not recognize the role of professions outside the medical profession in promoting and maintaining health. Changes are resulting from new legislation, but health promotion is likely to continue at an unhurried pace.

> In order to survive in the competitive world of health services, prevention must have specially designated budgetary provisions. When curative and preventive services have to compete for the same budgetary allocation, curative services will usually win. The man with cancer of the lung cannot be denied the expensive and heroic services we have to offer, in spite of the fact that he has only an 8 to 10 percent chance that he will be alive in five years. His treatment cannot be denied or deferred, although it would be more logical to provide an extensive antismoking program for young persons. The antismoking program, if it is to succeed, must have separate funding and separate staff, and the same is true of most of our preventive programs. (Matthews, 1984, p. 8)

A similar situation exists in Great Britain, where health care is ultimately governed by political decisions concerning how much money to spend on the National Health Service. As Kline (1984) noted, this results in an emphasis on responding to life-threatening conditions and an underdevelopment of prevention and improvement of quality of life through medical interventions. Although more of a free-market system, such as is found in Canada or to a greater extent the United States, leads to a better record of interventions concerned with quality of life (e.g., hip replacements), prevention still lags behind. In Canada prevention has been unable to attain even equivalent status with other health services, and in the United States less than 5 percent of health-care dollars go toward prevention (Knowles, 1977).

There are some signs that employers with health-care plans are beginning to recognize that emphasizing health-promoting and disease-preventing activities has long-term cost-reducing benefits (Norris, 1981). William S. Cohen (1985), a U.S. Senator (R-Maine) on the Special Committee on Aging, noted several features of the work environment that make it well suited for preventive effort:

> (a) Most employees go to the workplace on a regular schedule, facilitating *regular* participation in the programs; (b) contact with co-workers can provide reinforcing social support, which is believed by many to be a primary force in sustaining a life-style

change; (c) the workplace offers many opportunities for environmental supports, such as health food in the cafeteria and office policies regarding smoking; (d) opportunities abound for positive reinforcement for individuals participating in the programs; (e) programs in the workplace are generally less expensive for the employee than comparable programs in the community; and (f) programs in the workplace are convenient. (p. 215)

Pyle (1979) noted the trend for large corporations to provide in-house fitness programs for their employees. He compiled a profile of a typical program, based on interviews with directors and managers of about 30 of the most comprehensive programs in the United States, including the oldest continuing program (Western Electric's) and some that have received substantial public attention (Kimberly-Clark's and General Foods's). On average, he found that the surveyed programs required a budget of 500 dollars annually for each participant. This typically provided three rooms, a director, and equipment for a program consisting of personally prescribed endurance, flexibility, and strength exercise regimens in three 35-minute segments each week. Pyle noted that most programs began with participation of executive staff only. Although there was a general commitment to provide universal accessibility, the expense and the fact that the results of specific programs were largely undocumented deterred most employers from large-scale expansion. This is a major drawback of these programs. Changes in work environments are slow to come about and at the moment seem inevitably to involve a minority of the population.

SUMMARY

This chapter raised issues concerning the implementation of public programs intended to provide health benefits. Such programs are often opposed because of the Western emphasis on individual freedoms. To some extent, these programs are coercive in that they usurp the decision-making capabilities of individuals (e.g., fluoridation, seatbelt legislation). Nevertheless, it is clear that vested interests, such as powerful industrial lobbies, have a substantial impact on health-related aspects of society (e.g., pollution, motivation to smoke and drink), and informed and active public policies represent one of the only ways to counterbalance these influences.

The health-care system itself poses some obstacles to improvement, such as a lack of overall organization, profit-orientation, and inadequate attempts at self-evaluation. Problems also arise in the provision of information and balancing the demands for health-care services with the resources available. Although no ideal system for provision of both treatment and preventive health services may exist, it appears that a balance of the needs of providers and recipients requires some elements of a free-market system and some of a collective one. Health Maintenance Organizations are a promising development in the United States. Because both HMOs and employers have a long-term financial investment in the health of their members and employees, these organizations have found it increasingly possible to place more emphasis on both prevention and psychological interventions than have traditional health-care facilities, which are generally responding to immediate needs.

The economic analysis of medical treatment points to preventive interventions and psychological care as likely to be cost-effective treatments. Although the value of preventive interventions has been well known for many years, they have not been used widely in the United States or Canada. Some prevention programs are beginning to be used by employers in the workplace.

Chapter Eight

Programs for
Lifestyle Change

In preceding chapters, we have discussed preventive interventions intended to modify specific risk factors for particular diseases. These have often targeted populations specifically at risk or already suffering from a disease, for whom behavioral changes can prevent occurrence, recurrence, or exacerbation of a health problem. Another approach to prevention is to institute larger scale programs that reduce risk more generally across the population, preferably by forestalling the development of negative habits. These efforts have led to the development of a new field, social marketing of health behavior (Frederiksen, Solomon, & Brehony, 1984).

Although these programs are still in their infancy, they are quite varied. Some, such as smoking-prevention programs, target specific risk factors that may entail multiple risks, as smoking elevates the incidence of numerous lung diseases, cardiovascular disease, and a variety of cancers. These programs typically focus on high-risk groups, children or adolescents who are near the usual age of onset for smoking. Both primary and secondary prevention takes place within this context, for some attempts are made to deter any occurrence of the behavior, but other efforts are directed toward modifying the behavior if it exists.

Another prototype of general prevention is the screening model, which attempts to initiate appropriate medical treatment for those who unknowingly require it. Community- or school-based tuberculosis tests, routine Pap tests, and education to encourage breast or testicular self-examinations are examples of these secondary prevention programs. Particular populations may be sought out for some of these programs; in other instances, they are intended to encompass everyone.

Multiple risk factors are targeted by yet another group of programs. These primary prevention programs represent attempts on the broadest scale to encourage health by altering a variety of components of lifestyle. Although programs like the Stanford Heart Disease Prevention Project may be particularly concerned with risk for one type of disease, they are extensive interventions that modify behaviors thought to be linked to several health risks (e.g., smoking, diet, activity level).

We will describe several projects that illustrate the methods and problems in these broadly based prevention projects.

SMOKING PREVENTION

The last decade has seen a rapid growth in public consciousness of several behavioral patterns associated with increased risk of disease. Attention has been expressly concentrated on smoking, diet, and activity level. Recent work in the prevention of smoking provides a model for other research and interventions. Careful methodology has been combined with a sound theoretical basis to develop effective, practical programs, which could readily be implemented in many settings.

Development of Smoking Prevention Programs

Few people begin to smoke after the age of 20. Smoking usually begins in adolescence, initiating a harmful habit that is difficult to reverse (Russell, 1971). Since smoking control programs reach a miniscule proportion of the population (Stachnik & Stoffelmayr, 1981) and are characterized by high recidivism (Auger, Wright, & Simpson, 1972; Bernstein, 1969), prevention is the most appropriate approach. Although cessation rates of 70 percent are about average and a rate of 100 percent is common, within 6 months 75 to 80 percent of the individuals who quit are smoking again (Shiffman, Read, Maltese, Rapkin, & Jarvik, 1985). Shiffman et al. quoted Mark Twain: "Quitting smoking is easy—I've done it a hundred times" (p. 472).

Early deterrent programs were based on education about the long-term dangers to health, such as cancer, heart disease, and chronic lung disease. These efforts have had an impact, in that most people believe that smoking is detrimental to health, but they have not been successful, in that they have failed to influence the incidence of smoking. Many children still begin to smoke, particularly at around the seventh grade level

(Evans et al., 1978; Piper, Jones, & Matthews, 1974; Thompson, 1978). Educational efforts dealing with long-term risks fail to recognize the difficulties in controlling behavior based on future-oriented considerations, which are particularly problematic with children and adolescents. Similar limitations of purely educational programs have been noted in other applications, such as changing nutritional habits (Jeffery, Pirie, Rosenthal, Gerber, & Murray, 1982).

Recent efforts have turned to the more immediate and more powerful social influences on smoking. Peers, parents, and the media have been found to be the overriding influences to begin smoking (Evans et al., 1978). Accordingly, several prevention programs, grouped under the rubric of *social-psychological* approaches, have incorporated elements based on counteracting these influences (Flay, Hansen, Johnson, & Sobel, 1983; Luepker, Johnson, Murray, & Pechacek, 1983; McAlister, Perry, & Maccoby, 1979; Perry, Killen, Telch, Slinkard, & Danaher, 1980; Telch, Killen, McAlister, Perry, & Maccoby, 1982). They include elements based on research in the areas of persuasive communications, social inoculation, social learning, attribution, commitment, and decision-making theories (Flay et al., 1985). Detailed reviews of this literature and its methodological problems have concluded that dramatic advances have been made over the previous educational campaigns, but reviewers have nevertheless remained cautious in predicting long-term consequences, since 3-year follow-up data are the longest yet available (Botvin & Wills, 1985; Flay, in press; Flay et al., 1985).

Implications for Other Prevention Efforts

The shift in focus that is evident in smoking-control research provides a general paradigm worth emulating in other prevention efforts. Following the failure of initial, purely educational efforts to effect significant changes in smoking behavior, work was not abandoned, but became more analytical. Instead of assuming that mere awareness would lead people to act in a health-promoting manner, researchers analyzed the factors that influence decision-making concerning smoking. These analyses were then followed by more targeted programs, attempting to influence these specific factors.

This evolution in approach parallels that in the adherence literature, discussed earlier. In treatment settings, a laissez-faire attitude, in which it is left up to the patient whether or not to "accept" (i.e., follow) treatment recommendations, is increasingly recognized as failing to take into account the variables that affect the patient's decision and subsequent behavior. In most cases, provision of information is insufficient. If the patient concurs with the treatment regimen, then the next step in treatment becomes recognizing and dealing with the obstacles to adherence, just as preventing smoking requires recognizing and dealing with the variables that affect that behavior. A glaring example of the inadequacy of provision of information in altering engrained habits is the U.S. National Safety Council's public educational campaign to increase use of seatbelts in automobiles. Despite public service advertising time and space amounting to 51 million dollars, no increase in safety belt use was achieved (Lewy, 1980). This campaign may, however, have been partly responsible for the evolution of a public climate that would support the recent passage of mandatory seatbelt legislation in several states. Nevertheless, as we noted earlier, sufficient support for new laws to be passed does not necessarily imply a public that will comply with those laws without stringent enforcement. This problem with informational efforts underlines the need for a functional analysis of the behavior of interest, whether it is smoking, adherence to a medical regimen, use of safety precautions, or consumption of alcohol, in order to devise more effective programs intended to affect all types of behaviors.

The Waterloo Smoking Prevention Project

Under the direction of Alan Best of the Health Studies Department at the University of Waterloo, Ontario, 22 elementary schools have participated in one of the most intensive, and methodologically most rigorous, investigations of smoking prevention to date (Flay et al., 1985). Details of the study illustrate (1) the type of program that may provide the most hope for altering smoking patterns, (2) the factors that are important in many prevention programs, and (3) the necessary elements of sound research concerning the effectiveness of such interventions.

Three major program components were delivered in six 1-hour weekly sessions to sixth-grade students. Sessions were held during the first 3 months of the year, with two maintenance sessions provided later on. In addition, three booster sessions were held, two in seventh grade and one in eighth grade. It was reasoned that the increase in peer pressure with age would require updating of the original content of the program in the booster sessions to make it salient to maturing students.

1. Information concerning smoking was provided via a small-group-discussion and research format that required the students to search out and share with each other relevant data. The experimenters eschewed didactic presentation because they felt information that the students themselves found and presented would be more convincing, more understandable to themselves and their peers, and more relevant to their

own belief systems. Information on topics such as the health risks of smoking and tactics used by advertisers to encourage smoking was discussed and repeated throughout the program using multiple media to encourage attention, comprehension, and retention.

2. The second component dealt with social influences. Rather than simply educate the students concerning these influences, the program solicited from them (and bolstered with additional ideas) ways to resist pressures to smoke. Students generated responses that they could make to peers pressuring them to smoke (e.g., "No thank you, I don't smoke"), and a variety of responses were repeated, refined, and elaborated. Specific social coping skills, in particular interpersonal tactics, were then rehearsed through role playing.

3. Decision-making and commitment constituted the final component. Students were asked to consider all of the information from the sessions and to make public commitments, which were announced to classmates.

The booster sessions in seventh grade involved small groups of students in developing their own smoking prevention programs and presenting portions of them to classmates. The eighth grade session was a discussion of social benefits and consequences of smoking, pressures and influences to smoke, and a decision-making process.

Important Program Elements

Several aspects of this program are particularly notable as an example of a preventive intervention. First of all, the study took aim at the population for whom intervention was likely to have the most payoff. Rather than institute a community-wide campaign, the investigators targeted sixth-grade to eighth-grade students, who are most likely to be just beginning to smoke, thereby maximizing the likelihood of program impact and requiring fewer resources.

A second notable characteristic was the use of both questioning and information-gathering by the subjects, which provided an efficient means of tailoring the program to the specific needs of the participants. Involving students in challenging interactions reduced the likelihood that they would simply allow information to pass "in one ear and out the other." Another significant component was the deliberate focus on skills training and provision of rehearsal, both essential components of a behavioral change program (from a cognitive-behavioral point of view) (Meichenbaum & Genest, 1980).

Finally, it is worth noting that the sessions of small groups of peers were extremely well targeted. The behavior of interest— smoking—was known to be partly a function of the outcomes of social interactions among peers; these interactions were planned and rehearsed during the treatment, thus undermining coercive elements that might otherwise lead to smoking. It is hard to imagine a more efficient method of influencing such events.

Design of the Study

Eleven pairs of schools matched for socioeconomic status, size, and urban/rural location were designated, with one school in each pair assigned to the treatment and one to the control condition. This is a large number of units for study, a notable improvement upon previous studies, most of which used only one school for each condition. With one school per condition, the school environments, which may differ, are completely confounded with treatments, so that it is not possible to have confidence that any group differences result only from treatment differences. Illustrating the problems that can occur, Flay et al. (1985) noted that in one study the most successful treatment occurred in a school with a lower pretest smoking rate than others (Hurd, Johnson, Pechacek, Bast, Jacobs, & Luepker, 1980), and in another, the school that received the treatment was recognized as a "problem" school for smoking (McAlister, Perry, Killen, Maccoby, & Slinkard, 1980).

In the Best study, students in both conditions were pretested the week before the program began and posttested immediately following the program, at the end of the sixth grade, and at the beginning and end of the seventh grade. Long-term follow-up testing has yet to be reported.

Testing consisted of a questionnaire concerning demographics, self-reports of smoking behavior, and reports of smoking patterns of parents, siblings, friends, and teachers. Accurate self-reports were encouraged by having students submit saliva samples for thiocyanate testing, following exposure to a videotape showing how smoking can be measured by laboratory analysis. At the time of pretesting, the program and control schools were found to be equivalent in smoking, gender, and prevalence of family and peer smoking. This demonstrated pretreatment equivalence allows more confidence that any group's differences result from the treatment's effects, not from chance differences between subjects in the two groups.

Results and Implications

Results from the study are complex, consisting of both longitudinal and cross-sectional analyses with subjects classified according to five levels of initial experience, ranging from "never smoked" to "regular smoker." Overall, the treatment program showed a significant and regularly increasing (overtime) effect on smoking behavior (compared to the behavior of the no-treatment group). The biggest influence was, interestingly, on those subjects at highest risk for chronic smoking: those with prior smoking experience and those with smoking peer and family models. For example, by the end of the seventh grade, 14 percent of the control subjects who initially were regular smokers had quit, whereas 33 percent of regularly smoking treatment subjects had quit. Similarly, 16 percent of the controls who had "experimented" with smoking had quit by this time, compared to 71 percent of the treatment subjects.

Such results from a well-designed study are particularly encouraging. It is hoped that the long-term follow-up data will continue on this positive note.

> The ability of the program to have its greatest impact on the children at greatest social risk is gratifying, since in a sense it is they who need a program most. . . . It might prove useful to add components designed to affect directly the various models. For example, a complementary program to assist parents in quitting might be envisioned. . . . Our ability to identify individuals at greater risk creates the possibility of additional, supplementary programming for them. (Flay et al., 1985, p. 56)

OBESITY

A comprehensive review of the available literature concerning obesity led Stuart, Mitchell, and Jensen (1981) to declare that "for the time being at least, etiological factors appear to be beyond our control" (p. 333). This unfortunate state of affairs has led to emphasis on treatment. Treatment of obesity consitutes both treatment of an existing problem and prevention of secondary problems, which may be life-threatening.

The literature on obesity and its treatment is voluminous and has been the subject of thorough review (e.g., Leon, 1976; Stuart et al., 1981; Wilson & Brownell, 1980). Early approaches to management resemble other preventive and treatment programs that we have reviewed: Dietary recommendations were made and patients were left to adhere to these or not (Atkins, 1972; Pennington, 1954). They seldom did. In 1959, Stunkard and McLaren-Hume reported that 72 percent of obese patients in controlled studies had lost less than 20 lbs., and only 8 percent lost over 40 lbs. Significant changes in diet are sufficiently unpleasant that few dieters stay with them for long. Those who do may experience weight loss, but are unwilling or unable to sustain the punitive regimens and regain quickly. "Almost any fat person can lose weight: few can keep it off" (Schachter & Rodin, 1974, p. 1).

Behavioral approaches to weight management have flourished since the early work by Richard Stuart (1967), who has been responsible for many of the behavioral management aspects of the Weight Watchers program. Agras (1984) noted that a behavioral approach has been demonstrated to be more effective than various types of placebos and attention-control treatments, traditional forms of dietary counseling, and an appetite suppressant (fenfluramine). Nevertheless, it has been pointed out that many programs have not been successful (Stuart, 1980; Stunkard, 1977). Stuart's review of the factors responsible for the variety of findings in the behavioral treatment literature returned to the same sort of problem that characterizes dietary prescription attempts. Many programs have oversimplified the extremely difficult task of initiating and sustaining lifestyle changes:

> Investigators have, in effect, offered participants in their research an implied promise that they can be "fat-free forever" by participating in a short course in behavioral self-management. Sadly, while the promise can be glibly made, its delivery is controverted by all that we currently know about the complexity of the problem of obesity. . . . So long as behavior researchers and therapists continue to regard their technology as a powerful brand of magic that is effective whether delivered in whole or in part, and so long as basic program plans omit consideration of the essential nature of the disorders that are the targets of intervention, less than satisfying outcomes will be the norm rather than the exception. (Stuart, 1980, pp. 166, 188)

Effective treatments have utilized combinations of treatment elements offered throughout the stages of weight loss and maintenance. Included are self-monitoring, alteration of stimulus conditions that cue eating, alterations in eating style, modification of caloric intake, nutritional education, programmed and monitored increases in activity, and systematic use of reinforcement to strengthen many of these behaviors (Agras, 1984).

Maintenance has been the biggest problem. Various methods of enhancing long-term effects have been attempted, including the use of booster sessions, involvement of family members in treatment, and teaching self-control procedures. Findings are inconsistent, with some studies reporting significant results, and others finding no benefits in such procedures. Use of a self-help manual has also been tested. In one study, the *Slim Chance in a Fat World* volume (Stuart & Davis, 1972) was found to be as effective in producing weight loss when combined with minimal therapist contact as was full therapist contact, with both conditions superior to no-treatment (Lindstrom, Balch, & Reese, 1976). A related maintenance strategy currently being tested makes use of extended contact through the mail or by telephone (Cameron, personal communication, University of Waterloo; Perri, Shapiro, Ludwig, Twentyman, & McAdoo, 1984).

Although this is one of the most active areas of research in health psychology, it is clear that much work remains to be done to fulfill early, optimistic predictions concerning behavioral treatments of obesity (e.g., Stunkard, 1975). As Brownell (1982) noted, the need is to apply behavior therapy principles to development and investigation of multifaceted programs. In this way the full range of treatment approaches can be utilized (e.g., very low calorie diet, appetite suppressants) in powerful combinations, while making use of behavioral means to increase adherence and maintenance of gains (e.g., Wadden, Stunkard, Brownell, & Day, 1984). Agras (1982) pointed out that the long-term impact of treatment on physical variables such as weight has been investigated, but long-term behavioral changes have not. Since it is recognized that weight changes require behavioral change, it seems myopic to neglect investigation of the extended fate of the behavioral changes that are initiated by treatment.

ACTIVITY LEVEL

Whereas many preventive efforts are directed at reducing or eliminating negative risk factors, attempts have also been made to increase healthy behaviors. Most noteworthy of these is the promotion of physical activity. Extensive evidence has accumulated that exercise improves both physical and mental health (Martin & Dubbert, 1982; Martin et al., 1984; Morris, Everitt, Pollard, Chave, & Semmence, 1980; Nagle & Montoye, 1981). Popular acceptance of the value of exercise has led to a well-documented fitness explosion; yet few people exercise sufficiently or regularly enough to experience significant improvement in fitness levels (Bucher, 1974; Dishman, 1982; Martin & Dubbert, 1982). To develop and maintain cardiorespiratory fitness and recommended body composition in adults, a regimen of 15 to 60 minutes of fairly intense, continuous, aerobic exercise is required three to five times per week (American College of Sports Medicine, 1978). These levels are attained in a small proportion of the population, and many studies have found that change in this behavior pattern is as difficult to accomplish as most other lifestyle changes we have discussed (Martin et al., 1984).

PARTICIPaction—A Community-Based Intervention

One of the more interesting attempts to modify physical activity levels is a Canadian program that began as an experiment in the authors' home community and was subsequently adopted across the country

(Keir & Lauzon, 1980). In 1971, a private nonprofit organization, called PARTICIPaction, was established, funded primarily by the Canadian government. Its mandate was to employ marketing methods to promote fitness: (1) making consumers aware of a "product," (2) changing the attitude of the audience and educating them about their alternatives concerning the "product," and (3) inducing the consumers to "buy the package" by taking the first step toward change of habits (Keir & Lauzon, 1980). Here are examples of messages from these three steps as they were presented in advertising displayed in public transit facilities; on milk cartons; in multiple newspaper spot ads, television and radio spots; and so forth:

Product Awareness

Jog to the back of the bus. If you're like most Canadians, it will be the only real exercise you get today.

Walk, don't run, to catch the bus. The shape you're in, you might not make it. Swim, cycle, play squash, run, ski to get in shape. *Then* run to the bus.

A 30-year-old Canadian is in the same shape as a 60-year-old Swede.

This last item, lifted from some statistics that were published around the time PARTICIPaction was initiated, promoted friendly international competitions between several Canadian and Swedish communities, each of which would attempt, for example, to have the highest proportion of their citizenry walk at least 1 km on the same day.

Attitude Change

Fitness. In your heart you know it's right.

Three times a week I take my body out and give it a good run—wind her up and let her go. It's good for your heart and lungs and everything.

Habit Change

Set your goal to walk a block a day. An easy way to get a little fitter. [We still stare at this message on our milk cartons each morning at breakfast.]

PARTICIPaction salutes Sam Fuller on his greatest moment in sport. (Sam Fuller has just been convinced by his wife to walk around the block.)

Rigorous controls were not employed in the trial presentation and assessment of the project in Saskatoon, a midsized western Canadian city.

Nevertheless, the data concerning changes in the initial community were considered sufficiently impressive to lead to distribution of the package Canada-wide. Despite our skepticism concerning poorly controlled data collection, we too find the numbers impressive. For example, a study completed 3 years after the program was initiated (Jackson, 1974) documented such findings as these: (1) 94 percent of the Saskatoon population was aware of PARTICIPaction's campaign—surely a proportion to cause an advertiser to gloat; (2) there was an increase of 16 percent in the number of people who were regularly physically active during the campaign (from 25 to 41 percent); (3) 67 percent were involved in some form of physical activity, the highest rate of any Canadian metropolitan center; and (4) numerous indices of participation in specific sports experienced dramatic gains (e.g., sales of cross-country ski equipment more than doubled; YMCA classes filled).

In the years since its trial in Saskatoon, the PARTICIPaction program has become part of daily life in Canada. Canadians are exhorted to become active in every setting, with messages ranging from humorous to goading, encouraging to competitive. The full range of techniques employed by commercial advertisers has been employed.

In addition, community agencies, local governments, and corporations have become involved. Kraft Foods, for example, integrated a home fitness test kit and information package into its salad dressing campaign. And competition has moved from the realm of the elite athlete to become almost an accepted duty of the average citizen. On municipal walkathon days many employers and schools provide a break during which everyone is urged to walk, run, or jog at least 1 km; phone banks are established to receive calls from data-collectors who verify the distance logged; and media and local government officials hype the competition between rivalrous communities. Although short-term efforts such as walkathons cannot increase fitness in themselves, the intention is to provide occasions during which the maximum number of people undertake one small step toward increasing activity and to increase awareness of the fitness issue. Similar techniques have been adopted in more rigorously controlled studies, which we will describe later.

ALCOHOL AND DRUG ABUSE—POLICY ISSUES

Excessive alcohol consumption and abuse of other potentially harmful substances are widely recognized to constitute major health problems. Yet very little systematic investigation of the factors influencing alcohol consumption and of preventive interventions has taken place (Alden, 1980). Although substance abuse has ground in common with other problems we have described (adherence problems, the importance

of social influences on behavior, etc.), this area also has unique characteristics, such as severe physiological dependency, genetic contributions,
and, in the case of drug abuse, criminal implications, which we will not
attempt to review in this limited forum.

We will, however, take note of one controversial alcohol abuse prevention measure, which touches upon a far-reaching social issue. Based
on the finding that alcohol consumption is not, as a disease model of
alcoholism would suggest, bimodal (that is, divided into two groups, the
drinkers and nondrinkers) but continuous across the population (many
different levels of drinking exist, from none to moderate to excessive),
researchers at the Addiction Research Foundation in Toronto have proposed a very simple means of reducing alcoholism (Popham, Schmidt, &
deLint, 1975): shifting the whole distribution curve of consumption
downward (reducing levels of consumption across the population),
which would result in fewer individuals at the upper, most detrimental
levels of consumption. Unfortunately, many measures by governments
that might have accomplished this downward shift have had little effect
on the alcohol use distribution curve: private versus state dispensing of
liquor or control of the number of outlets, hours of sale, and types of
drinking establishments (Popham et al., 1975; Smart, 1977). Evidence
concerning legal drinking age is mixed: Although data concerning effects
on alcoholism are inconsistent, lower drinking ages have been clearly
associated with increases in alcohol-related traffic collisions and fatalities
(Alden, 1980). Price, however, has a consistent and systematic effect. As
cost relative to other goods rises, average consumption and alcoholism
incidence decline (Popham et al., 1975; Seeley, 1960; Smart, 1977).
There are, of course, limits to the positive impact from increasing costs.
Other contextual factors, such as liberal versus conservative community
attitudes and "wet" versus "dry" areas, interact with cost in determining
drinking patterns. Nevertheless, Popham et al.'s (1975) comments are
cogent: "Governments theoretically have at their disposal a powerful
instrument to control the prevalence of hazardous drinking and alcoholism. However, at the present time there are apt to be formidable political
and emotional obstacles to the use of this instrument" (p. 142).

This suggestion highlights a challenge that we have raised in other
contexts. In many cases the ability to influence the health of the population is dependent not so much upon whether it is theoretically possible
to have an impact as upon policy decisions that involve far more than just
health-related matters. In the case of much of traditional medicine, the
decision-making process is more straightforward: Whether one should
carry out an appendectomy depends largely upon the status of the
appendix; whether to treat a patient with a new antitumor drug depends

upon assessment of relative risk and benefits—less simple, but still manageable within the usual decision-making framework. Contrast such problems with the decision whether or not to reduce the rate of alcoholism and alcohol-related automobile injuries and deaths (often to unimpaired victims) by artificially inflating the cost of alcohol for everyone. In this instance one may know full well that it is possible not just to treat a problem, but very effectively to prevent large numbers of people from ever experiencing severe disability or from being killed through no fault of their own. Yet the decision to take the necessary action would have broad social and political implications, not the least of which are the issues of personal freedoms, economic considerations for individuals and industries, and the likelihood that such a measure might prove so unpopular as to be overturned in a political backlash.

Similar, difficult policy decisions are increasingly required, as it becomes evident that some of the means for improving health and reducing mortality require major social and regulatory changes. Furthermore, effectiveness of a preventive intervention is generally measured by the degree of compliance with which it meets. As a result, a high degree of voluntariness is incompatible with effectiveness; or, in other words, to succeed, an intervention must be highly persuasive and comparatively irresistible. The ethical concerns this raises have received scant attention in the psychological literature (Faden & Faden, 1978). Lest the alcohol price issue seem like too extreme an example, consider the simple behavioral act of buckling a seatbelt in an automobile before driving. The risk of serious or fatal injury is 3.4 times as great when safety belts are not worn. *Up to 18,000 fatalities could be avoided each year* with proper use of seatbelts (Robertson, 1976). How could use be increased? Two simple strategies have proven effective with 60-80 percent of the population. Ignition interlock systems and mandatory belt-use laws both are extremely effective means of increasing use. Seatbelt laws are in effect in most Canadian provinces and in other parts of the world. But United States state governments have long resisted such legislation; similarly, when the interlock system was introduced on 1974 model cars, it was quickly reversed by federal ruling (Lewy, 1980). As we noted earlier, the situation shows some recent signs of change, with legislation now in place in some jurisdictions and pending in others. When prevention programs involve direct and perhaps coercive control of behavior, health issues are not always given primary consideration.

This is illustrated clearly in the issue of speed limit laws. In the mid-1970s, a 55-m.p.h. highway speed limit was enacted in the United States. The new limit was widely enforced and was credited with saving countless lives. Although some drivers protested, there was sufficient public support to retain the lower limit. Although one would like to think this represented a raising of health-consciousness among the public, it seems now that economic incentives were paramount. The lowering of the limit took place during the oil embargo, when inefficient use of fuel was seen to be a danger. Individuals were also motivated to reduce consumption by skyrocketing prices. When, in 1986, prices dropped to under 70 cents a gallon, the economic incentive was reduced, and states began to fight against the federally imposed edict to lower limits (Thunder Road, 1986). Several states reduced fines for speeding and some dropped their enforcement levels. In the spring of the year, several court challenges of the federal right to impose the lower limit were pending. Whatever the outcome of these battles, the fact that they arose at all indicates the relative strength of economic, as opposed to health-related, motives for public policy decisions.

SCREENING PROGRAMS

Mass inoculation against disease is the prototype of successful preventive medicine.

> During the first decade after its introduction, measles immunization in the United States averted 23,707,000 cases of measles, prevented 2400 deaths and 7900 cases of mental retardation, saved 1,352,000 hospitalization days and 12,182,000 physician visits, reduced school absenteeism by 78 million days, and added 709,000 years of productive life. Every dollar spent on measles immunization yields an estimated $9 benefit. Similar cost-benefit analysis for rubella immunization in the United States revealed a ratio of 23. (Chang, 1981, p. 323)

What has led to such widespread implementation of this preventive procedure? The effectiveness of public inoculation efforts has depended to some extent upon strategies that are available to other preventive efforts, such as public education and attitude influences. The benefits of inoculation and the risks of diseases that are protected against have been established and received general public acceptance. This is also true, however, of smoking, yet compliance rates are very different. The major problem in the inoculation system is also universal to preventive programs—getting people to show up for the vaccine. The widely used solution with inoculation is to incorporate it into routines that involve most of the population, such as postnatal check-ups and school health programs.

This strategy has been attempted with some success in other contexts, but preventing disease by not smoking or by controlling diet, exercising, or adopting similar measures requires extended efforts that do not become habitual without persistence. Furthermore, many inoculations require only one decision to be made and one action to be taken, whereas the person avoiding or quitting smoking may be faced with making the same difficult decision hundreds or thousands of times, and the health-pursuing jogger must overcome lethargy, inertia, and competing time demands perhaps scores of times before running becomes a routine. Even then, it is possible to experience relapses or setbacks that require reinitiation of the positive habit formation.

Finally, some immunizations, such as for measles, have been required of everyone (e.g., all children before school entrance) by legislation. We have already noted the policy difficulties in legislating many types of preventive actions. It is interesting that a medically invasive procedure, with low but nevertheless recognized risks and potentially uncomfortable or serious side effects, would be legally required whereas use of seatbelts, with no side effects or risks and similar benefits, is considered by some an undue imposition on the rights of the individual.

DELAY IN SEEKING TREATMENT

The similarities and differences between mass inoculation and the preventive actions we have been discussing highlight some of the critical variables in public health promotion. These issues are emphasized in the area of delay in seeking diagnosis and treatment of physical disease.

Delay is considered to be particularly important in the case of cancer, since it has been associated with poorer prognosis. Blackwell (1963), reviewing the literature on delay, indicated that methodological problems in the literature precluded drawing many useful conclusions. She found, however, that there is substantial evidence that people do significantly delay seeking diagnosis when they suspect the presence of cancer. Greer (1976) studied patients who delayed at least 3 months between symptom discovery and first medical consultation. He found that the principle reasons given for delay by patients were fear of cancer and a fatalistic attitude toward the outcome. Ignorance played a small role. Greer also found that diagnostic errors and deficiencies in administrative channels of communication contributed to delay.

An example of a program attempting to influence delay was reported by Turner et al. (1984). Half of a sample of 28,788 women registered at 28 teaching practices in greater Belfast randomly received a booklet on breast self-examination from their general practitioners at the start of the study period and again 1 year later. During the 2 years of follow-up, the frequency of breast abnormalities was identical in the two groups. The types of tumors detected in the two groups differed, however: (1) The intervention group more frequently presented with early malignant tumors (53.6 percent) than the control group (24.3 percent); (2) there was a lower incidence of involvement of multiple sites in the intervention group; and (3) average tumor size was smaller in the intervention group.

Turner et al.'s minimal intervention seems sufficiently practical and efficacious to merit widespread consideration. Further evidence for the value of educational efforts in dealing with this problem is provided by a study by Alagna and Reddy (1984). Seventy-three women attending a health fair were asked to complete an attitude questionnaire before attempting to locate tumors on a model of a human female torso. The torso had seven tumors implanted in the breasts, four superficially and three deeply. On average, three tumors were discovered. Only one subject found all of them and five women did not find any.

When Alagna and Reddy examined the attitudes of their subjects, they found that women who were confident about their ability to perform a breast self-examination (BSE) on the dummy had the best technique and actually did find the most tumors. This finding remained even when prior experience with performing BSEs was accounted for. Variables that correlated with inefficient BSE techniques were fear and embarrassment at performing the examination procedure, a fatalistic attitude, and the conviction that a doctor should be the one to conduct a breast examination. The authors concluded that mass distribution of BSE literature designed to increase knowledge of the technique may be effective. Not surprisingly, it seems that women need to feel confident that they can be proficient at BSE in order to use the technique effectively.

COMMUNITY INTERVENTION

Public health groups have long attempted to alter health-related behaviors by educational campaigns aimed at the general populace. Until the early 1970s, however, there had been few large-scale, multifactor community interventions that were intensively studied in well-controlled designs. The Stanford Three Community Study (Maccoby, Farquhar, Wood, & Alexander, 1977) and the Finnish North Karelia Project (Puska et al., 1981), both begun in 1972, were the vanguard of a series of projects, for most of which final data will be unavailable until the 1990s. These studies have an audaciously ambitious goal: to reduce the risk of heart disease in an entire community.

Together, there are 10 comparable community-based cardiovascular disease prevention projects, including close to 2 million subjects in Australia, South Africa, Switzerland, the Federal Republic of Germany, and the United States (Farquhar, Maccoby, & Solomon, 1984). Although the expressed aim of these experimental interventions is to reduce cardio-vascular disease, the behavioral targets are sufficiently broad (e.g., nutri-tion, exercise, smoking) that, if the interventions are effective, they should affect the occurrence of a variety of conditions. Data from these projects can provide policy planners with essential information concern-ing the potential value of community campaigns and practical considera-tions involved in their implementation. Because of the far-reaching impact of this type of study, we will detail the elements of one of the initial efforts, for which fairly complete data are available.

The Stanford Three Community Study

With heart disease risk reduction as the central goal, the Stanford Three Community Study undertook to document the impact of interven-tion procedures on the complex variables that comprise that risk, as well as to study the process of change in order to enable refinements.

Design and Implementation

Three California communities, each with a population near 15,000, took part in the study: two (Gilroy and Watsonville) on an experimental basis and one (Tracy) as a control. This design sacrificed some of the experimental rigor of random assignment (of either individuals or towns) to conditions in order to accommodate to the practicalities of directing an intervention at whole communities within the constraints of finite resources.

The citizens of Gilroy and Watsonville may have been surprised to find themselves suddenly subjected for 3 years to an intensive, profes-sional, multimedia campaign, including several hours of television and radio programing, over 100 radio and 50 television commercials, weekly newspaper columns, newspaper ads, billboards, mailed materials, calen-dars, and so forth. In order to be able to assess the relative contributions of a media-only campaign and one involving more personal contact, in Watsonville additional intensive contact was made with those individuals who were assessed at the baseline period to be at highest risk of heart disease. These subjects were offered group sessions or individual home counseling over a 10-week period.

The campaign itself provided information and urged individuals to take actions that would result in achieving ideal weights, reducing or eliminating smoking, increasing physical activity, and reducing consump-tion of refined sugar, salt, cholesterol, saturated fats, and alcohol. Media presentations were based on (1) social learning principles, involving modeling and cueing of appropriate behavior and skills, which were used to help determine format of presentations, (2) the literature on persuasion and attitude change, which assisted in formulating the messages, and (3) work by Cartwright (1949) on mass means of stimulating action, which was used in building action cues and skills training into the mass media (Maccoby & Alexander, 1980). Materials were pretested with audience samples in another community, information was gathered from owners and managers of the media to be used, and marketing data was collected on media usage patterns.

Farquhar et al. (1984) have stressed the importance of making systematic use of relevant theoretical models to design and implement community-based change. They detail the contributions of three frameworks to the Stanford project: communication-behavior change (CBC), social marketing, and community organization:

> The CBC framework is based on a social-psychological perspective relevant to individual and group learning. This perspective is particularly useful in the development of the contents of education materials and the sequence in which they are delivered. The social marketing framework is especially applicable to the practical issues of how to design and distribute educational products. The community organization framework has special applicability to the process of diffusion of communication via organizations and helps establish a basis for long-term maintenance of health education programs. (Farquhar et al., 1984, p. 438)

Farquhar et al.'s (1984) paper provides an excellent, detailed summary of the necessary steps involved in planning, executing, and evaluating a community intervention study, as well as guidelines to assist in all stages. It, and related material from the Stanford project, are essential source materials for future efforts in this sphere (Farquhar, 1978; Farquhar et al., 1977; Maccoby et al., 1977; Maccoby & Solomon, 1981; Meyer, Maccoby, & Farquhar, 1977; Meyer, Nash, McAlister, Maccoby, & Farquhar, 1980). Another valuable resource for planning and policy making is a recent volume by Berwick, Cretin, and Keeler (1980).

Preliminary figures indicate that the costs should not be a deterrent to community interventions. Information for the Stanford study is not yet available, but the Finnish (North Karelia) project spent about 50 to 75 cents per person in the target communities each year, only 40 percent of which was a program cost (the remainder were experimental costs). This compares with a cost of between 10 cents and 1 dollar per American per year for advertising each widely marketed consumer item (Berwick et al., 1980).

Results

The media campaign in the Stanford study clearly increased awareness and knowledge about heart disease risk factors. In the two experimental towns, scores on a knowledge test administered at baseline and after 1 and 2 years showed an overall increase of about 31 percent, compared to 6 percent for the control town.

More important than informational differences, however, were comparisons on risk of heart disease and change in specific risk-related behaviors. Overall risk for heart disease was assessed prior to intervention and after 1, 2, and 3 years of the project. Age, sex, plasma cholesterol, systolic blood pressure, and relative weight were combined to yield a quantitative measure. About 550 subjects between the ages of 35 and 59 were assessed in each town. Whereas risk of heart disease increased marginally in the control town during the 3 years of the study (+3.3 percent), in the two experimental towns it decreased significantly (-8.8 percent and -12.8 percent; $p < .01$). Comparable risk reduction was observed in the Finnish study (Puska et al., 1981).

Examination of specific behavioral changes reveals that some behaviors seemed quite susceptible to modification through the media campaign whereas others were not. For example, significant reductions in consumption of dietary fats and cholesterol were obtained in the experimental towns compared to the control town, and these were reflected in the physiological indices, which showed clinically important decreases in blood pressure and small but significant decreases in serum cholesterol. By comparison, smoking was relatively unaffected, except among those who participated in the individual or small-group instruction sessions, and no changes were evident in physical activity levels or in weight. Those changes that were obatined tended to be maintained, and some were extended further in the 3rd year of the program, although the campaign itself was reduced in this final year (Meyer et al., 1980; Williams, Fortmann, Farquhar, Mellen, & Varady, 1981).

The absence of change in physical activity ostensibly contrasts with the PARTICIPaction results, which were, as we noted earlier, also achieved through a community campaign. The PARTICIPaction campaign, however, was more focused than the Three Community Study and included more interpersonal and direct contact elements, which the latter avoided in order to separate cleanly the intensive face-to-face contact group from the media-only group. The difference in the PARTICIPaction and Stanford findings and the absence of other effects are elucidated by comments made by Maccoby and Alexander (1980):

Learning how to modify complex habitual behaviors can be as difficult as learning to perform well in athletic competition or learning not to lose one's temper under provocation. Acquisition of such skills is enhanced when there is feedback of the results of practice. Ideally, there is initial modeling and then guided practice at the appropriate time tailored to individuals, and an individual perception of accomplishment or rewards. Mass media may not readily provide all of this. They can, however, effectively provide the initial modeling . . . and encourage the development of community organization and support systems to deliver the necessary individual guided practice. (p. 368)

The Stanford Five City Project

The Three Community Study results led to initiation of a larger study, involving two experimental and three control California cities (Farquhar, in press; Farquhar et al., 1984). In addition to attempting to replicate and extend the results from the previous project, this study is developing a protocol for independent community adoption of the campaign. Stanford involvement is being kept minimal, consisting primarily of assessment, design, and production of the mass media components; assistance in organization and promotion of community programs; and training of community leaders. Educational activities are being conducted by community members.

Other changes in the format include targeting a larger age range (12-74), using larger communities, allowing a 9-year intervention period, and focusing on cost-effectiveness and generalizability. Results from this project should be influential in determining the extent to which community-based prevention programs are accepted (Berwick et al., 1980; Hulley & Fortmann, 1981).

LAST WORDS

We have concluded our survey of the purview of health psychology with a look at the most far-reaching type of program, community prevention. Although health psychologists have been involved in diverse efforts, this area seems to epitomize their aims and professional expertise, involving analysis and synthesis of systems for affecting human behavior to enhance health, not just by treating illness but by preventively utilizing knowledge of the contingencies that affect health and illness.

Although we have taken a critical look at the knowledge base of health psychology and the practices related to health care, it is clear that progress has been rapid and accelerating since the beginnings of this field only a few years ago. More research is being done, and the basis of clinical treatment is broadening to include psycho-social components of health and illness in many areas.

In the case of particular illnesses, there is a pressing need for carefully controlled studies that experimentally examine the potential benefits for patients of behavioral interventions. Early reports of successes with biofeedback and other operant methods, for example, have not always been replicated. In other cases, laboratory paradigms have been simplistically and unsuccessfully applied to more complex clinical settings. As we noted, if clinical practice proceeds too far ahead of the database, there is a danger of an overgeneralized discounting of new approaches. There are data clearly supporting particular types of psychological interventions for some problems (e.g., chronic pain, acute and chronic stress). The promise shown in other areas deserves exploration (e.g., cardiovascular disease, cancer).

In the investigation of preventive efforts and health-enhancement, rapid developments have often led to the opposite type of problem. Here, often knowledge is well ahead of practice because the system for implementation of these new developments is lacking, and they come into conflict with existing systems (e.g., medicine and clinical psychology have been treatment-oriented, not prevention-oriented). Thus, although there have been successful demonstrations of the health-enhancing, disease-reducing value of preventing smoking, for example, the means to implement experimental programs are largely absent.

It is uncommon for a review of health psychology to pay much attention to policy issues. Psychologists are trained to be researchers and clinicians. Pursuit of their roles, therefore, generally involves little policy development. Yet our overview has repeatedly touched on policy issues. Our rationale has been that in some respects it is the psychologists involved in health research and programs that have the best perspective for making changes in existing systems. We have argued that if the developments occurring in the field are to yield benefits for the population at large, in many cases informed policy change is needed.

So we end not by simply echoing the ubiquitous calls of every reviewer for more research, more training, and, of course, more funding. Instead, we would exhort those who study this field—from the outside or the inside—to reach for greater health by personal and professional contributions toward informed, rational health-related public policies. The fulfillment of health psychology's promise depends upon it.

References

Aagaard, G. N. (1983). Psychological aspects of hypertension. In J. E. Carr & H. A. Dengerink (Eds.), *Behavioral science in the practice of medicine* (pp. 249-262). New York: Elsevier.

Ackerman, S. H., & Weiner, H. (1976). Peptic ulcer disease: Some considerations for psychosomatic research. In O. W. Hill (Ed.), *Modern trends in psychosomatic medicine* (Vol. 3, pp. 363-381). London: Butterworths.

Ad Hoc Committee on Classification of Headache. (1962). Classification of headache. *Journal of the American Medical Association, 179*, 717-718.

Ader, R. (1977). The role of developmental factors in susceptibility to disease. In Z. J. Lipowski, D. R. Lipsit, & P. C. Whybrow (Eds.), *Psychosomatic medicine: Current trends and clinical applications* (pp. 58-67). New York: Oxford University Press.

Admire, J. B., Roccella, E. J., & Haines, C. M. (1984). Hypertension control: Meeting the 1990 objectives for the nation. *Public Health Reports, 99*(3), 300-307.

Agras, W. S. (1982). Weight reduction and blood pressure management: The generalized and enduring effects of two behavior-change procedures. In R. B. Stuart (Ed.), *Adherence, compliance and generalization in behavioral medicine* (pp. 239-257). New York: Brunner/Mazel.

Agras, W. S. (1984). The behavioral treatment of somatic disorders. In W. D. Gentry (Ed.), *Handbook of behavioral medicine* (pp. 479-530). New York: Guilford.

Agras, W. S., & Jacob, R. G. (1979). Hypertension. In O. F. Pomerleau & J. P. Brady (Eds.), *Behavioral medicine: Theory and practice* (pp. 205-232). Baltimore: Williams & Wilkins.

Ahles, T. A., Cohen, R. E., Little, D., Balducci, L., Dubbert, P. M., & Keane, T. (1984). Towards a behavioral assessment of anticipatory symptoms associated with cancer chemotherapy. *Journal of Behavioral Therapy and Experimental Psychiatry, 15*(2), 141-145.

Alagna, S. W., & Reddy, D. M. (1984). Predictors of proficient technique and successful lesion detection in breast self-examination. *Health Psychology, 3*(2), 113-127.

Alden, L. (1980). Preventive strategies in the treatment of alcohol abuse: A review and a proposal. In P. O. Davidson & S. M. Davidson (Eds.), *Behavioral medicine: Changing health lifestyles* (pp. 256-278). New York: Brunner/Mazel.

Alexander, A. B., & Smith, D. D. (1979). Clinical applications of electromyographic biofeedback. In R. H. Gatchel & K. P. Price (Eds.), *Clinical applications of biofeedback: Appraisal and status* (pp. 112-133). New York: Pergamon.

Alexander, F. (1950). *Psychosomatic medicine.* New York: Norton.

Alexander, F., French, T., & Pollock, G. (1968). *Psychosomatic specificity.* Chicago: University of Chicago Press.

Allen, H. M. (1984). Consumers and choice: Cost containment strategies for health care provision. *Health Psychology, 3,* 411-430.

Allman, W. F. (1985, October). Staying alive in the 20th century. *Science 85, 6,* 30-37.

American College of Sports Medicine. (1978). Position statement on the recommended quantity and quality of exercise for developing and maintaining fitness in healthy adults. *Medicine and Science in Sports, 10,* 7-10.

American Psychological Association, Division of Health Psychology, Public Information Committee (1985). Health psychology: New perspectives. (Published as an insert in *The Health Psychologist, 7*(1).)

American Psychological Association Task Force on Health Research. (1976). Contributions to health research: Patterns, problems and potential. *American Psychologist, 31,* 263-274.

Anderson, B. L., Karlsson, J. A., Anderson, B., & Tewfik, H. H. (1984). Anxiety and cancer treatment: Response to stressful radiotherapy. *Health Psychology, 3,* 535-551.

Anderson, K. O., & Masur, F. T. (1983). Psychological preparation for invasive medical and dental procedures. *Journal of Behavioral Medicine, 6*(1), 1-40.

Anderson, T. P., Cole, T. M., Gullickson, G., Hudgens, A., & Roberts, A. H. (1977). Behavior modification of chronic pain: A treatment program of a multidisciplinary team. *Journal of Clinical Orthopedics, 129,* 96-100.

Andrasik, F., Coleman, D., & Epstein, L. H. (1982). Biofeedback: Clinical and research considerations. In D. M. Doleys, R. L. Merideth, & A. R. Ciminero

(Eds.), *Behavioral medicine: Assessment and treatment strategies* (pp. 83-116). New York: Plenum.

Andrasik, F., & Holroyd, K. A. (1980). A test of specific and nonspecific effects in the biofeedback treatment of tension headache. *Journal of Consulting and Clinical Psychology, 48,* 575-586.

Andrasik, F., & Holroyd, K. A. (1983). Specific and nonspecific effects in the biofeedback treatment of tension headache: 3-year follow-up. *Journal of Consulting and Clinical Psychology, 51,* 634-636.

Anisman, H., & Zacharko, R. M. (1983). Stress and neo-plasia: Speculations and caveats. *Behavioral Medicine Update, 5,* 27-35.

Antonovsky, A. (1979). *Health, stress, and coping.* San Francisco: Jossey-Bass.

Appels, A., & Mulder, P. (1984). Imminent myocardial infarction: A psychological study. *Journal of Human Stress, 10,* 129-134.

Atkins, D. (1972). *The diet revolution.* New York: Bantam.

Auger, T., Wright, E., & Simpson, R. (1972). Posters as smoking deterrents. *Journal of Applied Psychology, 56,* 169-171.

Avia, M. D., & Kanfer, F. H. (1980). Coping with aversive stimulation: The effects of training in a self-management context. *Cognitive Therapy and Research, 4,* 73-81.

Bakal, D. A. (1975). Headache: A biopsychological perspective. *Psychological Bulletin, 82,* 369-382.

Bakal, D. A. (1979). *Psychology and medicine: Psychobiological dimensions of health and illness.* New York: Springer.

Baron, J. M. (1962). Gastric secretion in relation to subsequent duodenal ulcer and family history. *Gut, 3,* 158-161.

Barrett, B. H. (1962). Reduction in rate of multiple tics by free operant conditioning methods. *Journal of Nervous and Mental Disease, 135,* 187-195.

Beck, A. T., Rush, A. J., Shaw, B. F., & Emery, G. (1979). *Cognitive therapy of depression.* New York: Guilford.

Beck, N. C., & Hall, D. (1978). Natural childbirth: A review and analysis. *Obstetrics and Gynecology, 52,* 371-379.

Beck, N. C., & Siegel, L. J. (1980). Preparation for childbirth and contemporary research on pain, anxiety, and stress reduction: A review and critique. *Psychosomatic Medicine, 42,* 429-447.

Becker, H. (1979). Psychodynamic aspects of breast cancer differences in younger and older women. *Psychotherapy and Psychodynamics, 32,* 287-296.

Becker, M. H. (Ed.). (1974). The health belief model and personal health behavior. *Health Education Monographs, 2*(4), iii-v, 1-147.

Becker, M. H. (1976). Sociobehavioral determinants of compliance. In D. L. Sackett & R. B. Haynes (Eds.), *Compliance with therapeutic regimens* (pp. 40-50). Baltimore: The Johns Hopkins University Press.

Beckman, H., & Frankel, R. (1984). The effect of physician behavior on the collection of data. *Annals of Internal Medicine, 10,* 692-696.

Belloc, N. B., & Breslow, L. (1972). Relationship of physical health status and health practices. *Preventive Medicine, 1,* 409-421.

Benson, H., Shapiro, D., Tursky, B., & Schwartz, G. E. (1971). Decreased systolic blood pressure through operant conditioning techniques in patients with essential hypertension. *Science, 173,* 740-742.

Bernstein, D. (1969). Modification of smoking behavior: An evaluative review. *Psychological Bulletin, 71,* 418-440.

Berwick, D., Cretin, S., & Keeler, E. (1980). *Cholesterol, children and heart disease: An analysis of alternatives.* New York: Oxford University Press.

Bieliauskas, L. A. (1983). Considerations of depression and stress in the etiology of cancer. *Behavioral Medicine Update, 5,* 23-26.

Bing, E. (1969). *Six practical lessons for an easier childbirth.* New York: Bantam.

Blackwell, B. (1963). The literature of delay in seeking medical care for chronic illness. *Health Education Monographs, 16,* 3-31.

Blackwell, B. (1976). Treatment adherence. *British Journal of Psychiatry, 129,* 513-531.

Blanchard, E. B. (1985, Winter-Spring). On public funding for health psychology. *The Health Psychologist, 7,* 1.

Blanchard, E. B., Andrasik, F., Ahles, T. A., Teders, S. J., & O'Keefe, D. (1980). Migraine and tension headache: A meta-analytic review. *Behavioral Therapy, 11,* 613-631.

Blanchard, E. B., Andrasik, F., Neff, D. F., Saunders, N. L., Arena, J. G., Pallmeyer, T. P., Teders, S. J., Jurish, S. E., & Rodichok, L. D. (1983). Four process studies in the behavioral treatment of chronic headache. *Behavioral Research and Therapy, 21,* 209-220.

Blanchard, E. B., & Epstein, L. H. (1977). The clinical utility of biofeedback. In M. Hersen, R. M. Eisler, & P. M. Miller (Eds.), *Progress in behavior modification* (Vol. 4, pp. 163-249). New York: Academic.

Blanchard, E. B., & Epstein, L. H. (1978). *A biofeedback primer.* Reading, MA: Addison-Wesley.

Blanchard, E. B., Miller, S. T., Abel, G. G., Haynes, M. R., & Wicker, R. (1979). Evaluation of biofeedback in the treatment of borderline essential hypertension. *Journal of Applied Behavior Analysis, 12,* 99-109.

Block, A. R. (1982). Multidisciplinary treatment of chronic low back pain: A review. *Rehabilitation Psychology, 27,* 51-63.

Block, A. R., Kremer, E., & Gaylor, M. (1980). Behavioral treatment of chronic pain: Variables affecting treatment efficacy. *Pain, 8,* 367-375.

Blonston, G. (1984). Cancer: The new synthesis: Prevention. *Science 84, 5*(7), 36-39.

Blumenthal, H. T. (1978, September). The cancer lottery. *Harper's*, pp. 12-21.

Blumenthal, J. A., O'Toole, L. S., & Haney, T. (1984). Behavioral assessment of the Type A behavior pattern. *Psychosomatic Medicine, 46*(5), 415-423.

Body count on the highway. (1984, November). *Consumer Reports*, pp. 663-666.

Boffey, P. (1984, September 18). Are the statistics telling the truth? *New York Times*, pp. C1, C3, C5.

Botvin, G., & Wills, T. A. (1985). Personal and social skills training: Cognitive-behavioral approaches to substance abuse prevention. In C. Bell & R. Battjes (Eds.), *Prevention research: Deterring drug abuse among children and adolescents*. Washington, DC: NIDA Research Monograph.

Bowers, J. Z. (1971). Changes in the supply and characteristics of American doctors in the twentieth century. In G. McLaughlin & T. McKeown (Eds.), *Medical history and medical care* (pp. 19-23). London: Oxford University Press.

Bowers, K. S., & Kelly, P. (1979). Stress, disease, psychotherapy, and hypnosis. *Journal of Abnormal Psychology, 88*, 490-505.

Bradley, L. A. (1983). Coping with chronic pain. In T. G. Burish & L. A. Bradley (Eds.), *Coping with chronic disease: Research and applications* (pp. 339-379). New York: Academic.

Bradley, L. A., & Burish, T. G. (1983). Coping with chronic disease: Current status and future directions. In T. G. Burish & L. A. Bradley (Eds.), *Coping with chronic disease: Research and applications* (pp. 475-482). New York: Academic.

Bradley, L. A., Prokop, C. K., Gentry, W. D., Van der Heide, L. H., & Prieto, E. J. (1981). Assessment of chronic pain. In C. K. Prokop & L. A. Bradley (Eds.), *Medical psychology: Contributions to behavioral medicine* (pp. 92-117). New York: Academic.

Bradshaw, P. W., Ley, P., Kincey, J. A., & Bradshaw, J. (1975). Recall of medical advice: Comprehensibility and specificity. *British Journal of Social and Clinical Psychology, 14*, 55-62.

Broitman, S. A., Vitale, J. J., & Gottlieb, L. S. (1983). Ethanolic beverage consumption, cigarette smoking, nutritional status, and digestive tract cancers. *Seminars in Oncology, 10*, 322-329.

Brooks, G. R., & Richardson, F. C. (1980). Emotional skills training: A treatment program for duodenal ulcer. *Behavior Therapy, 11*, 198-207.

Brownell, K. D. (1982). Obesity: Understanding and treating a serious, prevalent and refractory disorder. *Journal of Consulting and Clinical Psychology, 50*, 820-840.

Brucker, B. S. (1983). Spinal cord injuries. In T. G. Burish & L. A. Bradley (Eds.), *Coping with chronic disease: Research and applications* (pp. 285-311). New York: Academic.

Brucker, B. S., & Ince, L. P. (1977). Biofeedback as an experimental treatment for postural hypotension in a patient with a spinal cord lesion. *Archives of Physical Medicine and Rehabilitation, 58,* 49-53.

Brudny, J., Korein, J., Levidow, L., Grynbaum, B., Lieberman, A., & Friedmann, L. (1974). Sensory feedback therapy as a modality of treatment in central nervous system disorders of voluntary movements. *Neurology, 24,* 925-932.

Bruhn, J. G., Philips, B. U., & Wolf, S. (1972). Social readjustment and illness patterns: Comparisons between first, second, and third generation Italian Americans living in the same community. *Journal of Psychosomatic Research, 16,* 387-394.

Bruhn, J. G., Philips, B. U., & Wolf, S. (1982). Lessons from Roseta 20 years later: A community study of heart disease. *Southern Medical Journal, 75,* 575-580.

Bruhn, J. G., & Wolf, S. (1978). Update on Roseta, Pa.: Testing a prediction. *Psychosomatic Medicine, 40,* 86.

Bucher, C. A. (1974). National adult physical fitness survey: Some implications. *Journal of Health, Physical Education, Recreation, 45,* 25-31.

Budzynski, T. H., & Stoyva, J. M. (1969). An instrument for producing deep muscle relaxation by means of analog information feedback. *Journal of Applied Behavior Analysis, 2,* 231-237.

Budzynski, T. H., Stoyva, J. M., & Adler, C. S. (1970). Feedback-induced muscle relaxation: Application to tension headache. *Journal of Behavior Therapy and Experimental Psychiatry, 1,* 205-211.

Budzynski, T. H., Stoyva, J. M., Adler, C. S., & Mullaney, D. J. (1973). EMG biofeedback and tension headache: A controlled outcome study. *Psychosomatic Medicine, 35,* 484-496.

Burack, R., & Carpenter, R. (1983). The predictive value of the presenting complaint. *Journal of Family Practice, 16,* 749-754.

Burish, T. G., & Bradley, L. A. (Eds.). (1983). *Coping with chronic disease: Research and applications.* New York: Academic.

Burish, T. G., & Redd, W. H. (1983). Behavioral approaches to reducing conditioned responses to chemotherapy in adult cancer patients. *Behavioral Medicine Update, 5,* 12-16.

Burnham, J. C. (1984). Change in the popularization of health in the United States. *Bulletin of the History of Medicine, 58,* 183-197.

Bush, H. (1984). Cancer: The new synthesis: Cure. *Science 84, 5,* 34-35.

Byrne, P. S., & Long, B. E. (1976). *Doctors talking to patients: A study of the verbal behavior of general practitioners consulting in their surgeries.* Southampton, England: Hobbs.

Caffrey, B. (1968). Reliability and validity of personality and behavioral measures in a study of coronary heart disease. *Journal of Chronic Heart Diseases, 21,* 191-204.

Cairns, D., & Pasino, J. (1977). Comparison of verbal reinforcement and feedback in the operant treatment of disability due to chronic low back pain. *Behavior Therapy, 8*, 621-630.

Cairns, D., Thomas, L., Mooney, V., & Pace, J. B. (1976). A comprehensive treatment approach to chronic low back pain. *Pain, 2*, 301-308.

Caldwell, J. R., Cobb, S., Dowling, M. D., & de Jongh, D. (1970). The dropout problem in antihypertensive treatment. *Journal of Chronic Diseases, 22*, 579-592.

Calhoun, K. S., & Burnette, M. M. (1984). Etiology and treatment of menstrual disorders. *Behavioral Medicine Update, 5*(4), 21-26.

Callahan, D. (1977). Health and society: Some ethical imperatives. In J. H. Knowles (Ed.), *Doing better and feeling worse: Health in the United States* (pp. 23-33). New York: Norton.

Cameron, R. (1978). The clinical implementation of behavioral change techniques: A cognitively oriented conceptualization of therapeutic "compliance" and "resistance." In J. P. Foreyt & D. P. Rathjen (Eds.), *Cognitive behavior therapy: Research and application* (pp. 233-250). New York: Plenum.

Cameron, R., & Meichenbaum, D. (1982). The nature of effective coping and the treatment of stress related problems: A cognitive-behavioral perspective. In L. Goldberger & S. Breznitz (Eds.), *Handbook of stress: Theoretical and clinical aspects* (pp. 695-710). New York: Free Press.

Canada's amazing health history: Let's murder the medical officer [Edited text of film]. (1984). *Canadian Journal of Public Health, 75*, 344-347.

Caron, H. S., & Roth, H. P. (1968). Patients' cooperation with a medical regimen: Difficulties in identifying the noncooperator. *Journal of the American Medical Association, 203*, 922-926.

Carr, J. E., & Maxim, P. E. (1983). Communication research and the doctor-patient relationship. In J. E. Carr & H. A. Dengerink (Eds.), *Behavioral science in the practice of medicine* (pp. 133-161). New York: Elsevier.

Carter, S. (1976). Immunotherapy of cancer in man. *American Scientist, 64*, 418-423.

Cartwright, D. (1949). Some principles of mass persuasion. *Human Relations, 2*, 253-267.

Case, R., Heller, S., Case, N., & Moss, A. (1985). Type A behavior and survival after acute myocardial infarction. *The New England Journal of Medicine, 312*, 737-741.

Caspersen, C., Powell, K., & Christenson, G. (1985). Physical activity, exercise, and physical fitness: Definitions and distinctions for health-related research. *Public Health Reports, 100*, 126-131.

Cassell, E. J. (1979). Changing ideas of causality in medicine. *Social Research, 46*, 728-743.

Chang, R. S. (1981). Immunization. In R. S. Chang (Ed.), *Preventive health care* (pp. 323-341). Boston: G. K. Hall.

Chappell, M. N., Stefano, J. J., Rogerson, J. S., & Pike, F. H. (1936). The value of group psychological procedures in the treatment of peptic ulcer. *American Journal of Digestive Disease and Nutrition, 3,* 813-817.

Chesney, M. A. (1984, August). *Behavioral factors in coronary heart disease separating benign from malignant.* Paper presented at the annual meeting of the American Psychological Association, Toronto, Ontario.

Chesney, M. A., & Shelton, J. L. (1976). A comparison of muscle relaxation and electromyogram biofeedback treatments for muscle contraction headache. *Journal of Behavior Therapy and Experimental Psychiatry, 7,* 221-225.

Chobanian, A. V. (1980). The problem in perspective. In R. B. Haynes, M. E. Mattson, & T. O. Engelretson, Jr. (Eds.), *Patient compliance to prescribed antihypertensive medication regimens: A report of the National Heart, Lung, and Blood Institute* (NIH Publication No. 81-2102). Bethesda, MD: Department of Health and Human Services, Public Health Service, National Institutes of Health.

Cinciripini, P. M., & Floreen, A. (1982). An evaluation of a behavioral program for chronic pain. *Journal of Behavioral Medicine, 5,* 375-389.

Cobb, S., & Rose, R. M. (1973). Psychosomatic disease in air traffic controllers: Hypertension, diabetes, and peptic ulcer. *Journal of the American Medical Association, 224,* 489-492.

Cogan, R., Henneborn, W., & Klopfer, F. (1976). Predictors of pain during prepared childbirth. *Journal of Psychosomatic Research, 20* 523-533.

Cohen, J. B., Syme, S. L., Jenkins, C. D., Kagan, A., & Zyzanski, S. J. (1979). Cultural context of Type A behavior and risk for CHD: A study of Japanese American males. *Journal of Behavioral Medicine, 2,* 375-384.

Cohen, W. S. (1985). Health promotion in the workplace: A prescription for good health. *American Psychologist, 40,* 213-216.

Cook, W. W., & Medley, D. M. (1954). Proposed hostility and pharisaic-virtue scales for the MMPI. *Journal of Applied Psychology, 38,* 414-418.

Cooney, J. L., & Zeichner, A. (1985). Selective attention to negative feedback in Type A and Type B individuals. *Journal of Abnormal Psychology, 94,* 110-112.

Cooper, B. S., & Rice, D. P. (1976). The economic cost of illness revisited. *Social Security Bulletin, 39,* 21-36.

Costa, P. T., Zonderman, A. B., McCrae, R. R., & Williams, R. B. (in press). Content and comprehensiveness in the MMPI: An item factor analysis in a normal adult sample. *Journal of Personality and Social Psychology.*

Cox, D. J., Freundlich, A., & Meyer, R. J. (1975). Differential effectiveness of electromyograph feedback, verbal relaxation instructions, and medication placebo with tension headaches. *Journal of Consulting and Clinical Psychology, 43,* 892-899.

Coyne, J. C., & Lazarus, R. S. (1980). Cognitive style, stress perception, and coping. In I. L. Kutash & L. B. Schlesinger (Eds.), *Handbook on stress and anxiety: Contemporary knowledge, theory, and treatment* (pp. 144-158). San Francisco: Jossey-Bass.

Cummings, N. A. (1977). Prolonged (ideal) versus short-term (realistic) psychotherapy. *Professional Psychology, 8,* 491-501.

Cummings, N. A., & Follette, W. T. (1976). Brief psychotherapy and medical utilization. In H. Dorken and Associates (Eds.), *The professional psychologist today* (pp. 165-174). San Francisco: Jossey-Bass.

Cunningham, A. J. (1985). The influence of mind on cancer. *Canadian Psychology, 26,* 13-29.

Dattore, P. J., Shontz, F. C., & Coyne, L. (1980). Premorbid personality differentiation of cancer and non-cancer groups: A test of the hypothesis of cancer proneness. *Journal of Consulting and Clinical Psychology, 48,* 388-394.

Davidson, P. O. (1976). Therapeutic compliance. *Canadian Psychological Review, 17*(4), 247-259.

Davidson, P. O., & Schrag, A. R. (1969). Factors affecting the outcome of child psychiatric consultations. *American Journal of Orthopsychiatry, 39,* 774-778.

Davis, M. S. (1967). Predicting non-compliant behavior. *Journal of Health and Social Behavior, 8,* 265-271.

DeLongis, A., Coyne, J. C., Dakof, G., Folkman, S., & Lazarus, R. S. (1982). Relationship of daily hassles, uplifts, and major life events to health status. *Health Psychology, 1,* 119-136.

Dembroski, T. M., & MacDougall, J. M. (in press). Beyond global Type A: Relation of paralinguistic attributes, hostility, and anger in coronary heart disease. In T. Field, P. McCabe, & N. Schneiderman (Eds.), *Stress and coping.* Hillsdale, NJ: Lawrence Erlbaum.

Dembroski, T. M., MacDougall, J. M., & Shields, J. L. (1977). Physiologic reactions to social challenge in persons evidencing the Type A coronary-prone behavior pattern. *Journal of Human Stress, 3,* 2-10.

Dembroski, T. M., MacDougall, J. M., Shields, J. L., Petitto, J., & Lushene, R. (1978). Components of the Type A coronary-prone behavior pattern and cardiovascular responses to psychomotor performance challenge. *Journal of Behavioral Medicine, 1,* 159-176.

Dembroski, T. M., MacDougall, J. M., Williams, R., Haney, T., & Blumenthal, J. (1985). *Components of Type A, hostility, and anger-in relationship to angiographic findings.* Unpublished manuscript, Eckerd College, Stress and Cardiovascular Research Center, St. Petersburg, FL.

Dengerink, H. A. J., & Bakker, C. B. (1983). Behavioral research in health care. In J. E. Carr & H. A. Dengerink (Eds.), *Behavioral science in the practice of medicine* (pp. 21-42). New York: Elsevier.

Department of Health and Human Services. (1980). *Promoting health/preventing disease: Objectives for the nation.* Washington, DC: U.S. Government Printing Office.

Department of Health and Human Services. (1983, Sept.-Oct.). Promoting health/preventing disease: Public health service implementation plans for attaining objectives for the nation. *Public Health Reports, 98*(Supp. 5).

Derogatis, L. R., Abeloff, M. D., & Melisaratos, N. (1979). Psychological coping mechanisms and survival time in metastatic breast cancer. *Journal of the American Medical Association, 242,* 1504-1508.

Dick-Read, G. (1953). *Childbirth without fear: The principles and practice of natural childbirth.* New York: Harper.

DiMatteo, M. R., Taranta, A., Friedman, H. S., & Prince, L. M. (1980). Predicting patient satisfaction from physicians' nonverbal communication skills. *Medical Care, 18,* 376-387.

Dishman, R. K. (1982). Compliance/adherence in health-related exercise. *Health Psychology, 1,* 237-267.

Dishman, R. K., Sallis, J., & Orenstein, D. (1985). The determinants of physical activity and exercise. *Public Health Reports, 100,* 159-171.

Dohrenwend, B. S., & Dohrenwend, B. P. (Eds.). (1974). *Stressful life events: Their nature and effects.* New York: Wiley.

Dohrenwend, B. S., & Dohrenwend, B. P. (1978). Some issues in research on stressful life events. *The Journal of Nervous and Mental Disease, 166,* 7-15.

Dohrenwend, B. S., Krasnoff, L., Askenasy, A. R., & Dohrenwend, B. P. (1978). Exemplification of a method for scaling life events: The PERI Life Events Scale. *Journal of Health and Social Behavior, 19,* 205-229.

Doyle, B. J., & Ware, J. E., Jr. (1977). Physician conduct and other factors that affect consumer satisfaction with medical care. *Journal of Medical Education, 52,* 793-801.

Edwards, R. (1963, January). Indoctrination: A respectable technique in health education. *Journal of Health, Physical Education, Recreation, 34*(1), 44-45, 66.

Eisenberg, L. (1977). The search for care. In J. H. Knowles (Ed.), *Doing better and feeling worse: Health in the United States* (pp. 235-246). New York: Norton.

Elder, S. T., Ruiz, Z. B., Deabler, H. L., & Dillenkoffer, R. L. (1973). Instrumental conditioning of diastolic blood pressure in essential hypertensive patients. *Journal of Applied Behavior Analysis, 6,* 377-382.

Eliot, R. S., & Buell, J. C. (1981). Environmental and behavioral influences in the major cardiovascular disorders. In S. M. Weiss, J. A. Herd, & B. H. Fox (Eds.), *Perspectives on behavioral medicine* (pp. 25-39). New York: Academic.

Epstein, L. H., & Masek, B. J. (1978). Behavioral control of medicine compliance. *Journal of Applied Behavior Analysis, 11,* 1-9.

Epstein, M., & Oster, J. (1984). *Hypertension: A practical approach.* Philadelphia: W. B. Saunders.

Evans, R. I., Rozelle, R. M., Mittelmark, M. B., Hansen, W. B., Bane, A. L., & Havis, J. (1978). Deterring the onset of smoking in children: Knowledge of immediate physiological effects and coping with peer pressure, media pressure and parent modelling. *Journal of Applied Social Psychology, 8,* 126-135.

Faden, R. R., & Faden, A. I. (1978). The ethics of health education as public health policy. *Health Education Monographs, 6,* 180-197.

Fahrion, S., Norris, P., Green, A., & Green, E. (1984). *Bio-behavioral treatment of central hypertension: A group outcome study.* Topeka, KS: The Menninger Foundation.

Farquhar, J. W. (1978). The community-based model of life-style intervention trials. *American Journal of Epidemiology, 108,* 103-111.

Farquhar, J. W. (in press). The Stanford Five City Project: An overview. In J. D. Matarazzo, N. E. Miller, A. J. Herd, & S. M. Weiss (Eds.), *Behavioral health: A handbook of health enhancement and disease prevention.* New York: Wiley.

Farquhar, J. W., Maccoby, N., & Solomon, D. S. (1984). Community applications of behavioral medicine. In W. D. Gentry (Ed.), *Handbook of behavioral medicine* (pp. 437-478). New York: Guilford.

Farquhar, J. W., Maccoby, N., Wood, P. D., Alexander, J. K., Breitrose, H., Brown, B. A., Jr., Haskell, W. L., McAlister, A. L., Meyer, A. J., Nash, J. D., & Stern, M. P. (1977). Community education for cardiovascular health. *Lancet, 1,* 1192-1195.

Faust, J., & Melamed, B. G. (1984). Influence of arousal, previous experience, and age on surgery preparation of same day surgery and in-hospital pediatric patients. *Journal of Consulting and Clinical Psychology, 52,* 359-365.

Fears, T. R., Scotto, J., & Schneiderman, M. A. (1976). Skin cancer, melanoma, and sunlight. *American Journal of Public Health, 66*(5), 461-464.

Fishman, A. (1982). *Arteriosclerosis 1981* (Vol. 1: Report of the Working Group on Arteriosclerosis of the National Heart, Lung, and Blood Institute). Washington, DC: U.S. Department of Health and Human Services.

Flay, B. R. (in press). What do we know about the social influences approach to smoking prevention? Review and recommendations. In C. Bell & R. Battjes (Eds.), *Prevention research: Deterring drug abuse among children and adolescents.* Washington, DC: NIDA Research Monograph.

Flay, B. R., Hansen, W. B., Johnson, C. A., & Sobel, J. L. (1983). *Involvement of children in motivating parents to quit smoking with a television program.* Presented at a meeting of the American Psychological Association, Anaheim, CA.

Flay, B. R., Ryan, K. B., Best, J. A., Brown, K. S., Kersell, M. W., d'Avernas, J. R., & Zanna, M. P. (1985). Are social-psychological smoking prevention programs effective? The Waterloo study. *Journal of Behavioral Medicine, 8,* 37-59.

Flor, H., & Turk, D. C. (1984). Etiological theories and treatments for chronic back pain I: Somatic models and interventions. *Pain, 19,* 105-121.

Fordyce, W. E. (1976). *Behavioral methods for chronic pain and illness.* St. Louis: Mosby.

Fordyce, W. E., Fowler, R. S., Lehmann, J. F., DeLateur, B. J., Sand, P. L., & Trieschmann, R. B. (1973). Operant conditioning in the treatment of chronic pain. *Archives of Psychological Medicine, 54,* 399-408.

Forster, F. (1978). *Reflex epilepsy.* Springfield, IL: Charles C Thomas.

Fortin, F., & Kirouac, S. A. (1976). A randomized controlled trial of preoperative patient education. *International Journal of Nursing Studies, 13,* 11-24.

Fox, B. H. (1978). Premorbid psychological factors as related to cancer incidence. *Journal of Behavioral Medicine, 1,* 45-134.

Francis, V., Korsch, B. M., & Morris, M. J. (1969). Gaps in doctor-patient communication: Patients' response to medical advice. *New England Journal of Medicine, 280,* 535-540.

Frank, J. D. (1974). *Persuasion and healing.* Baltimore: Johns Hopkins University Press.

Frank, K. A., Heller, S. S., Kornfeld, D. S., Sporn, A. A., & Weiss, M. D. (1978). Type A behavior pattern and coronary angiographic findings. *Journal of the American Medical Association, 240,* 761-763.

Frankel, B. L., Patel, D. J., Horwitz, D., Friedewald, W. T., & Gaarder, K. R. (1978). Treatment of hypertension with biofeedback and relaxation techniques. *Psychosomatic Medicine, 40,* 276-293.

Frankenhaeuser, M. (1978). *Coping with job stress: A psychological approach* (p. 532). Stockholm: University of Stockholm.

Frankenhaeuser, M. (1980). Psychobiological aspects of life stress. In S. Levine & H. Ursin (Eds.), *Coping and health.* New York: Plenum.

Franz, S. I. (1913). On psychology and medical education. *Science, 38,* 555-566.

Frederiksen, L., Solomon, L., & Brehony, K. (Eds.). (1984). *Marketing health behavior: Principles, techniques, and applications.* New York: Plenum.

Fried, R., Rubin, S. R., Carlton, R. M., & Fox, M. C. (1984). Behavioral control of intractable idiopathic seizures: I. Self-regulation of end-tidal carbon dioxide. *Psychosomatic Medicine, 46,* 315-331.

Friedewald, W. (1985). Physical activity research and coronary heart disease. *Public Health Reports, 100,* 115-117.

Friedman, M., & Powell, L. H. (1984). The diagnosis and quantitative assessment of Type A behavior: Introduction and description of the videotaped structured interview. *Integrative Psychiatry, 2,* 123-136.

Friedman, M., & Rosenman, R. H. (1959). Association of specific overt behavior pattern with blood and cardiovascular findings. *Journal of the American Medical Association, 169,* 1286-1296.

Friedman, M., & Rosenman, R. H. (1974). *Type A behavior and your heart.* New York: Knopf.

Friedman, M., Thoreson, C. E., Gill, J. J., Powell, L. H., Ulmer, D., Thompson, L., Price, V. A., Rabin, D. D., Breall, W. S., Dixon, T., Levy, R., & Bourg, E. (1984). Alteration of Type A behavior and reduction in cardiac recurrences in postmyocardial infarction patients. *American Heart Journal, 108,* 237-248.

Friedman, M., Thoresen, C. E., Gill, J. J., Ulmer, D., Thompson, L., Powell, L. H., Price, V., Elek, S. R., Rabin, D. D., Breall, W. S., Piaget, G., Dixon, T., Bourg, E., Levy, R. A., & Tasto, D. L. (1982). Feasibility of altering Type A behavior pattern after myocardial infarction. Recurrent Coronary Prevention Project Study: Methods, baseline results and preliminary findings. *Circulation, 66,* 87-92.

Frum, D. (1984, October). A little learning. *Saturday Night,* pp. 34-45.

Gately, M. S. (1968). To be taken as directed. *Journal of the Royal College of General Practitioners, 5,* 298-311.

Genest, M. (1981). Preparation for childbirth: Evidence of efficacy. *Journal of Obstetric, Gynecological, and Neonatal Nursing, 10*(2), 82-85.

Genest, M. (1983). Coping with rheumatoid arthritis. *Canadian Journal of Behavioural Science, 15,* 392-408.

Genest, M., & Turk, D. C. (1979). A proposed model for behavioral group therapy with pain patients. In D. Upper & S. M. Ross (Eds.), *Behavioral group therapy: An annual review* (pp. 237-276). Champaign, IL: Research Press.

Gentry, W. D., & Kobasa, S. C. (1984). Social and psychological resources mediating stress-illness relationships in humans. In W. D. Gentry (Ed.), *Handbook of behavioral medicine* (pp. 87-116). New York: Guilford.

Gerbert, B. (1984). Perceived likeability and competence of simulated patients: Influence on physicians' management plans. *Social Science and Medicine, 18*(12), 1053-1059.

Gil, K. M. (1984). Coping effectively with invasive medical procedures: A descriptive model. *Clinical Psychology Review, 4,* 339-362.

Gillum, R. F., & Barsky, A. J. (1974). Diagnosis and management of patient noncompliance. *Journal of the American Medical Association, 223,* 1563-1567.

Glasgow, M., Gaarder, K. R., & Engel, B. T. (1982). Behavioral treatment of high blood pressure II: Acute and sustained effects of relaxation and systolic blood pressure biofeedback. *Psychosomatic Medicine, 44,* 155-170.

Glass, D. C. (1977). Behavior patterns, stress and coronary disease. Hillsdale, NJ: Lawrence Erlbaum.

Glass, D. C., & Carver, C. S. (1980). Environmental stress and the Type A response. In A. Baum & J. E. Singer (Eds.), *Advances in environmental psychology: Vol. 2. Applications of personal control*. Hillsdale, NJ: Lawrence Erlbaum.

Glass, D. C., Krakoff, L. R., Contrada, R., Hilton, W. F., Kehoe, K., Mannucci, E. G., Collins, C., Snow, B., & Elting, E. (1980). Effect of harassment and competition upon cardiovascular and catecholamine responses in Type A and Type B individuals. *Psychophysiology, 17,* 453-463.

Glass, D. C., Snyder, M. L., & Hollis, J. J. (1974). Time urgency and the Type A coronary-prone behavior pattern. *Journal of Applied Social Psychology, 4,* 125-140.

Goetz, A. A., Duff, J. F., & Bernstein, J. E. (1980). Health risk appraisal: The estimation of risk. *Public Health Reports, 95,* 119-126.

Goldband, S., Katkin, E. S., & Morrell, M. A. (1979). Personality and cardiovascular disorder: Steps toward demystification. In I. G. Sarason & C. D. Spielberger (Eds.), *Stress and anxiety* (Vol. 6). New York: Wiley.

Goldenberg, D. A., Hodges, V., Hersh, T., & Jinich, H. (1980). Biofeedback therapy for fecal incontinence. *American Journal of Gastroenterology, 74,* 342-345.

Goldman, L., & Cook, E. (1984). The decline in ischemic heart disease mortality rates. An analysis of the comparative effects of medical interventions and changes in lifestyle. *Annals of Internal Medicine, 101,* 825-836.

Goldsmith, G. A. (1981). Life style and health. In R. S. Chang (Ed.), *Preventive health care* (pp. 33-44). Chicago: Year Book Medical Publishers.

Goldstein, I. B., Shapiro, D., Thananopavarn, C., & Sambhi, M. P. (1982). Comparison of drug and behavioral treatments of essential hypertension. *Health Psychology, 1,* 7-26.

Gonder-Frederick, L., Cox, D., Pohl, S., & Carter, W. (1984). Patient blood glucose monitoring: Use, accuracy, adherence, and impact. *Behavioral Medicine Update, 6*(1), 12-16.

Gottlieb, H., Strite, L. C., Koller, R., Madorsky, A., Hockersmith, V., Kleeman, M., & Wagner, J. (1977). Comprehensive rehabilitation of patients having chronic low back pain. *Archives of Physical Medicine and Rehabilitation, 58,* 101-108.

Graham, D. T. (1972). Psychosomatic medicine. In N. S. Greenfield & R. A. Sternbach (Eds.), *Handbook of psychophysiology* (pp. 839-924). New York: Holt, Rinehart & Winston.

Graham, D. T., Lundy, R. M., Benjamin, L. S., Kabler, J. D., Lewis, W. C., Kunish, N. S., & Graham, F. K. (1962). Specific attitudes in initial interviews with patients having different "psychosomatic diseases." *Psychosomatic Medicine, 24,* 257-266.

Graves, P. L., & Thomas, C. B. (1981). Themes of interaction in medical students' Rorschach responses as predictors of midlife health or disease. *Psychosomatic Medicine, 43,* 215-225.

Green, E., & Green, A. (1979). General and specific applications of thermal biofeedback. In J. V. Basmajian (Ed.), *Biofeedback: Principles and practice for clinicians* (pp. 253-269). Baltimore: Williams & Wilkins.

Green, H. R., & O'Toole, K. M. (1982). Early gastric cancer. *Annals of Internal Medicine, 97,* 272-273.

Greenhoot, J. H., & Sternbach, R. A. (1974). Conjoint treatment of chronic pain. In J. J. Bonica (Ed.), *International symposium on pain: Vol. 4. Advances in neurology* (pp. 595-603). New York: Raven.

Greer, S. (1976). Psychological aspects: Delay in the treatment of breast cancer. *Proceedings of the Royal Society of Medicine, 67,* 470-473.

Greer, S. (1979). Psychological enquiry: A contribution to cancer research. *Psychological Medicine, 9,* 81-89.

Gumbiner, R. (1975). *HMO: Putting it all together.* St. Louis: Mosby.

Hager, J. L., & Surwit, R. S. (1978). Hypertension self-control with a portable feedback unit or meditation-relaxation. *Biofeedback and Self-Regulation, 3,* 269-276.

Halberstam, J. L., Zaretsky, H. H., Brucker, B. S., & Guttman, A. (1971). Avoidance conditioning of motor responses in elderly brain-damaged patients. *Archives of Physical Medicine and Rehabilitation, 52,* 318-336.

Hall, J. A., Roter, D. L., & Rand, C. S. (1981). Communication of affect between patient and physician. *Journal of Health and Social Behavior, 22,* 18-30.

Haney, C. A. (1971). Psychological factors involved in medical decision making. In R. H. Coombs & C. E. Clark (Eds.), *Psychosocial aspects of medical training* (pp. 404-423). Springfield, IL: Charles C Thomas.

Harrell, T., & Beiman, I. (1978). Cognitive-behavioral treatment of the irritable colon syndrome. *Cognitive Therapy and Research, 2,* 371-374.

Haybittle, J. (1983). Is breast cancer ever cured? *Reviews on Endocrine-Related Cancer, 14,* 13-18.

Haynes, R. B. (1976). A critical review of the "determinants" of patient compliance with therapeutic regimens. In D. L. Sackett & R. B. Haynes (Eds.), *Compliance with therapeutic regimens* (pp. 26-39). Baltimore: Johns Hopkins University Press.

Haynes, R. B. (1979). Strategies to improve compliance with referrals, appointments, and prescribed medical regimens. In R. B. Haynes, D. W. Taylor, & D. L. Sackett (Eds.), *Compliance in health care* (pp. 121-143). Baltimore: Johns Hopkins University Press.

Haynes, R. B. (1982). Improving patient compliance: An empirical view. In R. B. Stuart (Ed.), *Adherence, compliance and generalization in behavioral medicine* (pp. 56-78). New York: Brunner/Mazel.

Haynes, S. G., Feinleib, M., & Kannel, W. B. (1980). The relationship of psychosocial factors to coronary heart disease in the Framingham Study: III Eight-year incidence of coronary heart disease. *American Journal of Epidemiology, 111,* 37-58.

Haynes, S. G., Feinleib, M., Levine, S., Scotch, N., & Kannel, W. B. (1978). The relationship of psychosocial factors to coronary heart disease in the Framingham Study: II. Prevalence of coronary heart disease. *American Journal of Epidemiology, 107,* 384-402.

Haynes, S. G., Levine, S., Scotch, N., Feinleib, M., & Kannel, W. B. (1978). The relationship of psychosocial factors to coronary heart disease in the Framingham Study: I Methods and risk factors. *American Journal of Epidemiology, 107,* 362-381.

Haynes, S. N., Griffin, P., Mooney, D., & Parise, M. (1975). Electromyographic biofeedback and relaxation instructions in the treatment of muscle contraction headaches. *Behavior Therapy, 6,* 672-678.

Healey, K. M. (1968). Does preoperative instruction make a difference? *American Journal of Epidemiology, 68,* 62-67.

Heide, F. J., & Mahoney, M. J. (1980). Cognitive strategies for medical disorders. In J. M. Ferguson & C. B. Taylor (Eds.), *The comprehensive handbook of behavioral medicine: Vol. 3. Extended applications and issues* (pp. 99-111). New York: SP Medical and Scientific Books.

Henneborn, W. J., & Cogan, R. (1975). The effect of husband participation on reported pain and probability of medication during labor and birth. *Journal of Psychosomatic Research, 19,* 215-222.

Herd, J. A. (1984). Cardiovascular disease and hypertension. In W. D. Gentry (Ed.), *Handbook of behavioral medicine* (pp. 222-281). New York: Guilford.

Herd, J. A., & Weiss, S. M. (1984). Overview of hypertension: Its treatment and prevention. In J. D. Matarazzo, S. M. Weiss, J. A. Herd, N. E. Miller, & S. M. Weiss (Eds.), *Behavioral Health: A handbook of health enhancement and disease prevention* (pp. 789-805). New York: Wiley.

Hersen, M., & Barlow, D. (1976). *Single case experimental designs: Strategies for studying behavior change.* New York: Pergamon.

Hettler, B., Janty, C., & Moffat, C. (1977). A comparison of seven methods of health hazard appraisal. *Proceedings of the Thirteenth Annual Meeting, Society of Prospective Medicine.* San Diego: Society of Prospective Medicine.

Hinkle, L. E., Jr. (1977). The concept of "stress" in the biological and social sciences. In Z. J. Lipowski, D. R. Lipsitt, & P. C. Whybrow (Eds.), *Psychosomatic medicine* (pp. 27-49). New York: Oxford University Press. (Reprinted from *Science, Medicine and Man,* 1973, *1,* 31-48.)

Hirsch, I., Matthews, M., Rawlings, S., Broughton, J., Breyfogle, R., Simonds, J., Kossoy, K., England, J., Weidmeyer, H., Little, R., & Goldstein, D. (1983). Home capillary blood glucose monitoring (HBGLM) for diabetic youths: A one-year follow-up of 98 patients. *Diabetes, 32,* 16A.

Holmes, T. H. (1979). Development and application of a quantitative measure of life change magnitude. In J. E. Barrett, R. M. Rose, & G. L. Klerman (Eds.), *Stress and mental disorder* (pp. 37-53). New York: Raven.

Holmes, T. H., & Masuda, M. (1974). Life change and illness susceptibility. In B. S. Dohrenwend & B. P. Dohrenwend (Eds.), *Stressful life events: Their nature and effects* (pp. 49-72). New York: Wiley.

Holmes, T. H., & Rahe, R. H. (1967). The social readjustment rating scale. *Journal of Psychosomatic Research, 11,* 213-218.

Holroyd, K. A. (1979). Stress, coping, and the treatment of stress-related illness. In J. M. McNamara (Ed.), *Behavioral approaches to medicine* (pp. 191-226). New York: Plenum.

Holroyd, K. A., & Andrasik, F. (1982). Do the effects of cognitive therapy endure? A two-year follow-up of tension headache sufferers treated with cognitive therapy or biofeedback. *Cognitive Therapy and Research, 6,* 325-334.

Holroyd, K. A., Andrasik, F., & Noble, J. A. (1980). A comparison of EMG biofeedback and a credible pseudotherapy in treating tension headache. *Journal of Behavioral Medicine, 3,* 29-39.

Holroyd, K. A., Andrasik, F., & Westbrook, T. (1977). Cognitive control of tension headache. *Cognitive Therapy and Research, 1,* 121-133.

Holroyd, K. A., & Lazarus, R. S. (1982). Stress, coping, and somatic adaptation. In L. Goldberger & S. Breznitz (Eds.), *Handbook of stress: Theoretical and clinical aspects* (pp. 21-35). New York: Free Press.

Holroyd, K. A., & Penzien, D. B. (1982). Cognitive change underlying the effectiveness of biofeedback training. *Cognitive Behavior Therapy Newsletter, 4,* 6-10.

Holt, R. R. (1982). Occupational stress. In L. Goldberger & S. Breznitz (Eds.), *Handbook of stress: Theoretical and clinical aspects* (pp. 419-444). New York: Free Press.

Horner, R. (1971). Establishing use of crutches by a mentally retarded spina bifida child. *Journal of Applied Behavior Analysis, 4,* 183-189.

House, J. S., McMichael, A. J., Wells, J. A., Kaplan, B. H., & Landerman, L. R. (1979). Occupational stress and health among factory workers. *Journal of Health and Social Behavior, 20,* 139-160.

Howard, J. H., Cunningham, D. A., & Rechnitzer, P. A. (1976, March). Health patterns associated with Type A behavior: A managerial population. *Journal of Human Stress, 2,* 24-33.

Hudgens, R. W. (1974). Personal catastrophe and depression: A consideration of the subject with respect to medically ill adolescents, and a requiem for retrospective life-events studies. In B. S. Dohrenwend & B. P. Dohrenwend (Eds.), *Stressful life events: Their nature and effects* (pp. 119-134). New York: Wiley.

Hughes, C. C., & Kennedy, D. A. (1983). Beyond the germ theory: Reflections on relations between medicine and the behavioral sciences. In J. L. Ruffino (Ed.), *Advances in social science* (Vol. 1). New York: Gordon & Breach.

Hulka, B. S., Cassel, J. C., Kupper, L. L., & Burdette, J. A. (1976). Communications, compliance and concordance between physicians and patients with prescribed medication. *American Journal of Public Health, 66,* 847-853.

Hulley, S. G., & Fortmann, S. P. (1981). Clinical trials changing behavior to prevent cardiovascular disease. In S. M. Weiss, J. A. Herd, & B. H. Fox (Eds.), *Perspectives on behavioral medicine* (pp. 89-98). New York: Academic.

Hurd, P. D., Johnson, C. A., Pechacek, T. F., Bast, L. P., Jacobs, D. R., & Luepker, R. V. (1980). Prevention of cigarette smoking in seventh grade students. *Journal of Behavioral Medicine, 3,* 15-28.

Hutchings, D. F., & Reinking, R. H. (1976). Tension headache: What form of therapy is most effective? *Biofeedback and Self-Regulation, 7,* 183-190.

Hyland, J. M., Novotny, E. S., Coyne, L., Travis, J. W., & Pruyser, H. (1984). Coping with difficult-to-treat cancer patients. *Bulletin of the Menninger Clinic, 48,* 329-341.

Ignelzi, R. J., Sternbach, R. A., & Timmermans, G. (1977). The pain ward follow-up analysis. *Pain, 3,* 277-280.

Ince, L. P. (1969). Escape and avoidance conditioning of responses in the plegic arm of stroke patients: A preliminary study. *Psychonomic Science, 16,* 49-50.

Ince, L. P., Brucker, B. S., & Alba, A. (1977). Conditioning bladder responses in patients with spinal cord lesions. *Archives of Physical Medicine and Rehabilitation, 58,* 59-65.

Inter-Society Commission for Heart Disease Resources. (1970). Primary prevention of atherosclerotic diseases. *Circulation, 42,* A55-A95.

Inui, T., Yourtee, E., & Williamson, J. (1976). Improved outcomes in hypertension after physician tutorials: A controlled trial. *Annals of Internal Medicine, 84,* 644-651.

Jackson, J. (1974). *Diffusion of an innovation: An exploratory study of the consequences of sport participation: Canada's campaign at Saskatoon.* Unpublished doctoral dissertation, University of Alberta, Edmonton.

Janis, I. L. (1958). *Psychological stress: Psychoanalytic and behavioral studies of surgical patients.* New York: Wiley.

Janis, I. L. (1969). *Stress and frustration.* New York: Harcourt Brace Jovanovich.

Janis, I. L. (1984). The patient as decision maker. In W. D. Gentry (Ed.), *Handbook of behavioral medicine* (pp. 326-358). New York: Guilford.

Janis, I. L., & Mann, L. (1977). *Decision making.* New York: Free Press.

Jeffery, R. W., Pirie, P. L., Rosenthal, B. S., Gerber, W. M., & Murray, D. M. (1982). Nutrition education in supermarkets: An unsuccessful attempt to influence knowledge and product sales. *Journal of Behavioral Medicine, 5,* 189-200.

Jemmott, J. B., III, & Locke, S. E. (1984). Psychological factors, immunologic mediation, and human susceptibility to infectious diseases: How much do we know? *Psychological Bulletin, 95*, 78-108.

Jenkins, C. D., Rosenman, R. H., & Friedman, M. (1968). Replicability of rating the coronary-prone behavior pattern. *British Journal of Preventive and Social Medicine, 22*, 16-22.

Jenkins, C. D., Rosenman, R. H., & Zyzanski, S. J. (1974). Prediction of clinical coronary heart disease by a test for the coronary-prone behavior pattern. *New England Journal of Medicine, 290*, 1271-1275.

Jessup, B. A., Neufeld, R. W., & Merskey, H. (1979). Biofeedback therapy in headache and other pain: An evaluative review. *Pain, 7*, 225-270.

Johnson, J. E., & Leventhal, H. (1974). Effects of accurate expectations and behavioral instructions on reactions during a noxious medical examination. *Journal of Personality and Social Psychology, 19*, 180-182.

Joyce, C. R., Caple, G., Mason, M., Reynolds, E., & Mathews, J. A. (1969). Quantitative study of doctor-patient communications. *Quarterly Journal of Medicine, 38*, 183-194.

Kalb, B. (1978). The effects of biofeedback relaxation training on speech and writing skills of cerebral palsy children and adolescents. *Dissertation Abstracts International, 38*, 6218B.

Kane, R. L. (Ed.). (1974a). *The challenges of community medicine.* New York: Springer.

Kane, R. L. (1974b). Disease control: What is really preventable? In R. L. Kane (Ed.), *The challenges of community medicine* (pp. 123-144). New York: Springer.

Kanfer, F. H., & Seidner, M. L. (1973). Self-control factors enhancing tolerance of aversive stimulation. *Journal of Personality and Social Psychology, 20*, 55-64.

Kannel, W. B., & Dawber, T. R. (1973). Hypertensive cardiovascular disease: The Framingham Study. In K. E. Onesti, & J. H. Moyer (Eds.), *Hypertension: Mechanisms and management* (pp. 93-110). New York: Grune & Stratton.

Kanner, A. D., Coyne, J. C., Schaefer, C., & Lazarus, R. S. (1981). Comparisons of two modes of stress measurement: Daily hassles and uplifts versus major life events. *Journal of Behavioral Medicine, 4*, 1-39.

Kaplan, N. M. (1980). The control of hypertension: A therapeutic breakthrough. *American Scientist, 68*, 537-545.

Kaplan, R. M. (1984). The connection between clinical health promotion and health status. *American Psychologist, 39*, 755-765.

Kaplan, R. M., Atkins, C. J., & Lenhard, L. (1982). Coping with a stressful sigmoidoscopy: Evaluation of cognitive and relaxation preparations. *Journal of Behavioral Medicine, 5*(1), 67-82.

Karmel, M. (1965). *Thank you, Dr. Lamaze: A mother's experiences in painless childbirth.* New York: Doubleday.

Kazdin, A. (1981). Drawing valid inferences from case studies. *Journal of Consulting and Clinical Psychology, 2*, 183-192.

Keefe, F. J. (1982). Behavioral assessment and treatment of chronic pain: Current status and future directions. *Journal of Consulting and Clinical Psychology, 50*, 896-911.

Keefe, F. J., Block, A. R., Williams, R. B., & Surwit, R. S. (1981). Behavioral treatment of chronic low back pain: Clinical outcome and individual differences in pain relief. *Pain, 11*, 221-232.

Keefe, F. J., & Bradley, L. A. (1984). Behavioral and psychological approaches to the assessment and treatment of chronic pain. *General Hospital Psychiatry, 6*, 49-54.

Keir, S., & Lauzon, R. (1980). Physical activity in a healthy lifestyle. In P. O. Davidson & S. M. Davidson (Eds.), *Behavioral medicine: Changing health lifestyles* (pp. 334-350). New York: Brunner/Mazel.

Kendall, P. C., Williams, L., Pechacek, T. F., Graham, L. E., Shisslak, C., & Herzoff, N. (1979). Cognitive-behavioral and patient education intervention in cardiac catheterization procedures: The Palo Alto medical psychology project. *Journal of Consulting and Clinical Psychology, 47*, 49-58.

Kimmel, H. D. (1967). Instrumental conditioning of autonomically mediated behavior. *Psychological Bulletin, 67*(5), 337-345.

King, T. C. (1974). Environmental health: Effluence, affluence, and influence. In R. L. Kane (Ed.), *The challenges of community medicine* (pp. 237-260). New York: Springer.

Kissen, D. M. (1966). The significance of personality in lung cancer in men. *Annals of New York Academy of Science, 125*, 820-826.

Kline, R. (1984). Rationing health care. *British Medical Journal, 289*, 143-144.

Klopfer, B. (1957). Psychological variables in human cancer. *Journal of Projective Techniques, 21*, 331-340.

Knowles, J. H. (Ed.). (1977). *Doing better and feeling worse: Health in the United States.* New York: Norton.

Kohlenberg, R. J., & Cohn, T. (1981). Self-help treatment for migraine headaches: A controlled outcome study. *Headache, 21*, 196-200.

Kondo, C. Y., & Canter, A. (1977). True and false electromyograph feedback: Effect on tension headache. *Journal of Abnormal Psychology, 86*, 93-95.

Korsch, B. M., Gozzi, E. K., & Francis, V. (1968). Gaps in doctor-patient communication, I: Doctor-patient interaction and patient satisfaction. *Pediatrics, 42*, 871-885.

Korsch, B. M., & Negrete, V. N. (1972). Doctor-patient communication. *Scientific American, 227*, 66-74.

Kowal, S. J. (1955). Emotions as a cause of cancer: 18th and 19th century contributions. *The Psychoanalytic Review, 42*, 217-227.

Krantz, D. S., & Deckel, A. W. (1983). Coping with coronary heart disease and stroke. In T. G. Burish & L. A. Bradley (Eds.), *Coping with chronic disease: Research and applications* (pp. 85-112). New York: Academic.

Krantz, D. S., & Glass, D. C. (1984). Personality, behavior patterns, and physical illness: Conceptual and methodological issues. In W. D. Gentry (Ed.), *Handbook of behavioral medicine* (pp. 38-86). New York: Guilford.

Krantz, D. S., & Manuck, S. B. (1984). Acute psychophysiologic reactivity and risk of cardiovascular disease: A review and methodologic critique. *Psychological Bulletin, 96*(3), 435-464.

Lacey, J. I. (1967). Somatic response patterning of stress: Some revisions of activation theory. In M. Appley & R. Trumbull (Eds.), *Conference on psychological stress* (pp. 14-37). New York: Appleton-Century-Crofts.

Lacey, J. I., Bateman, D. E., & Van Lehn, R. (1953). Autonomic response specificity: An experimental study. *Psychosomatic Medicine, 15*, 8-21.

Lalonde, M. (1974). *A new perspective on the health of Canadians*. Ottawa: Ministry of Health and Welfare.

Lamaze, F. (1958). *Painless childbirth: Psychoprophylactic method* (L. R. Celestin, Trans.). London: Burke Publishing.

Lang, P. J. (1977). Imagery in therapy: An information processing analysis of fear. *Behavior Therapy, 8*, 862-886.

Langer, E. J., Janis, I. L., & Wolfer, J. A. (1975). Reduction of psychological stress in surgical patients. *Journal of Experimental Social Psychology, 1*, 155-165.

Lazarus, R. S. (1966). *Psychological stress and the coping process*. New York: McGraw-Hill.

Lazarus, R. S. (1975). Psychological stress and coping in adaptation and illness. In Z. J. Lipowski, D. R. Lipsitt, & P. C. Whybrow (Eds.), *Psychosomatic medicine: Current trends and clinical applications* (pp. 14-26). New York: Oxford University Press.

Lazarus, R. S., & Cohen, J. B. (1977). Environmental stress. In I. Altman & J. F. Wohlwill (Eds.), *Human behavior and environment* (Vol. 2, pp. 90-124). New York: Plenum.

Lazarus, R. S., & DeLongis, A. (1983). Psychological stress and coping in aging. *American Psychologist, 38*, 245-254.

Lazarus, R. S., & Folkman, S. (1984). *Stress, appraisal, and coping*. New York: Springer.

Lazarus, R. S., & Launier, R. (1978). Stress-related transactions between person and environment. In L. A. Pervin & M. Lewis (Eds.), *Perspective in interactional psychology* (pp. 287-327). New York: Plenum.

LeBaron, S., & Zeltzer, L. (1984a). Assessment of acute pain and anxiety in children and adolescents by self-reports, observer reports, and a behavior checklist. *Journal of Consulting and Clinical Psychology, 52*, 729-738.

LeBaron, S., & Zeltzer, L. (1984b). Behavior intervention for reducing chemotherapy-related nausea and vomiting in adolescents with cancer. *Journal of Adolescent Health Care, 5,* 178-182.

Lehrer, P. (1983). Clinical biofeedback: Efficacy and mechanisms. *Contemporary Psychology, 28,* 824-826.

Leon, G. R. (1976). Current directions in the treatment of obesity. *Psychological Bulletin, 83,* 557-578.

Leon, G. R., Butcher, J., Kleinman, M., Goldberg, A., & Almagor, M. (1981). Survivors of the Holocaust and their children: Current status and adjustment. *Journal of Personality and Social Psychology, 41,* 503-516.

LeShan, L. (1959). Psychological states as factors in the development of malignant disease: A critical review. *Journal of the National Cancer Institute, 22,* 1-18.

LeShan, L. (1964). The world of the patient in severe pain of long duration. *Journal of Chronic Diseases, 17,* 119-126.

Leventhal, H. (1970). Findings and theory in the study of fear communications. In L. Berkowitz (Ed.), *Advances in experimental psychology* (Vol. 5, pp. 119-186). New York: Plenum.

Leventhal, H. (1973). Changing attitudes and habits to reduce risk factors in chronic disease. *American Journal of Cardiology, 31,* 571-580.

Leventhal, H. (1984). Rewards and adolescent health behavior: Promise or promise missed. *Health Psychology, 3*(4), 347-349.

Leventhal, H., & Everhart, D. (1979). Emotion, pain, and physical illness. In C. Izard (Ed.), *Advances in experimental social psychology* (Vol. 13). New York: Plenum.

Leventhal, H., & Hirschman, R. S. (in press). Social psychology and prevention. In G. S. Sanders & J. Suls (Eds.), *Social psychology of health and illness.* Hillsdale, NJ: Lawrence Erlbaum.

Leventhal, H., Meyer, D., & Gutmann, M. (1980). The role of theory in the study of compliance to high blood pressure regimens. In R. B. Haynes, M. E. Mattson, & T. O. Engebretson (Eds.), *Patient compliance to prescribed antihypertensive medication regimens: A report to the National Heart, Lung, and Blood Institute.* Bethesda, MD: National Heart, Lung, and Blood Institute.

Leventhal, H., & Nerenz, D. R. (1983). A model for stress research with some implications for the control of stress disorders. In D. Meichenbaum & M. E. Jaremko (Eds.), *Stress reduction and prevention* (pp. 5-38). New York: Plenum.

Leventhal, H., Safer, M., & Panagis, F. D. (1983). The impact of communications on the self-regulation of health beliefs, decisions and behavior. *Health Education Quarterly, 10,* 3-29.

Leventhal, H., Zimmerman, R., & Gutmann, M. (1984). Compliance: A self-regulation perspective. In W. D. Gentry (Ed.), *Handbook of behavioral medicine* (pp. 369-436). New York: Guilford.

Levine, M. E. (1979). Three answers from experience. *American Journal of Nursing, 10,* 1992-1995.

Levy, R., & Moskowitz, J. (1982). Cardiovascular research: Decades of progress, a decade of promise. *Science, 217,* 121-129.

Levy, S. M. (1984, August). *Immunological correlates of behavior and prognosis in breast cancer: Intervention implications.* Paper presented at the annual meeting of the American Psychological Association, Toronto.

Levy, S. M. (1985). *Behavior and cancer.* San Francisco: Jossey-Bass.

Levy, S. M. (1986, March 18). *Natural immunity and cancer: The role of behaviour as a biological response modifier.* Address to the 18th Banff International Conference on Behavioural Science, Banff, Alberta.

Lewis, C. E. (1974). Health services research: Asking the painful questions. In R. L. Kane (Ed.), *The challenges of community medicine* (pp. 69-86). New York: Springer.

Lewy, R. (1980). *Preventive primary medicine: Reducing the major causes of mortality.* Boston: Little, Brown.

Ley, P. (1977). Psychological studies of doctor-patient communication. In S. Rachman (Ed.), *Contributions to medical psychology* (Vol. 1, pp. 9-42). Oxford: Pergamon.

Ley, P., Bradshaw, P. W., Eaves, D. E., & Walker, C. M. (1973). A method for increasing patients' recall of information presented to them. *Psychological Medicine, 3,* 217-220.

Ley, P., Bradshaw, P.W., Kincey, J.A., & Atherton, S.T. (1976). Increasing patients' satisfaction with communications. *British Journal of Social and Clinical Psychology, 15,* 403-413.

Ley, P., & Spelman, M. S. (1967). *Communicating with the patient.* St. Louis: Warren H. Green.

Ley, P., Whitworth, M. A., Skilbeck, C. E., Woodward, R., Pinset, R. J., Pike, L. A., Clarkson, M. E., & Clark, P. B. (1976). Improving doctor-patient communication in general practice. *Journal of the Royal College of General Practitioners, 26,* 720-724.

Lindeman, C. A., & Van Aernam, B. (1971). Nursing intervention with the presurgical patient—The effects of structured and unstructured preoperative teaching. *Nursing Research, 20,* 319-331.

Lindstrom, L. L., Balch, P., & Reese, S. (1976). In person versus telephone treatment of obesity. *Journal of Behavior Therapy and Experimental Psychiatry, 7,* 367-369.

Lipid Research Clinics Program. (1984). The lipid research clinics coronary primary prevention trial results II: The relationship of reduction in incidence of coronary heart disease to cholesterol lowering. *Journal of the American Medical Association, 251,* 365-374.

Lipowski, Z. J. (1977). Psychosomatic medicine in the seventies: An overview. *American Journal of Psychiatry, 134,* 233-244.

Litt, I. F., & Cuskey, W. R. (1984). Satisfaction with health care: A predictor of adolescents' appointment keeping. *Journal of Adolescent Health Care, 5,* 196-200.

Locke, S. E., & Hornig-Rohan, M. (1983). *Mind and immunity: Behavioral immunology.* New York: Institute for Advancement of Health.

Locke, S. E., Kraus, L., Leserman, J., Hurst, M. W., Heisel, S., & Williams, M. (1984). Life change stress, psychiatric symptoms, and natural killer cell activity. *Psychosomatic Medicine, 46,* 441-453.

Loeser, J. D. (1980). Low back pain. In J. J. Bonica (Ed.), *Pain* (pp. 363-377). New York: Raven.

Lubar, J. F., & Bahier, W. W. (1976). Behavioral management of epileptic seizures following EEG biofeedback training of the sensorimotor rhythm. *Biofeedback and Self-Regulation, 1,* 77-104.

Lubin, J. H., Richter, B. S., & Blot, W. J. (1984). Lung cancer risk with cigar and pipe use. *Journal of the National Cancer Institute, 73*(2), 377-381.

Luepker, R. V., Johnson, C. A., Murray, D. M., & Pechacek, T. F. (1983). Prevention of cigarette smoking: Three year follow-up of an education program for youth. *Journal of Behavioral Medicine, 6,* 53-62.

Luft, H. S. (1978). How do health-maintenance organizations achieve their "savings"? *New England Journal of Medicine, 298,* 1136-1143.

Lynn, S. J., & Freedman, R. R. (1979). Transfer and evaluation of biofeedback treatment. In A. P. Goldstein & F. Kanfer (Eds.), *Maximizing treatment gains: Transfer enhancement in psychotherapy* (pp. 445-484). New York: Academic.

Maccoby, N., & Alexander, J. (1980). Use of media in lifestyle programs. In P. O. Davidson & S. M. Davidson (Eds.), *Behavioral medicine: Changing health lifestyles* (pp. 351-370). New York: Brunner/Mazel.

Maccoby, N., Farquhar, J. W., Wood, P. D., & Alexander, J. K. (1977). Reducing the risk of cardiovascular disease: Effects of a community-based campaign on knowledge and behavior. *Journal of Community Health, 3,* 100-114.

Maccoby, N., & Solomon, D. S. (1981). The Stanford community studies in heart disease prevention. In R. Rice & W. Paisley (Eds.), *Public communications campaigns.* Beverly Hills, CA: Sage.

Mace, D. R. (1971). Communication, interviewing, and the physician-patient relationship. In R. H. Coombs & C. E. Clark (Eds.), *Psychosocial aspects of medical training* (pp. 380-403). Springfield, IL: Charles C Thomas.

Mahoney, M. J. (1977). Reflections on the cognitive-learning trend in psychotherapy. *American Psychologist, 32,* 5-13.

Mahoney, M. J., & Kazdin, A. E. (1979). Cognitive behavior modification: Misconceptions and premature evacuations. *Psychological Bulletin, 86,* 1044-1049.

Mahrer, A. R. (1980). The treatment of cancer through experiential psychotherapy. *Psychotherapy: Theory, Research and Practice, 17,* 335-342.

Malament, I. B., Dunn, M. E., & Davis, R. (1975). Pressure sores: An operant conditioning approach to prevention. *Archives of Physical Medicine and Rehabilitation, 56,* 161-165.

Martin, J. E., & Dubbert, P. M. (1982). Exercise applications and promotion in behavioral medicine: Current status and future directions. *Journal of Consulting and Clinical Psychology, 50,* 1004-1017.

Martin, J. E., Dubbert, P. M., Kattell, A. D., Thompson, J. K., Raczynski, J. R., Lake, M., Smith, P. O., Webster, J. S., Sikora, T., & Cohen, R. E. (1984). Behavioral control of exercise in sedentary adults: Studies 1 through 6. *Journal of Consulting and Clinical Psychology, 52,* 795-811.

Mason, J. W. (1975a). A historical view of the stress field, part I. *Journal of Human Stress, 1,* 6-12.

Mason, J. W. (1975b). A historical view of the stress field, part II. *Journal of Human Stress, 1,* 22-26.

Mason, J. W., Sachar, E. J., Fishman, J. R., Hamburg, D. A., & Handlon, J. H. (1965). Corticosteroid responses to hospital admission. *Archives of General Psychiatry, 13,* 1-8.

Matarazzo, J. D. (1982). Behavioral health challenge to academic, scientific and professional psychology. *American Psychologist, 37,* 1-4.

Matthews, K. A., Glass, D. C., Rosenman, R. H., & Bortner, R. W. (1977). Competitive drive, Pattern A, and coronary heart disease: Further analysis of some data from the Western Collaborative Group Study. *Journal of Chronic Diseases, 30,* 489-498.

Matthews, V. L. (1984, June). *What's past is prologue. Future issues in public health.* Presented at the annual meeting of the Canadian Public Health Association, Calgary, Alberta.

McAlister, A., Perry, C., Killen, J., Maccoby, N., & Slinkard, L. A. (1980). Pilot study of smoking, alcohol and drug abuse prevention. *American Journal of Public Health, 70,* 719-721.

McAlister, A., Perry, C., & Maccoby, N. (1979). Adolescent smoking: Onset and prevention. *Pediatrics, 63,* 650-658.

McCaffrey, R., & Blanchard, E. (1985). Stress management approaches to the treatment of essential hypertension. *Annals of Behavioral Medicine, 7*(1), 5-12.

McCarroll, J., & Haddon, W. (1962). A controlled study of fatal automobile accidents in New York City. *Journal of Chronic Diseases, 15,* 811-826.

McEvoy, L., & Land, G. (1981). Lifestyle and death patterns of the Missouri RLDS church members. *American Journal of Public Health, 71,* 1350-1356.

McKeachie, W. (1974, March). The decline and fall of the laws of learning. *Educational Training,* pp. 7-11.

McKenzie, R. E., Ehrisman, W. J., Montgomery, P. S., & Barnes, R. H. (1974). The treatment of headache by means of electroencephalographic biofeedback. *Headache, 14,* 164-172.

McKeown, T. (1971a). A historical appraisal of the medical task. In G. McLachlan & T. McKeown (Eds.), *Medical history and medical care* (pp. 29-55). London: Oxford University Press.

McKeown, T. (1971b). A sociological approach to the history of medicine. In G. McLachlan & T. McKeown (Eds.), *Medical history and medical care* (pp. 3-16). London: Oxford University Press.

McLanahan, S., & Sørensen, A. (1984). Life events and psychological well-being: A reexamination of the theoretical and methodological issues. *Social Science Research, 13,* 111-128.

Meagher, R. B., Jr. (1982). Cognitive behavior therapy in health psychology. In T. Millon, C. Green, & R. Meagher (Eds.), *Handbook of clinical health psychology* (pp. 499-520). New York: Plenum.

Mechanic, D. (1972). Social psychological factors affecting the presentation of bodily complaints. *New England Journal of Medicine, 288,* 1132-1139.

Mechanic, D. (1974). Discussion of research programs on relations between stressful life events and episodes of physical illness. In B. S. Dohrenwend & B. P. Dohrenwend (Eds.), *Stressful life events: Their nature and effects* (pp. 87-97). New York: Wiley.

Meichenbaum, D. H. (1977). *Cognitive-behavior modification: An integrative approach.* New York: Plenum.

Meichenbaum, D. H., & Genest, M. (1980). Cognitive-behavior modification: An integration of cognitive and behavioral methods. In F. Kanfer & A. Goldstein (Eds.), *Helping people change* (2nd ed., pp. 390-422). New York: Pergamon.

Meichenbaum, D. H., & Gilmore, J. B. (1984). The nature of unconscious processes: A cognitive-behavioral perspective. In K. S. Bowers & D. Meichenbaum (Eds.), *The unconscious reconsidered* (pp. 273-298). New York: Wiley.

Melamed, B. G. (1977). Psychological preparation for hospitalization. In S. Rochma (Ed.), *Contribution to medical psychology* (Vol. 1, pp. 43-74). Oxford: Pergamon.

Melzack, R. (Ed.). (1983). *Pain measurement and assessment.* New York: Plenum.

Melzack, R., & Wall, P. (1982). *The challenge of pain.* New York: Basic Books.

Merluzzi, T. V., Glass, C. R., & Genest, M. (Eds.). (1981). *Cognitive assessment.* New York: Guilford.

Mervis, J. (1984, October). Policy institute tackles smoking behavior. *APA Monitor, 15*(10), 7.

Messerli, M. L., Garamendi, C., & Romano, J. (1980). Breast cancer: Information as a technique of crisis intervention. *American Journal of Orthopsychiatry, 50,* 728-731.

Meyer, A. J., Maccoby, N., & Farquhar, J. W. (1977). The role of opinion leadership and the diffusion of innovations in a cardiovascular health education campaign. In D. Nimmo (Ed.), *Communication yearbook I.* New Brunswick, NJ: Transaction Books.

Meyer, A. J., Nash, J. D., McAlister, A. L., Maccoby, N., & Farquhar, J. W. (1980). Skills training in a cardiovascular health education campaign. *Journal of Consulting and Clinical Psychology, 48,* 129-142.

Middaugh, S. J. (1982). Muscle training. In D. M. Doleys, R. L. Meredith, & A. R. Ciminero (Eds.), *Behavioral medicine: Assessment and treatment strategies* (pp. 145-171). New York: Plenum.

Middaugh, S. J., & Miller, M. C. (1980). Electromyographic feedback: Effect on voluntary muscle contractions in paretic subjects. *Archives of Physical Medicine and Rehabilitation, 61,* 24-29.

Miller, N. E. (1969). Learning of visceral and glandular responses. *Science, 163,* 434.

Miller, N. E. (1975). Applications of learning and biofeedback to psychiatry and medicine. In A. M. Freedman, H. I. Kaplan, & B. J. Sadock (Eds.), *Comprehensive textbook of psychiatry—II* (pp. 349-365). Baltimore: Williams & Wilkins.

Miller, N. E. (1986, March 17). *The role of the brain in the health of the body.* Keynote address to the 18th Banff International Conference on Behavioural Science, Banff, Alberta.

Miller, N. E., & Dworkin, B. R. (1977). Critical issues in therapeutic applications of biofeedback. In G. E. Schwartz & J. Beatty (Eds.), *Biofeedback: Theory and research* (pp. 129-162). New York: Academic.

Millon, T. (1982). On the nature of clinical health psychology. In T. Millon, C. Green, & R. Meagher (Eds.), *Handbook of clinical health psychology* (pp. 1-27). New York: Plenum.

Milsum, J. W. (1980). Lifestyle changes for the whole person: Stimulation through health hazard appraisal. In P. O. Davidson & S. M. Davidson (Eds.), *Behavioral medicine: Changing health lifestyles* (pp. 116-150). New York: Brunner/Mazel.

Moos, R. M. (Ed.). (1977). *Coping with physical illness.* New York: Plenum.

Morris, J. N., Everitt, M. G., Pollard, R., Chave, S. P. W., & Semmence, A. M. (1980). Vigorous exercise in leisure-time: Protection against coronary heart disease. *Lancet, 2,* 1207-1210.

Morris, T., Buckley, M., & Blake, S. (1984). Defining psychological responses to a diagnosis of cancer. In M. Watson & T. Morris (Eds.), *Psychological aspects of cancer* (pp. 55-64). Oxford: Pergamon.

Mostofsky, D. I. (1981). Recurrent paroxysmal disorders of the central nervous system. In S. M. Turner, K. S. Calhoun, & H. E. Adams (Eds.), *Handbook of clinical behavior therapy* (pp. 447-474). New York: Wiley.

Mostofsky, D. I., & Iguchi, M. Y. (1982). Behavior control of seizure disorders. In D. M. Doleys, R. L. Meredith, & A. R. Ciminero (Eds.), *Behavioral medicine: Assessment and treatment strategies* (pp. 251-268). New York: Plenum.

Multiple Risk Factor Intervention Trial Group. (1979). The MRFIT behavior pattern study: 1. Study design procedures and reproducibility of behavior pattern judgments. *Journal of Chronic Diseases, 32,* 293-305.

Myers, R., Taljaard, J., & Penman, K. (1977). Alcohol and road traffic injury. *South African Medical Journal, 52,* 328-330.

Nacht, M. B., Wolf, S. L., & Coogler, C. E. (1982). Use of electromyographic biofeedback during the acute phase of spinal cord injury. A case report. *Physical Therapy, 62,* 290-294.

Nagle, F., & Montoye, H. (Eds.). (1981). *Exercise, health and disease.* Springfield, IL: Charles C Thomas.

National Cancer Institute. (1981). *Decade of Discovery* (Pub. 81-2323). Bethesda, MD: National Institutes of Health.

National Center for Health Statistics. (1983). *Health, United States, 1983* (DHHS Publication No. PHS 84-1232). Washington, DC: U.S. Government Printing Office.

National Institutes of Health. (1981). *The public and high blood pressure* (DHHS Publication No. NIH 81-2118). Washington, DC: U.S. Government Printing Office.

Nelson, S., & Stapp, J. (1983). Research activities in psychology. *American Psychologist, 38,* 1321-1329.

Nerenz, D. R., Leventhal, H., & Love, R. R. (1982). Factors contributing to emotional distress during cancer chemotherapy. *Cancer, 50,* 1020-1027.

Newberry, B. H., Liebelt, A. G., & Boyle, D. A. (1984). Variables in behavioral oncology: Overview and assessment of current issues. In B. H. Fox & B. H. Newberry (Eds.), *Impact of psychoendocrinal systems in cancer and immunity* (pp. 86-146). New York: C. J. Hogrefe.

Newman, R. I., Seres, J. L., Yospe, L. P., & Garlington, B. (1978). Multidisciplinary treatment of chronic pain: Long-term follow-up of low back pain patients. *Pain, 4,* 283-292.

Newton, B. W. (1982-1983). The use of hypnosis in the treatment of cancer patients. *American Journal of Clinical Hypnosis, 25,* 104-113.

Norris, E. (1981, October). Firms cite victories in battle over rising health care costs. *Business Insurance,* pp. 33-35.

Norton, J. C. (1982). *Introduction to medical psychology.* New York: Free Press.

Nouwen, A., & Solinger, J. W. (1979). The effectiveness of EMG biofeedback training in low back pain. *Biofeedback and Self-Regulation, 4,* 103-111.

Olbrisch, M. E. (1977). Psychotherapeutic interventions in physical health: Effectiveness and economic efficiency. *American Pscyhologist, 32,* 761-777.

Ort, R. S., Ford, A. B., & Liske, R. E. (1964). The doctor-patient relationship as described by physicians and medical students. *Journal of Health and Human Behavior, 5,* 25-34.

Orton, I. K., Beiman, I., & Ciminero, A. R. (1982). The behavioral assessment and treatment of essential hypertension. In D. M. Doleys, R. L. Meredith, & A. R. Ciminero (Eds.), *Behavioral medicine: Assessment and treatment strategies* (pp. 175-198). New York: Plenum.

Painter, J. R., Seres, J. L., & Newman, R. I. (1980). Assessing benefits of the pain center: Why some patients regress. *Pain, 8,* 101-113.

Patel, C. H. (1975, March 29). 12-month follow-up of yoga and biofeedback in the management of hypertension. *Lancet, 1,* 62-67.

Patel, C. H. (1977). Biofeedback-aided relaxation in the management of hypertension. *Biofeedback and Self-Regulation, 2,* 11-41.

Patel, C. H., Marmot, M. G., & Terry, D. J. (1981). Controlled trial of biofeedback-aided behavioural methods in reducing mild hypertension. *British Medical Journal, 6281,* 2005-2008.

Patel, C. H., & North, W. R. S. (1975, July 19). Randomized controlled trial of yoga and biofeedback in management of hypertension. *Lancet, 2,* 93-99.

Pearlin, L. I., Lieberman, M. A., Menaghan, E. G., & Mullan, J. T. (1981). The stress process. *Journal of Health and Social Behavior, 22,* 337-356.

Pennebaker, J. W. (1982). *The psychology of physical symptoms.* New York: Springer-Verlag.

Pennebaker, J. W. (1985). Traumatic experience and psychosomatic disease: Exploring the roles of behavioural inhibition, obsession, and confiding. *Canadian Psychology, 26*(2), 82-95.

Pennington, A. W. (1954). Treatment of obesity: Developments of the past 150 years. *American Journal of Digestive Disorders, 21,* 65-73.

Perkins, D. V. (1982). The assessment of stress using life events scales. In L. Goldberger & S. Breznitz (Eds.), *Handbook of stress: Theoretical and clinical aspects* (pp. 320-331). New York: Free Press.

Perri, M., Shapiro, R., Ludwig, W., Twentyman, C., & McAdoo, W. (1984). Maintenance strategies for the treatment of obesity: An evaluation of relapse prevention training and posttreatment contact by mail and telephone. *Journal of Consulting and Clinical Psychology, 52,* 404-413.

Perry, C. L., Killen, J., Telch, M. J., Slinkard, L. A., & Danaher, R. S. (1980). Modifying smoking behavior of teenagers: A school-based intervention. *American Journal of Public Health, 70,* 722-725.

Pettingale, K. W. (1984). Coping and cancer prognosis. *Journal of Psychosomatic Research, 28*(5), 363-364.

Pettingale, K. W. (1985). A review of psychological interactions in cancer patients. In M. Watson & T. Morris (Eds.), *Psychological aspects of cancer* (pp. 3-18). New York: Pergamon.

Piper, G. W., Jones, J. A., & Matthews, V. L. (1974). The Saskatoon smoking project: Results of the second year. *Canadian Journal of Public Health, 65,* 127-129.

Popham, R. E., Schmidt, W., & deLint, J. (1975). The prevention of alcoholism: Epidemiological studies of the effects of government control measures. *British Journal of Addictions, 70,* 125-144.

Powell, L. H. (1984). The Type A behavior pattern: An update on conceptual, assessment, and intervention research. *Behavioral Medicine Update, 6,* 7-10.

Powell, L. H., Friedman, M., Thoresen, C. E., Gill, J. J., & Ulmer, D. K. (1984). Can the Type A behavior pattern be altered after myocardial infarction? A second year report from the recurrent coronary prevention project. *Psychosomatic Medicine, 46,* 293-313.

Powles, J. (1974). On the limitation of modern medicine. In R. L. Kane (Ed.), *The challenges of community medicine* (pp. 89-122). New York: Springer.

Price, V. (1982). *Type A behavior pattern: A model for research and practice.* New York: Academic.

Puska, P., Tuomilehto, J., Salonen, J., Nissinen, A., Virtamo, J., Björkqvist, S., Koskela, K., Neittaanmäki, L., Takalo, T., Kottke, T., Maki, J., Sipila, P., & Varvikko, P. (1981). The North Karelia Project: Evaluation of a comprehensive community programme for control of cardiovascular diseases in 1972-1977 in North Karelia, Finland. *Public Health in Europe: WHO/EURO Monograph Series,* Copenhagen.

Pyle, R. L. (1979, January-February). Corporate fitness programs—How do they shape up? *Personnel,* pp. 58-67.

Rabkin, J. G., & Struening, E. L. (1976). Life events, stress, and illness. *Science, 194,* 1013-1020.

Rahe, R. H. (1974). The pathway between subjects' recent life changes and their near future illness reports: Representative results and methodological issues. In B. S. Dohrenwend & B. P. Dohrenwend (Eds.), *Stressful life events: Their nature and effects.* (pp. 73-86). New York: Wiley.

Rahe, R. H., & Arthur, R. J. (1978). Life change and illness studies: Past history and future directions. *Journal of Human Stress, 4,* 3-15.

Rayder, M. (1979). Problem: A new nurse asks why preoperative teaching isn't done. Three answers from experience. *American Journal of Nursing, 10,* 1992-1995.

Reading, A. E. (1979). Short-term effects of psychological preparation for surgery. *Social Science & Medicine—Medical Psychology & Sociology, 13A,* 641-654.

Rensberger, B. (1984). Cancer: The new synthesis: Cause. *Science 84, 5,* 28-33.

Review Panel on Coronary-Prone Behavior and Coronary Heart Disease. (1981). Coronary-prone behavior and coronary heart disease: A critical review. *Circulation, 63,* 1199-1215.

Reynolds, E., Joyce, C. R., Swift, J. L., Tooley, P. H., & Weatherall, M. (1965). Psychological and clinical investigation of the treatment of anxious outpatients with three barbiturates and placebo. *British Journal of Psychiatry, 111,* 84-95.

Robbins, L. C., & Hall, J. H. (1970). *How to practice prospective medicine.* Indianapolis: Methodist Hospital of Indiana.

Roberts, A. H., & Reinhardt, L. (1980). The behavioral management of chronic pain: Long-term follow-up with comparison groups. *Pain, 8,* 151-162.

Robertson, L. S. (1976). Estimates of motor vehicle seat belt effectiveness and use: Implications for occupant crash protection. *American Journal of Public Health, 66,* 859-864.

Rockey, P. H., Tompkins, R. K., Wood, R. W., & Wolcott, B. W. (1978). The usefulness of X-ray examinations in the evaluation of patients with back pain. *The Journal of Family Practice, 7,* 455-465.

Roemer, M. I. (1974). Can prepaid care succeed: A vote of confidence. *Prism, 2,* 13-67.

Rose, R. M. (1983). What are we talking about and who listens? A citation analysis of *Psychosomatic Medicine. Psychosomatic Medicine, 45,* 379-394.

Rosenman, R. H., Brand, R. J., Jenkins, C. D., Friedman, M., Straus, R., & Wurm, M. (1975). Coronary heart disease in the Western Collaborative Group Study: Final follow-up experience 8½ years. *Journal of the American Medical Association, 233,* 872-877.

Rosenman, R. H., Brand, R. J., Sholtz, R. I., & Friedman, M. (1976). Multivariate prediction of coronary heart disease during 8.5 year follow-up in the Western Collaborative Group Study. *American Journal of Cardiology, 37,* 902-910.

Rosenman, R. H., & Friedman, M. (1977). Modifying Type A behavior pattern. *Journal of Psychosomatic Research, 21,* 321-333.

Rosenman, R. H., Friedman, M., Straus, R., Wurm, M., Kositchek, R., Hahn, W., & Werthessen, N. T. (1964). A predictive study of coronary heart disease: The Western Collaborative Group Study. *Journal of the American Medical Association, 189,* 15-22.

Roskies, E. (1983). Stress management for Type A individuals. In D. Meichenbaum & M. E. Jaremko (Eds.), *Stress reduction and prevention* (pp. 261-288). New York: Plenum.

Roskies, E., & Avard, J. (1982). Teaching healthy managers to control their coronary-prone (Type A) behavior. In K. Blankstein & J. Polivy (Eds.), *Self-control and self-modification of emotional behavior* (pp. 163-181). New York: Plenum.

Roskies, E., Kearney, H., Spevack, M., Surkis, A., Cohen, C., & Gilman, S. (1979). Generalizability and durability of treatment effects in an intervention program for coronary-prone (Type A) managers. *Journal of Behavioral Medicine, 2,* 195-207.

Roskies, E., Seraganian, P., Oseasohn, R., Smilga, C., Martin, N., & Hanley, J. A. (in press). Treatment of psychological stress responses in healthy Type A men. In R. W. Neufeld (Ed.), *Advances in the investigation of psychological stress.* New York: Wiley.

Rosser, J. M., & Mossberg, H. E. (1977). *An analysis of health care delivery.* New York: Wiley.

Roter, D. (1977). Patient participation in the patient-provider interaction: The effects of patient question asking on the quality of interaction, satisfaction and compliance. *Health Education Monographs, 50,* 281-315.

Rothman, K., & Keller, A. (1972). Effect of joint exposure to alcohol and tobacco on risk of cancer of the mouth and pharynx. *Journal of Chronic Diseases, 25,* 711-716.

Rottkamp, B. C. (1976). A behavior modification approach to nursing therapeutics in body positioning of spinal cord-injured patients. *Nursing Research, 25,* 181-186.

Rowland, M., Fulwood, M., & Kleinman, J. C. (1983). Changes in heart disease risk factors. In National Center for Health Statistics, *Health, United States, 1983* (DHHS Publication No. PHS 84-1232) (pp. 13-24). Washington, DC: U.S. Government Printing Office.

Russell, M. A. H. (1971). Cigarette smoking: Natural history of a dependence disorder. *British Journal of Medical Psychology, 44,* 4-16.

Rybstein-Blinchik, E. (1979). Effects of different cognitive strategies on chronic pain experience. *Journal of Behavioral Medicine, 2,* 93-101.

Rybstein-Blinchik, E., & Grzesiak, R. C. (1979). Reinterpretive cognitive strategies in chronic pain management. *Archives of Physical Medicine and Rehabilitation, 60,* 609-612.

Sachs, D. A., Martin, J. E., & Fitch, J. L. (1972). The effect of visual feedback on a digital exercise in a functionally deaf cerebral palsied child. *Journal of Behavior Therapy and Experimental Psychiatry, 3,* 217-222.

Sachs, D. A., & Mayhall, B. (1971). Behavioral control of spasms using aversive conditioning with a cerebral palsied adult. *Journal of Nervous and Mental Disease, 152,* 362-363.

Sackett, D. L. (1976). The magnitude of compliance and noncompliance. In D. L. Sackett & R. B. Haynes (Eds.), *Compliance with therapeutic regimens* (pp. 9-39). Baltimore: Johns Hopkins University Press.

Sackett, D. L., & Haynes, R. B. (Eds.). (1976). *Compliance with therapeutic regimens.* Baltimore: Johns Hopkins University Press.

Sadusk, J. F., & Robbins, L. C. (1968). Proposal for health hazard appraisal in comprehensive health care. *Journal of the American Medical Association, 203,* 106-110.

Sand, P. L., Fordyce, W. E., & Fowler, R. S. (1973). Fluid intake behavior in patients with spinal-cord injury: Prediction and modification. *Archives of Physical Medicine and Rehabilitation, 54,* 254-262.

Sapolsky, H. M. (1980). The political obstacles to the control of cigarette smoking in the United States. *Journal of Health Politics, Policy and Law, 5,* 277-290.

Schachter, S., & Rodin, J. (1974). *Obese humans and rats.* Patomic, MD: Lawrence Erlbaum.

Schwartz, G. E., & Weinberger, D. A. (1980). Patterns of emotional responses to affective situations: Relations among happiness, sadness, anger, fear, depression, and anxiety. *Motivation and Emotion, 4,* 175-191.

Scott, L. E., & Clum, G. A. (1984). Examining the interaction effects of coping style and brief interventions in the treatment of postsurgical pain. *Pain, 20,* 279-291.

Scurry, M. T., & Levin, E. M. (1978-1979). Psychosocial factors related to the incidence of cancer. *International Journal of Psychiatry in Medicine, 9,* 159-177.

Seeley, J. R. (1960). Death by liver cirrhosis and the price of beverage alcohol. *Canadian Medical Association Journal, 83,* 1361-1366.

Selye, H. (1936). A syndrome produced by diverse nocuous agents. *Nature, 138,* 32.

Selye, H. (1982). History and present status of the stress concept. In L. Goldberger & S. Breznitz (Eds.), *Handbook of stress: Theoretical and clinical aspects* (pp. 7-17). New York: Free Press.

Seres, J. L., & Newman, R. I. (1976). Results of treatment of chronic low back pain at the Portland Pain Center. *Journal of Neurosurgery, 45,* 32-36.

Shaffer, J. W., Duszynski, K. R., & Thomas, C. B. (1982). Family attitudes in youth as a possible precursor of cancer among physicians: A search for explanatory mechanisms. *Journal of Behavioral Medicine, 5,* 143-164.

Shapiro, A. P., Schwartz, G. E., Redmond, D. P., Ferguson, D. C., & Weiss, S. M. (1977). Behavioral methods in the treatment of hypertension. A review of their clinical status. *Annals of Internal Medicine, 86,* 626-636.

Shapiro, D., & Goldstein, I. B. (1982). Biobehavioral perspectives on hypertension. *Journal of Consulting and Clinical Psychology, 50,* 841-858.

Shapiro, D., & Surwit, R. S. (1976). Learned control of psychological function and disease. In H. Leitenberg (Ed.), *Handbook of behavior modification and behavior therapy* (pp. 74-123). Englewood Cliffs, NJ: Prentice-Hall.

Shapiro, R. J. (1974). Therapist attitude and premature termination in family and individual therapy. *Journal of Nervous and Mental Disease, 159,* 101-107.

Shekelle, R. B., Gayle, M., Ostfeld, A. M., & Paul, O. (1983). Hostility, risk of coronary heart disease, and mortality. *Psychosomatic Medicine, 45,* 109-114.

Shekelle, R. B., Raynor, W. J., Ostfeld, A. M., Garron, D. C., Bieliauskas, L. A., Liu, S. C., Maliza, C., & Paul, O. (1981). Psychological depression and 17-year risk of death from cancer. *Psychosomatic Medicine, 43,* 117-125.

Shiffman, S., Read, L., Maltese, J., Rapkin, D., & Jarvik, M. E. (1985). Preventing relapse in ex-smokers: A self-management approach. In G. A. Marlatt & J. R. Gordon (Eds.), *Relapse prevention* (pp. 472-520). New York: Guilford.

Shoemaker, J. E., & Tasto, D. L. (1975). The effects of muscle relaxation on blood pressure of essential hypertensives. *Behavior Research and Therapy, 13,* 29-43.

Silver, B. V., & Blanchard, E. B. (1978). Biofeedback and relaxation training in the treatment of psychophysiological disorders: Or are the machines really necessary? *Journal of Behavioral Medicine, 1,* 217-238.

Silver, J. M. (1979, November). Medical terms—A two-way block? *Colloquy, The Journal of Physician-Patient Communications,* pp. 4-10.

Silverberg, E. (1983). Cancer statistics, 1983. *CA-A Cancer Journal for Clinicians, 33,* 9-25.

Sime, A. M. (1976). Relationship of preoperative fear, type of coping, and information received about surgery to recovery from surgery. *Journal of Personality and Social Psychology, 34,* 716-724.

Simonton, O. C., Matthews-Simonton, S., & Creighton, J. (1978). *Getting well again.* Los Angeles: JP Tarcher.

Simonton, O. C., Matthews-Simonton, S., & Sparks, T. F. (1980). Psychological intervention in the treatment of cancer. *Psychosomatics, 21,* 226-233.

Simonton, O. C., & Simonton, S. (1975). Belief systems and management of the emotional aspects of malignancy. *Journal of Transpersonal Psychology, 7,* 29-47.

Sklar, L. S., & Anisman, H. (1980). Social stress influences tumor growth. *Psychosomatic Medicine, 42,* 347-365.

Sklar, L. S., & Anisman, H. (1981). Stress and cancer. *Psychological Bulletin, 89,* 369-406.

Skrotzky, K., Gallenstein, J. S., & Osterrig, L. R. (1978). Effects of electromyographic feedback training on motor control in spastic cerebral palsy. *Physical Therapy, 58,* 547-552.

Slovic, P., Lichtenstein, S., & Fischhoff, B. (1980). Facts and fears: Understanding perceived risk. In R. C. Schwing & W. A. Albers, Jr. (Eds.), *Societal risk assessment. How safe is safe enough?* (pp. 181-214). New York: Plenum.

Smart, R. G. (1977). The relationship of availability of alcoholic beverages to per capita consumption and alcoholism rates. *Journal of Studies on Alcohol, 38,* 891-896.

Smith, S. D., Rosen, D., Trueworthy, R. C., & Lowman, J. T. (1979). A reliable method for evaluating drug compliance in children with cancer. *Cancer, 43,* 169-173.

Stachnik, T. J., & Stoffelmayr, B. E. (1981). Is there a future for smoking cessation programs? *Journal of Community Health, 7,* 47-56.

Statistics Canada. (1983, May). *In sickness and in health. Health statistics at a glance* (Catalogue No. 82-541). Ottawa: Statistics Canada.

Sternbach, R. A. (1974). *Pain patients: Traits and treatments.* New York: Academic.

Sternbach, R. A., & Rusk, T. N. (1973). Alternatives to the pain career. *Psychotherapy: Theory, Research and Practice, 10,* 321-324.

Sternlieb, J. J., & Munan, L. (1972). A survey of health problems, practices and needs of youth. *Pediatrics, 49,* 177-186.

Stevens, H. (1966). Paroxysmal choreoathetosis. *Archives of Neurology, 14,* 415-420.

Stewart, M. A. (1984). What is a successful patient-doctor interview? A study of interactions and outcomes. *Social Science in Medicine, 19,* 167-175.

Stewart, M. A., McWhinney, I. R., & Buck, C. W. (1975). How illness presents: A study of patient behavior. *The Journal of Family Practice, 2,* 411-414.

Stewart, R. B., & Cluff, L. F. (1972). A review of medication errors and compliance in ambulant patients. *Clinical Pharmacology and Therapeutics, 13,* 463-468.

Stimson, G. V. (1974). Obeying doctor's orders: A view from the other side. *Social Science and Medicine, 3,* 97-104.

Stoeckle, J. D., Zola, I. K., & Davidson, G. E. (1963). On going to see the doctor: The contribution of the patient to the decision to seek medical aid. *Journal of Chronic Diseases, 16,* 975-989.

Stoll, B. (1985). Psychoendocrine pathways and cancer prognosis. In M. Watson & T. Morris (Eds.), *Psychological aspects of cancer* (pp. 19-29). New York: Pergamon.

Stout, C., Morrow, J., Brandt, E., & Wolf, S. (1964). Unusually low incidence of death from myocardial infarction. Study of an Italian-American community in Pennsylvania. *Journal of the American Medical Association, 188,* 845-849.

Stuart, R. B. (1967). Behavioral control of overeating. *Behavioral Research and Therapy, 5,* 357-365.

Stuart, R. B. (1980). Weight loss and beyond: Are they taking it off and keeping it off? In P. O. Davidson & S. M. Davidson (Eds.), *Behavioral medicine: Changing health lifestyles* (pp. 151-194). New York: Brunner/Mazel.

Stuart, R. B., & Davis, B. (1972). *Slim chance in a fat world: Behavioral control of obesity.* Champaign, IL: Research Press.

Stuart, R. B., Mitchell, C., & Jensen, J. A. (1981). Therapeutic options in the management of obesity. In C. K. Prokop & L. A. Bradley (Eds.), *Medical psychology. Contributions to behavioral medicine* (pp. 321-353). New York: Academic.

Stunkard, A. J. (1975). From explanation to action in psychosomatic medicine: The case of obesity. *Psychosomatic Medicine, 37,* 195-236.

Stunkard, A. J. (1977). Behavioral treatments of obesity: Failure to maintain weight loss. In R. B. Stuart (Ed.), *Behavioral self-management* (pp. 317-350). New York: Brunner/Mazel.

Stunkard, A. J. (1979). Behavioral medicine and beyond: The example of obesity. In O. F. Pomerleau & J. P. Brady (Eds.), *Behavioral medicine: Theory and practice* (pp. 279-298). Baltimore: Williams & Wilkins.

Stunkard, A. J., & McLaren-Hume, M. (1959). The result of treatment for obesity. *Archives of Internal Medicine, 103,* 79-85.

Suinn, R. M. (1975). The cardiac stress management program for Type A patients. *Cardiac Rehabilitation, 5,* 13-15.

Suinn, R. M. (1982). Intervention with Type A behaviors. *Journal of Consulting and Clinical Psychology, 50,* 933-949.

Suinn, R. M., & Bloom, L. J. (1978). Anxiety management training for pattern A behavior. *Journal of Behavioral Medicine, 1,* 25-36.

Suinn, R. M., & Richardson, F. (1971). Anxiety-management training: A nonspecific behavior therapy program for anxiety control. *Behavior Therapy, 2,* 498-510.

Surwit, R. S. (1973). Biofeedback: A possible treatment for Raynaud's disease. *Seminars in Psychiatry, 5,* 483-490.

Surwit, R. S., & Feinglos, M. N. (1984). Relaxation-induced improvement in glucose tolerance is associated with decreased plasma cortisol. *Diabetes Care, 7,* 203-204.

Surwit, R. S., Shapiro, D., & Good, M. I. (1978). Comparison of cardiovascular biofeedback, neuromuscular biofeedback, and meditation in the treatment of borderline essential hypertension. *Journal of Consulting and Clinical Psychology, 46,* 252-263.

Susser, M. (1975). Prevention and health maintenance revisited. *Bulletin of the New York Academy of Medicine, 51,* 5-8.

Swanson, D. W., Maruta, T., & Swenson, W. M. (1979). Results of behavioral modification in treatment of chronic pain. *Psychosomatic Medicine, 41,* 55-61.

Swanson, D. W., Swenson, W. M., Maruta, T., & McPhee, M. C. (1976). Program for managing chronic pain I: Program description and characteristics of patients. *Mayo Clinic Proceedings, 51,* 401-408.

Syme, S. L. (1984). Sociocultural factors and disease etiology. In W. D. Gentry (Ed.), *Handbook of behavioral medicine* (pp. 13-37). New York: Guilford.

Szasz, T. S., & Hollender, M. H. A. (1956). A contribution to the philosophy of medicine: The basic models of doctor-patient relationship. *Archives of Internal Medicine, 97,* 585-592.

Tan, S. Y. (1982). Cognitive and cognitive-behavioral methods for pain control. *Pain, 12,* 201-228.

Telch, M. J., Killen, J. D., McAlister, A. L., Perry, C. L., & Maccoby, N. (1982). Long-term follow-up of a pilot project on smoking prevention with adolescents. *Journal of Behavioral Medicine, 5,* 1-8.

Thomas, C. B., & Duszynski, K. R. (1974). Closeness to parents and the family constellation in a prospective study of five disease states: Suicide, mental illness, malignant tumor, hypertension, and coronary heart disease. *Johns Hopkins Medical Journal, 134,* 251-270.

Thomas, L. (1977). On the science and technology of medicine. In J. H. Knowles (Ed.), *Doing better and feeling worse: Health in the United States* (pp. 35-46). New York: Norton.

Thompson, E. L. (1978). Smoking education programs 1960-76. *American Journal of Public Health, 68,* 250-257.

Thompson, R. J., Jr., & Matarazzo, J. D. (1984). Psychology in United States medical schools: 1983. *American Psychologist, 39,* 988-995.

Thompson, S. C. (1981). Will it hurt less if I can control it? A complex answer to a simple question. *Psychological Bulletin, 90,* 89-101.

Thunder road: States fight the 55-m.p.h. limit. (1986, May 5). *Time,* p. 31.

Trombly, C. (1966). Principles of operant conditioning: Related to orthotic training of quadriplegic patients. *American Journal of Occupational Therapy, 20,* 217-220.

Trotter, A. B., & Inman, D. A. (1968). The use of positive reinforcement in physical therapy. *Physical Therapy, 48,* 347-352.

Tulkin, S. R., & Frank, G. W. (1985). The changing role of psychologists in health maintenance organizations. *American Psychologist, 40,* 1125-1130.

Turk, D. C., & Flor, H. (1984). Etiological theories and treatments for chronic back pain II: Psychological models and interventions. *Pain, 19,* 209-233.

Turk, D. C., & Genest, M. (1979). Regulation of pain: The application of cognitive and behavioral techniques for prevention and remediation. In P. C. Kendall & S. D. Hollon (Eds.), *Cognitive behavioral intervention: Theory, research and procedures* (pp. 287-318). New York: Academic.

Turk, D. C., Meichenbaum, D. H., & Berman, W. H. (1979). Application of biofeedback for the regulation of pain: A critical review. *Psychological Bulletin, 86,* 1322-1338.

Turk, D. C., Meichenbaum, D. H., & Genest, M. (1983). *Pain and behavioral medicine: Theory, research and clinical practice.* New York: Guilford.

Turner, J., Blaney, R., Roy, D., Odling-Smee, W., Irwin, G., & Mackenzie, G. (1984). Does a booklet on breast self-examination improve subsequent detection rates? *Lancet, 2,* 337-339.

Turner, J. A., & Chapman, C. R. (1982). Psychological interventions for chronic pain: A critical review: II. Operant conditioning, hypnosis, and cognitive-behavioral therapy. *Pain, 12,* 23-46.

Tversky, A., & Kahneman, D. (1974). Judgment under uncertainty: Heuristics and biases. *Science, 185,* 1124-1131.

Urquhart, M., & Heilmann, K. (1984). *Risk watch: The odds of life.* New York: Facts on File Publications.

U.S. Bureau of the Census. (1975). *Historical statistics of the United States, colonial times to 1970, bicentennial edition, Part 2* (Stock No. 003-024-00120-9). Washington, DC: U.S. Government Printing Office.

Velvovski, I., Platonov, K., Plotitcher, V., & Chougom, E. (1960). *Painless childbirth through psychoprophylaxis.* Moscow: Foreign Language Publishing House.

Vincent, P. (1971). Factors influencing patient noncompliance: A theoretical approach. *Nursing Research, 20,* 509-516.

Visintainer, M. A., & Wolfer, J. A. (1975). Psychological preparation for surgical pediatric patients: The effect on children's and parents' stress responses and adjustment. *Pediatrics, 56*(2), 187-202.

von Baeyer, C. (1986). *Do psychological services reduce health care costs? An introduction and research summaries in nontechnical language.* Ottawa, Canada: Applied Division, Canadian Psychological Association.

von Baeyer, C., & Genest, M. (1985). Role of psychologists in Canadian pain centres. *Canadian Psychology, 26*(2), 140-147.

Votey, H., Jr. (1984). Recent evidence from Scandinavia on deterring alcohol impaired driving. *Accident Analysis and Prevention, 16,* 123-138.

Wadden, T. A., Luborsky, L., Greer, S., & Crits-Christoph, P. (1984). The behavioral treatment of essential hypertension: An update and comparison with pharmacological treatment. *Clinical Psychology Review, 4,* 403-429.

Wadden, T. A., Stunkard, A. J., Brownell, K. D., & Day, S. C. (1984). Treatment of obesity by behavior therapy and very low calorie diet: A pilot investigation. *Journal of Consulting and Clinical Psychology, 52,* 692-694.

Walde, A. (1981). Biofeedback therapy for fecal incontinence. *Annals of Internal Medicine, 95,* 146-149.

Wallen, J., Waitzkin, H., & Stoeckle, J. D. (1979). Physician stereotypes about female health and illness: A study of patient's sex and the informative process during medical interviews. *Women and Health, 4,* 135-146.

Watkins, J. D., Roberts, D. E., Williams, T. F., Martin, D. A., & Coyle, V. (1967). Observation of medication errors made by diabetic patients in the home. *Diabetes, 16,* 882-885.

Watson, C. G., & Schuld, D. (1977). Psychosomatic factors in the etiology of neoplasms. *Journal of Consulting and Clinical Psychology, 45,* 455-461.

Watson, D., & Kendall, P. C. (1983). Methodological issues in research on coping with chronic disease. In T. G. Burish & L. A. Bradley (Eds.), *Coping with chronic disease: Research and applications* (pp. 39-81). New York: Academic.

Watson, M., Pettingale, K., & Greer, S. (1985). Stress reactions and autonomic arousal in breast cancer patients. In M. Watson & T. Morris (Eds.), *Psychological aspects of cancer* (pp. 31-39). New York: Pergamon.

Weiner, H. (1984). What the future holds for psychosomatic medicine. *Psychotherapy and Psychosomatics, 42,* 15-25.

Weiner, H., Thaler, M., Reiser, M. F., & Mirsky, I. A. (1957). Etiology of duodenal ulcer I: Relation of specific psychological characteristics to rate of gastric secretion (serum pepsinogen). *Psychosomatic Medicine, 19,* 1-10.

Weinstock, C. (1977). Notes on "spontaneous" regression of cancer. *Journal of the American Society of Psychosomatic Dentistry and Medicine, 24,* 106-110.

Weisman, A. D., & Worden, J. W. (1975). Psychosocial analysis of cancer deaths. *Omega, 6,* 61-75.

Weiss, J. M. (1970). Somatic effects of predictable and unpredictable shock. *Psychosomatic Medicine, 32,* 397-408.

Weiss, J. M. (1984). Behavioral and psychological influences on gastrointestinal pathology: Experimental techniques and findings. In W. D. Gentry (Ed.), *Handbook of behavioral medicine* (pp. 174-221). New York: Guilford.

West, C. (1983). Ask me no questions. . . . An analysis of queries and replies in physician-patient dialogues. In S. Fisher & A. Todd (Eds.), *The social organization of doctor-patient communication* (pp. 75-106). Washington, DC: Center for Applied Linguistics.

West, C. (1984). Medical misfires: Mishearings, misgivings, and misunderstandings in physician-patient dialogues. *Discourse Processes, 7,* 107-134.

White, L., & Tursky, B. (1982). *Clinical biofeedback: Efficacy and mechanisms.* New York: Guilford.

Whitehead, W. E., & Bosmajian, L. S. (1982). Behavioral medicine approaches to gastrointestinal disorders. *Journal of Consulting and Clinical Psychology, 50,* 972-983.

Whitehead, W. E., Fedoravicius, A. S., Blackwell, B., & Wooley, S. (1979). A behavioral conceptualization of psychosomatic illness: Psychosomatic symptoms as learned responses. In J. R. McNamara (Ed.), *Behavioral approaches to medicine: Application and analysis* (pp. 65-99). New York: Plenum.

Wideman, M. V., & Singer, J. E. (1984). The role of psychological mechanisms in preparation for childbirth. *American Psychologist, 39,* 1357-1371.

Wiggins, J. G. (1976). Utilization and costs of mental health services. In H. Dorken and associates (Eds.), *The professional psychologist today* (pp. 175-206). San Francisco: Jossey-Bass.

Wildavsky, A. (1977). Doing better and feeling worse: The political pathology of health policy. In J. H. Knowles (Ed.), *Doing better and feeling worse: Health in the United States* (pp. 105-123). New York: Norton.

Williams, P. T., Fortmann, S. P., Farquhar, J. W., Mellen, S., & Varady, A. (1981). A comparison of statistical methods for evaluating risk factor changes in community-based studies: An example from the Stanford three community study. *Journal of Chronic Diseases, 34,* 565-571.

Williams, R. B., Jr. (1984a). Type A behavior and coronary heart disease: Something old, something new. *Behavioral Medicine Update, 6*(3), 29-35.

Williams, R. B., Jr. (1984b, September/October). An untrusting heart. *The Sciences,* pp. 31-36.

Williams, R. B., Jr., Haney, T. L., Lee, K. L., Kong, Y. H., Blumenthal, J. A., & Whalen, R. E. (1980). Type A behavior, hostility, and coronary atherosclerosis. *Psychosomatic Medicine, 42,* 539-549.

Wilson, G. T. (1984). Fear reduction methods and the treatment of anxiety disorders. In G. T. Wilson, C. M. Franks, K. D. Brownell, & P. C. Kendall (Eds.), *Annual review of behavior therapy. Theory and practice.* (Vol. 9, pp. 95-131). New York: Guilford.

Wilson, G. T., & Brownell, K. D. (1980). Behavior therapy for obesity: An evaluation of treatment outcome. *Advances in Behavior Research and Therapy, 3,* 49-86.

Wing, S. (1984). The role of medicine in the decline of hypertension-related mortality. *International Journal of Health Services, 14*(4), 649-666.

Wolfer, J. A., & Visintainer, M. A. (1979). Pre-hospital psychological preparation for tonsillectomy patients: Effects on children's and parents' adjustment. *Pediatrics, 64*(5), 646-655.

Yates, B. T. (1980). The theory and practice of cost-utility, cost-effectiveness, and cost-benefit analysis in behavioral medicine: Toward delivering more health care for less money. In J. M. Ferguson & C. B. Taylor (Eds.), *The comprehensive handbook of behavioral medicine* (Vol. 3, pp. 165-197). Jamaica, NY: Spectrum Publications.

Yates, B. T. (1984). How psychology can improve effectiveness and reduce costs of health services. *Psychotherapy, 21,* 439-451.

Zarsky, J. J. (1984). Hassles and health: A replication. *Health Psychology, 3,* 243-251.

Zegans, L. S. (1982). Stress and the development of somatic disorders. In L. Goldberger & S. Breznitz (Eds.), *Handbook of stress: Theoretical and clinical aspects* (pp. 134-152). New York: Free Press.

Zeltzer, L., & LeBaron, S. (1983). Behavioral intervention for children and adolescents with cancer. *Behavioral Medicine Update, 5,* 17-22.

Ziesat, H. A., Jr. (1981). Behavioral approaches to the treatment of chronic pain. In C. K. Prokop & L. A. Bradley (Eds.), *Medical psychology—Contributions to behavioral medicine* (pp. 291-305). New York: Academic.

Subject Index

Author Index

229

3747